Home educating our autistic spectrum children

of related interest

Asperger's Syndrome
A Guide for Parents and Professionals
Tony Attwood
ISBN 1 85302 577 1

Hitchhiking Through Asperger Syndrome
Lise Pyles
ISBN 1 85302 937 8

Caring for a Child with Autism
A Practical Guide for Parents
Martine Ives and Nell Munro
ISBN 1 85302 9963

Pretending to be Normal
Living with Asperger's Syndrome
Liane Holliday Willey
Foreword by Tony Attwood
ISBN 1 85302 749 9

Home educating our autistic spectrum children

Paths are made by walking

Edited by
Terri Dowty and Kitt Cowlishaw

Jessica Kingsley Publishers
London and Philadelphia

First published in the United Kingdom in 2002
by Jessica Kingsley Publishers Ltd
116 Pentonville Road
London N1 9JB, England
and
325 Chestnut Street
Philadelphia, PA 19106, USA

www.jkp.com

Copyright © Jessica Kingsley Publishers 2002

Library of Congress Cataloging in Publication Data
A CIP catalog record for this book is available from the Library of Congress

British Library Cataloguing in Publication Data
A CIP catalogue record for this book is available from the British Library

ISBN 1 84310 037 1

Printed and Bound in Great Britain by
Athenaeum Press, Gateshead, Tyne and Wear

Contents

Traveller, there are no paths—paths are made by walking

—Spanish proverb

The core human rights standards for education include respect of freedom. The respect of parents' freedom to educate their children according to their vision of what education should be has been part of international human rights standards since their very emergence.

—United Nations Commission on Human Rights Statement by Special Rapporteur on the Right to Education 8/4/99

Acknowledgments

My thanks to all of the authors, who have played such a major part in this challenging project; in particular, to Jackie Stout for her massive contribution and drafting of the 'school problems' chapter, and to Andrea Stephenson and Alan Phillips for their helpful input.

Thanks, also, to the members of the HE-SPECIAL-UK e-mail support list; to Anne of 'Spearhead' for her expert advice; to Perri Hart of Creators Syndicate for her rapid-response help in obtaining copyright permission; and to Jessica Kingsley and all of her staff for bearing with us.

On a personal note, my love and gratitude to Alison, Angie and Mary for all the emotional band-aid, to Ian for his constant support, and to Biggs and Ollie, who have given me the exciting journey called 'home education'.

—*Terri Dowty*

Editor's note

Some of our editorial decisions may surprise you, so a little explanation is in order.

Our book celebrates diversity. The authors speak in their own voices, using their own individual styles. The editing of their stories has therefore been multinational rather than mid-Atlantic.

American homeschoolers have a marvelous time: they live in apartments, take the elevator, learn math, practice the piano, enjoy television programs, have favorite colors, and go on vacations. English home educators, on the other hand, have a marvellous time: they live in flats, take the lift, learn maths, practise the piano, enjoy television programmes, have favourite colours and go on holidays.

As demonstrated in the preceding pair of sentences, our American writers use the serial comma, whereas our English writers omit it. These cultural differences have been respected in our book.

We hope you will keep an open mind as you read our stories. What at first sight appears to be an error may simply be an unfamiliar variant. What at first sight appears to be a disorder may simply be an unfamiliar mind.

—*Kittredge Cowlishaw*

1

Introduction

Terri Dowty

I had one of those grandmothers whose pearls of wisdom could make Confucius look like an amateur, at least in terms of output. We're not talking pocket-sized, chicken soup books here: Grandma was a ten-volume walking encyclopaedia of proverbs and epithets for every occasion. 'Don't put it down, put it away!' she cautioned, and 'Never economise on shoes or bras!' Probably the most influential for me, though, has been 'If you want a job done well, do it yourself.'

Now, while such self-reliance has obvious dangers when it comes to brain surgery or rewiring the house, where bringing up my children is concerned, I have generally found it a very sound piece of advice. I am, like every parent, the ultimate expert when the subject in question is my own children. How could it be otherwise? I have known them since long before any midwife fired their official starting pistols, and we have continued to shape each other's lives ever since.

I have a pretty shrewd idea of how they tick; I know how their eyebrows wiggle when they are fascinated, the chew of the lip that accompanies deep thought, the sideways glance that says 'Let me out of here.' This non-stop, silent communication puts me in a strong position to extend my parental activities to include educating them: I *know* how each of them grasps knowledge and I can see immediately when my attempts to explain or answer a question are futile. I also know, for instance, that one child needs diagrams and the written word, whereas the other needs a practical, physical activity to fix a concept in his mind.

By home educating, I can ensure that everything they do is interesting, purposeful and effective.

It would be hard for any school to compete with parents' profound knowledge of their children and, in our case, the only reasonable option seemed to be home education. As simple as that? Well, yes and no. Certainly, I can look back and see that time has proved it to be the best possible decision for all of us—but no, it wasn't easy at the outset. I am not one of life's natural bungee jumpers, so the period between making the decision and actually putting it into effect was fraught with panic induced by a little voice in my head assuring me that, this time, I really had taken leave of my senses.

Few home educators will be surprised by my anxiety. We all know just how difficult it can be to reclaim the responsibility for our children's education—or to decide not to relinquish it to a school in the first place. Parenthood is riddled with guilt, under-confidence and a sneaking fear that our children might be better off in more qualified hands. That is one of the reasons for writing this book: we believe that all parents are experts, that 'education' and 'school' are not synonyms, and that the intimate knowledge we each have of our children can be just as effective an educational catalyst as any curriculum, programme or specially designed institution.

In little more than a century, the idea that a school education is inevitably superior to anything an untrained parent can provide has become embedded in our collective subconscious. A child is to school as bread is to butter. Perhaps that was true to some extent in the days when knowledge was a restricted commodity; however, we now inhabit a world where access to information on any subject imaginable is only a library ticket or mouse click away. As our society changes, the sacred cow of education has come to resemble a rather less exotic domestic beast, prompting thousands of parents to take the leap of faith into providing it themselves, in co-operation with their children.

How families go about the business of education is very personal. Just as each child is unique, so is the educational path that will best suit him or her. In this book, we have twelve different families giving a dozen different answers to the same question. Some parents find that their child is happiest with a highly structured and predictable day; others prefer to follow their child's lead, providing resources and encouragement for the interests that arise spontaneously. As long as parents listen to their child and to their own well-honed instincts, there is no single, right way of home educating. Education can become a partnership, rather than a battle of wills.

This rather flies in the face of the current dogma that there is one essential core of knowledge without which one cannot possibly thrive. The nonsense of such an assertion is easy to demonstrate: how much of that vital curriculum that was spoon-fed to you at school still remains with you now? Has life really been unmanageable without all those things you forgot—or never understood in the first place? Did your failure to grasp the significance of the Tudors make you a bad receptionist or graphic designer? Has your indifference to the life cycle of the frog prevented you from becoming a computer programmer?

While there are inevitable mutterings about a 'broad and balanced' curriculum, there is no legal requirement upon a home educator to provide any such thing. Knowledge, like food, is only nourishing if it is actually absorbed. Time wasted on study which, to borrow William Morris's words, one finds neither useful nor beautiful is time which could be put to a far better purpose. Home education allows a child to do just that: to concentrate on the absorbing or essential and leave the rest.

Probably the question that home educators face most frequently, though, is about 'socialisation'—a strange word, really. We are now so ready to accept that school is the means by which children become socially competent that it is tempting to wonder how society managed to advance beyond grunting until the advent of compulsory mass schooling.

Socialisation—and education—are what all parents are providing as they gently draw their beloved baby into a relationship with the world, encouraging, explaining and protecting as the circumstances demand. For some children, particularly those on the autistic spectrum, that relationship is going to prove extremely challenging, but where it threatens to be overwhelming, parents can instead bring the world to the child in manageable, bite-sized pieces. Home education means that this process can continue for as long as a child needs.

By contrast, if we consider the experience of school from the point of view of a child who prefers large doses of his or her own company and is distressed by noise, the daily enforced contact with thirty loud, busy people simultaneously must often seem more like torture than a beneficial experience. We have to ask: what kind of 'socialisation' does school actually offer?

A home educator might well, in any case, turn the question upside down and ask: at what other stage of life will somebody have to spend years almost exclusively in the company of a large group of people whose common ground lies in having been born in the same year? And if those people are hostile, or even simply uncomprehending of one's individual, quirky way of being, is it not likely that any social messages will be negative enough to reduce even the most robust child's self-esteem to ashes?

While home education is no easy option, many parents find it preferable to the misery and stress of watching their child suffer the pain of bewildering rejection, or of being told in a thousand small ways and on a daily basis that he is 'failing' to meet the expectations of others.

Even if we believe that our children must learn to roll with the punches, children on the autistic spectrum are known to have difficulty in transferring any social skills thus acquired to other situations. In other words, learning to socialise at school equips one to socialise at school, but is not necessarily a lot of help anywhere else. What point, then, does the suffering serve? While parents may have other extremely pressing and understandable reasons for sending a child to school, it is hard to see how a case can be made for the social benefits it supposedly confers being one of them.

Home education allows a child to form relationships with anyone he or she chooses, at a manageable pace and within a real, mixed community. In this setting, an individual can be recognised as a whole, unique person, albeit an eccentric one, rather than viewed as a checklist of symptoms or dismissed as a bundle of deficits. Parents and other trusted adults are on hand to explain how a conversation has come unstuck, to suggest different approaches and to mediate between the child and a sometimes baffling world. The social skills thus learned can be carried into the future as applicable to the real world, not simply the restricted environment of school.

It should be said at this point that some parents question the need for a diagnosis of Asperger's syndrome—and even its validity. In an increasingly conformist society, we have seen the use of labels proliferate in the classroom to a point where it is sometimes hard to imagine how any child could ever meet the narrow specification for 'normal'. It is all too easy to attribute a pathology to a child whose individual way of being makes the institution of school unworkable. For those parents who find the label helpful, many come to find the diagnosis largely irrelevant in home education, and use it only to explain to others their child's behaviour in social situations where the common courtesies of tolerance and respect might otherwise be withheld.

So, how do parents set about this whole business of home educating their children? When I first started out with my own sons, I asked this question many times and grew frustrated with the enigmatic responses I encountered: 'Well, you just have to work out your own way.' 'Give it time and you'll find it's obvious.' However, after a year or two, when home educating had become second nature, I found myself making exactly the same kind of vague response, and understood why the question could not be answered directly.

There is no 'home education curriculum', no user manual. The saying 'If you meet the Buddha on the road, kill him!' springs to mind; if anyone can answer your question with any foolproof method, she is a fake who has not grasped the most important principle of home education: you must seek out the unique path that suits your particular family, even if it bears no resemblance to anything you see around you. It may take a period of trial and error before you find the right balance—and even then, it will shift to meet the varying needs of your growing, changing child.

What we have done in this book is to give you some samples of the very different forms home education has taken for a variety of families. They are not claiming to have found the ideal solution for any family except their own, but their stories may encourage you to think about what you hope to establish with your own child, or at least give you some clues about your own starting point.

We have also included a lively and straightforward chapter about the law relating to home education in England, Wales and Northern Ireland, written by an acknowledged legal expert, who also happens to be my husband and the fellow home educator of our children—a happy combination of factual knowledge and practical experience! Unfortunately, we are unable to address the law in Scotland, nor in the USA—where the law, in any case, varies from state to state—nor in any other jurisdiction. However, we have included a list of support organisations and other sources of advice in the *Finding support and information* section of this book.

If you feel that home education might just be a solution to your problems, but sheer terror is holding you back, then I would venture only one piece of advice: take it a bit at a time. By choosing to home educate, you are not bidding a final farewell to other options. If, a year from now, you believe your choice was a mistake, the schools will still be there. In fact, as you will hear, many parents have used a combination of school and home throughout their children's education.

In the end, the responsibility for your child's education rests with you. You have the power to make informed choices about how you will set about your task. Only you can know what makes up your own 'vision of what education should be'.

2

So, what's the problem with school?

All the contributors, with particular thanks to Jackie Stout, Andrea Stephenson and Alan Phillips

How would Terri's Grandma answer a question like this? Probably something involving sauce and ganders, or about one man's meat being another man's poison. It seems clear that, for some children, school does provide the kind of soil in which they can put down roots and flourish. For others, especially those on the autistic spectrum, it proves to be a difficult and frightening place, filled daily with confusion, anxiety and overwhelming sensory assault. At worst, it can become an environment inimical to mental health and emotional security.

To understand the serious difficulties which autistic children can experience at school, it is probably helpful if we take a little time to outline what we understand of autism, before moving on to discuss the effects it has on the everyday reality of a child's life.

It is generally agreed that autism is a developmental difference which affects a person's ability to communicate, to understand the feelings of others and to make relationships. 'The autistic spectrum' encompasses both severe autism at one end of the spectrum and Asperger's syndrome at the other. Before receiving a diagnosis of autism, a child is likely to have shown significant difficulties in the areas of social interaction, communication and imagination, and may also have very restricted activities and interests. Some children may enter the world with serious and obvious problems, while others may show no sign of autism until around age three or four.

Children affected by classic autism are often non-verbal and may be very withdrawn, while those with Asperger's syndrome usually have normal, or advanced, language abilities. They may speak fluently, albeit in a formal, stilted way, but appear insensitive by talking at great length and without noticing their listener's reactions. Social relationships can be further hampered by a difficulty in interpreting facial expressions or other subtle communications, and by a very literal understanding of language, which causes confusion about jokes or everyday phrases like 'I did it by the skin of my teeth.'

Children with Asperger's syndrome are likely to be of at least average intelligence, and may have outstanding intellectual abilities. Often, their interests involve arranging or memorising facts about a specialist subject, something at which they excel, but they may find it hard to think in the more abstract ways necessary to the study of philosophical or creative subjects.

An autistic child may find it difficult to identify and articulate his feelings, and is likely to demonstrate emotional pain in behaviour which may seem inexplicable to anyone but a loving parent. These demonstrations are easily misunderstood, or dismissed as pathological symptoms, rather than recognised as a desperate communication. The consequent downward spiral of frustration, misunderstanding and, sometimes, punishment can be highly toxic.

The most fundamental instinct of all parents—be they human, penguin or elephant—is to keep their young safe, but the human species has now become so clever with words and theories that any parent who takes this idea much beyond teaching the Green Cross Code is liable to be labelled as over-protective or neurotic. The use of pseudo-clinical 'put downs' seems to have grown in inverse proportion to respect for parental wisdom.

Some parents, though, believe that their child not only needs to be safe in an objective sense, but also needs to *feel* beyond all doubt that he is safe, whatever this may entail, if he is to grow into a confident, capable adult. Rejecting the blanket application of abstract theories about 'children in general' or 'children with autism', they instead choose to follow gut feeling and deep knowledge of their unique child.

> Tristan's outlook on life has always been tainted by fear. It is fear that colours his perceptions. Our challenge is to help him feel safe in the world.
>
> —Anne

Sadly, any guidelines for teaching such acutely sensitive children are not followed in all schools, and often do not draw on the specialist knowledge parents have of their children's needs, strengths and likely behaviour in a variety of situations. The consequent lack of understanding can have a dramatic effect on a child's self-esteem, the quality of his education and his ability to live up to his potential.

Parents' intimate knowledge of their child's learning style, preferences and sensitivities, as well as the subtle ways in which his individual level of autism is demonstrated, is often misunderstood, under-used, or even devalued by educational professionals. Many parents are accused of over-protectiveness or of having too close a relationship with their children. This seems to be a common experience for parents of a child with Asperger's syndrome. It may even be suggested by school staff that parents are not providing adequate home discipline for a child whom they perceive as lazy and unmotivated.

> Any parental input is often seen as amateur interference. It is assumed that we are inevitably biased in favour of our own children. When Alex was at school, this led to many misunderstandings. Some staff were very quick to read deviousness or delinquency into situations which were in fact due to his extreme naïveté and lack of self-preservation.
>
> —Grace

In school, there are many rules upon which teachers rely in order to maintain control. Conformity reassures teachers and parents alike that consistent learning is taking place in a well-controlled learning environment. This way of thinking is ingrained from our earliest experiences and reinforced over and over again, but it is not an attitude that lends itself to accommodating a minority.

In the name of fairness to all pupils, many simple and imaginative modifications requested by parents are often denied to children with real needs. Less homework, the use of a keyboard or a calculator, allowing a child to meet his teacher before the first day of a new term, a support assistant to help a child get from one class to the next, written homework instructions or copies of class notes—all these basic steps could help an autistic child make it through the school day with less stress.

> Treating everyone the same was the crude and very unfair sort of 'fairness' that most schools subscribe to. Their idea of fairness dictated that Stephen would not be allowed to use a fountain pen, as the school had banned them, despite the fact that he found writing difficult, but easiest with such a pen.
>
> —Elizabeth

The challenges that school can present to a non-verbal autistic child are enormous: he may not be able to communicate even his simplest needs. All too often, the resulting frustration is expressed in behaviour that is misunderstood and may lead to his being physically restrained or isolated, setting up a vicious circle of anger and despair.

Some children are inappropriately placed in schools for children with moderate to severe learning difficulties, which may or may not have specialist units for autistic children. A non-verbal child who does not 'perform', and who cannot tell a teacher that he does not understand what is expected of him, risks being written off, leaving him with little direction or stimulus to learn.

> Greg was so severely autistic that experts predicted he would never be able to talk. Schools and teachers seem to assume that because they don't get much, if anything, back from children like Greg, those children can't do things. Our experience is very different. There is far more going on for Greg than you might first think. He is capable of very intelligent thought, but it has taken a

lot of time, patience, understanding and love to discover that in him.

—Alan

Children with Asperger's syndrome may have fewer overt signs of problems than those with severe autism, but they nevertheless face tremendous challenges in their daily school life. Although their difficulties are subtle, they are no less real. For instance, they frequently have trouble with the planning and organisational skills required to complete projects. Writing an essay in class, even on a subject with which they are familiar, may be an impossibility.

> Alex sat through a whole creative writing lesson without putting pen to paper. At the end, his teacher said to him, 'Do you mean to tell me that thirty-one other children were able to write something on this subject, but you couldn't?' He gave her an honest, one-word answer: 'Yes!'
>
> —Grace

Alex has Asperger's syndrome. He probably does not respond well to time pressures; moreover, because the priorities of an autistic child can be very different from those of a neurotypical child, it may not have occurred to Alex that there would be any consequences of not completing his work. Possibly, he was unable to find the perfect way to begin his story, and so he sat for the entire period thinking about it. He may have thought the task unimportant, and therefore irrelevant.

When a child is home educated, a parent can allow a choice of topics and unlimited time to write. A more formal writing project can be built around the child's special interest in guitars, computers or film censorship, for example. As necessary, and when his own maturity allows the receiving and processing of new information, a child can be gently led toward improving his skills.

> Stephen was completely unable to write essays such as 'My Holiday' or 'My Family' or 'My Favourite...', which other pupils found easy. When I tried to find out why, he just said that such things were too private. Even now, at fourteen, he cannot write

about himself. Faced with 'personal writing, non-fiction' at GCSE, he resorted to a highly coloured and slightly fictional account in the humorous style of *Three Men in a Boat*. In this way, he was able to distance himself from the subject matter and make it more impersonal and therefore 'safe'. Because he was at home, we could negotiate this slight twisting of the requirements with him. Not all teachers in school would have been as flexible or as sympathetic.

—Elizabeth

Alex has done some very amusing creative writing which generally makes use of play on words. Because context doesn't distract him from noticing the multiple meanings of words, he can use this to create humour.

—Grace

Children with Asperger's syndrome tend to be underestimated intellectually, sometimes quite dramatically, unless they demonstrate a particular talent or interest; even then, their unique areas of expertise are sometimes regarded as flukes, rather than genuine indicators of their ability.

Alexandra was placed in a remedial reading class, not because she could not read, but in order to work in a smaller group of children. I personally didn't feel that she belonged with children who were having difficulty reading.

—Rachel

Mark was good at maths, but he couldn't colour in pictures, so he was stuck on the first maths workbook, on the concept of counting to five, for six months.

—Mark's Mum

Where a child's exceptional capacity for intense concentration on an engrossing topic goes unrecognised, or is thwarted by the school bell and the need to move on to another activity, he may feel exasperated. By contrast, at home he can spend as long as he likes on his quest for knowledge, and also avoid the tedium of working at a level well below his intellectual capabilities.

At school, outright conflict can arise because of a child's difficulty in interpreting body language and facial expressions. He may interrupt the teacher or another pupil to add his point of view and then talk at length until stopped, unaware that others are bored, angry or even laughing at him. The child perceives himself to be helpful when offering a correction in class, and has no clue as to why a teacher would not welcome accurate information.

> Alex cares passionately about getting things right and was always outraged when the teacher gave incorrect information. Once he was told he was wrong when he insisted that glass isn't a solid, which made him look stupid in front of the other children. When he took his science encyclopaedia to class the next day to show the teacher he was right, she just told him it would confuse the class to tell them glass wasn't solid.
>
> —Grace

Truth is vitally important to children with autism. Precise systems of thinking and behaving are essential tools for making sense of a very confusing world. Everything is distilled into facts, with the parts being more important than the whole. However, this tendency to take a narrow view means that shades of grey, nuances and contradictory ideas are hard to tolerate. A child may become extremely frustrated when others do not agree with his views, and feel irritated or hurt when his assumption that others share the same information as he does proves to be groundless.

This difficulty in 'thinking about thinking' makes it nearly impossible for children with autism to evaluate, interpret or understand the relevance of philosophical ideas. There is a puzzling contradiction between their often massive fund of factual knowledge and their difficulty in contributing to a class discussion or in writing an essay on an abstract topic. Children are often told they are lazy or commanded to 'think!' when they simply cannot process information in the same way as the majority in their class.

Environmental sensitivities, such as sounds, lights and touch, affect children with autism every day, whether they are in school or at home, causing pain, confusion, fear and sometimes anger. Something as simple as a school bell ringing every hour to signal the changing of classes can be so unpleasant to a child that he might spend the entire lesson preparing and waiting for the bell to ring, and consequently not concentrate.

> Robert sat with his hands over his ears, because he could not stand the tone of the teacher's voice. She thought he was extremely rude.
>
> —Andrea

> How did they expect me to concentrate with lizards scratching and a bird talking and a fish tank bubbling? If they didn't want me to pay attention to those things, they shouldn't have put them in the room.
>
> —Kevin

At home, a child can escape the whizzing, whirring, clacking, ringing, shuffling, snapping, shouting, screeching and bright lights of school. If he needs a period of quiet and solitude, then it is readily available. Gradually, he can relax and regain confidence in his ability to control his environment; this, in turn, leaves him free to think, to listen and to learn in the way that best suits him.

Another difficult aspect of school life can be working on tasks within a group, an activity demanding co-operation and an appreciation of others, which an autistic child simply may not possess.

> For one lesson, each table of six children was given a large sheet of paper on which to make a joint drawing. Alex started drawing on the section of paper immediately in front of him. The other children decided that the other end of the paper was to be the bottom of the picture, and when he refused to co-operate, one of them started rubbing out what he had drawn. At that point, he grabbed the other child's pencil and rubber, threw it across the room and pushed the child away. This was clearly an impossible task for Alex. He knew what he wanted to draw and was happy to get on with it. To participate in the group required more flexibility of thinking than he possessed. Probably his only other option

would have been to withdraw completely from any involvement in the task.

—Grace

Occasionally, a child will not be able to cope with a specific pressure and may act upon a physical impulse. If his vulnerability is discounted and he is merely punished for the outburst without any attempt to find the underlying cause, his confidence and ability to regain control are likely to take a nosedive.

More often, an autistic child will simply withdraw from conflict and become ultra-compliant, perhaps even the self-appointed policeman of the classroom—a position not likely to endear him to his classmates. He may become concerned and confused when one of his actions—or inactions—results in someone's becoming angry with him.

> Not understanding social signals makes Tristan very anxious. He is always asking, 'Are you upset? Angry? Happy?' If he thinks someone is even slightly upset or angry, whether they actually are or not, he has to apologise.
>
> —Anne

Dealing with the unpredictability of the world can cause a child such fear and anxiety that he retreats into repetitive or bizarre coping strategies that further alienate him from his classmates and teachers. He may 'perseverate', speaking loudly and in detail about the topic which is currently preoccupying him. Some autistic children withdraw from taxing situations by using self-stimulation techniques that distract them mentally, such as blinking, tapping, rocking or spinning.

> On a few occasions, when Kevin found the noise in our car too stimulating, he would voluntarily make rapid eye movements to distract himself. He explained, 'When I blink my eyes very fast, it blocks out disturbances from entering my consciousness.'
>
> —Jackie

Some children are able to make it through the school day, but then lose control emotionally upon reaching home.

Robert really let himself go—kicking the car, swearing, crying, banging about—being completely unbearable for at least two hours until he calmed down.

—Andrea

Even if a safe and supportive environment is found during the earlier years of school, the onset of adolescence all too often proves to be the watershed where any such containment breaks down entirely.

Homework is another aspect of school that poses a problem for autistic children. After exhausting hours away from home, navigating the obstacle course of school, a child must then make sense of and complete homework.

When Kevin was attending school, he was responsible for filling in a homework notebook every day. Because he often forgot to do this, his teachers agreed to check his notebook daily to make sure it was complete. Frequently, they forgot to check. If I asked about the problem, I would hear, 'Kevin needs to take responsibility for this.' He was clearly unable to, so I would keep an extra set of books at home, and 'phone the teacher for details of homework. After I began to home educate him, we no longer had these difficult demands to deal with.

—Jackie

The academic issues faced by children on the autistic spectrum are only the beginning of their troubles in school. While some are lucky enough to have a sympathetic teacher, it is more likely that their teachers will have little or no understanding. Teachers can find it very hard to relate to a pupil who may appear wilful, rude or openly disobedient, and it is not uncommon for a teacher to feel threatened by such a student.

It can be difficult for teachers to understand that a child may have an unusual vocabulary, an outstanding aptitude for computers and an incredible memory for obscure facts, but at the same time be unable to tie his shoelaces, follow directions, and remember to bring his homework and supplies to lessons. He may disrupt the classroom with odd questions or comments and challenge the authority of the teacher.

All of this happens completely inadvertently, and the child is left even more bewildered if he is treated as if it were deliberate.

> In Mark's first year of school, he had a kind, loving teacher who accepted his bizarre behaviour with equanimity. In the following year, his new teacher was very strict and refused to tolerate any deviation from the norm. She punished him by making him stand by the door whenever he did anything odd. He seemed to spend most of the day standing by the door. If I asked him what he had been punished for, he was never able to tell me. That's when he first began to talk about killing himself.
>
> —Mark's Mum

To be fair, it is not surprising if teachers become confused or exasperated by a child's inconsistent and erratic behaviour. The demands upon them to deliver a curriculum to an entire class leave precious little space to give the autistic child the individual attention that he needs, and their problems may be compounded by lack of classroom support.

Some children with autism may not be receiving suitable provision within school. There are various reasons for this, one of them being the lack of a firm diagnosis of autism. The National Autistic Society reports that sixty-five per cent of autistic children do not yet have a confirmed diagnosis. This would lead one to conclude that a significant number of undiagnosed children are receiving either a minimal amount of inappropriate support at school or none at all. Often, teaching and support staff have had little or no specific training to enable them to identify or recognise such children. This can lead to inappropriate labelling and consequent use of unsuitable strategies by teachers.

However, even a confirmed diagnosis of autism or Asperger's syndrome does not guarantee that suitable educational provision will be made. The help provided for children on the autistic spectrum is often patchy, varying considerably from one area to another subject to local budget constraints. Most parents of autistic children find that obtaining appropriate support is a long uphill battle.

Frustration and impatience expressed by busy teachers working under pressure inevitably influence the child's classmates, encouraging them to view him as an undesirable, and even inferior, member of the group. The scant supervision of children during break times, lesson changes or physical education provides the ideal opportunity for their dislike of the vulnerable autistic child to spill over into teasing and bullying. Because he is unable to interpret the cues that would otherwise warn him of impending trouble, he may well be unable to counter or deflect such abuse.

> Alex had a particular sensitivity to having someone else's saliva on him and would be very distressed if this occurred. He would become very insistent about washing it off. Some of the boys used to take great delight in blowing raspberries at him, because they discovered that this was the thing that could get him really worked up.
>
> —Grace

Even though he may be perceived as odd by his classmates, a child's sincere desire to make friends can often lead to his being 'set up' by other children. One boy, for instance, was told by two girls in his class that if he took his trousers down in class, they would be his friends. He did, and was puzzled when it earned him an exclusion for the day.

In a home education setting, parents can keep an eye on social interactions and intervene if necessary, at least until the autistic child is old enough and savvy enough, socially and emotionally, to have bypassed the childhood land mines so prevalent in schools.

Some children can tolerate school, and some schools are more sensitive and conscientious than others in meeting the needs of autistic children. However, despite the improvements now being suggested by caring teachers and medical experts, many parents feel that it is just not enough.

For the time being, it seems impossible for all schools to implement the vast changes necessary to make them the right places for autistic children to learn and grow. We can't wait for those changes. School simply does not feel like a safe place to our children, who are growing up fast. The best way we have found of ensuring they walk positively and confidently into the future is to home educate them.

The school system focuses on our children's deficits and implicitly encourages parents to do the same. Being outside that system allows us to learn to accept their totality—to celebrate and enjoy their strengths, as well as to support and help them with their difficulties. I think what we are all learning to do is to diminish their difficulties by building on their strengths.

—Grace

3

Square pegs don't fit round holes
Robert's story

Andrea Stephenson

Our son is now twelve years of age and has been home educated since the age of ten. He has been diagnosed as having Asperger's syndrome, attention deficit hyperactivity disorder (ADHD) and dyspraxia, as well as some eyesight difficulties. Unlike many parents of children on the autistic spectrum, we knew six weeks after his birth that Robert would be different.

I had waited until I was thirty before having my first child, hoping, like many other mothers, that I would be able to juggle the demands of a full-time career with raising a child. However, I was soon to discover that for me this would not be a possibility.

My elder sister, a nurse and mother of three children herself, was quick to point out that babies' eyes do not usually wobble from side to side as Robert's did. In any case, by the age of six weeks babies should have some control over their heads instead of still being floppy. Even though he was still only weeks old, we knew there was something wrong, although it would be several years before the labels were attached to him.

We visited the paediatrician for the first time when Robert was three months old, and he was duly enrolled into the NHS system: the world of paediatricians, audiologists, orthoptists, *etc.*; a world in which the professionals know best—or so I assumed.

When Robert was two, our second baby was born. By this time, Robert was displaying all the characteristics of severe autism, yet he still had no definite diagnosis; the doctors were unwilling to commit themselves. Although to me it was obvious what was wrong, convincing the professionals was another matter.

I had begun to despair at the lack of help that was available to us from the medical services. I decided that the only way to ensure that my son got the help he needed was to approach the local education authority (LEA). There was no time to waste; I hassled the LEA with telephone calls and letters until they agreed to assess Robert's special needs. In the event, this turned out to be an epic in itself, which was resolved only after the intervention of a county councillor.

At three years of age, Robert attended school for the first time. It was a thirty-eight–mile round trip from our home in an escorted taxi to the only full-time special needs school in the county. Even now, I look back at this and wonder why I thought it was the right thing to do. In the absence of anything else, it seemed to be the only thing to do at the time.

Robert later transferred to mainstream school, although not in September with his peers, but in the following May, when he was almost five years of age. The explanation for the delay was that the LEA needed time to organise the correct support—a process that seemed to take forever, despite the fact that they had known for the previous two years about Robert's difficulties.

The first three years of primary school, whilst not exactly problem free, passed without too much event. Robert was given a special support assistant in the classroom for thirteen hours per week. I remained closely involved with the school and became the school governor for special educational needs (SEN).

Then a new head teacher was appointed. He would have preferred that all children with special educational needs should be down the road at the special school, including my son. Not surprisingly, we did not see eye to eye on this, or on many other things. It proved impossible to educate him about the positive aspects of including disabled children in the school.

To make matters worse, the school became grant maintained and the relationship between the school and the LEA deteriorated. This made things more difficult, particularly for children with special needs. Once the school became autonomous, any intervention from the LEA was unwelcome, including advice from the specialist autism outreach teacher, who was an employee of the LEA.

The outreach teacher maintained her weekly visits to the school to see Robert, but her input was largely ignored. For example, Robert is particularly sensitive to sound, so the outreach teacher supplied earplugs for him to use to reduce the noise level. However, his class teacher threw them in the bin, saying that he wouldn't be able to hear her properly. On another occasion, the outreach teacher provided some specialist games that the special support assistant could use with Robert, but the class teacher wouldn't allow her to use them, declaring that there was 'no time for him to play silly games'.

When Robert went into junior school at age seven, his problems really began. His class teacher had totally unrealistic expectations of him. Whilst Robert is hyperlexic (he taught himself to read at age three) and extremely computer literate, he also has some very subtle difficulties, such as his sound sensitivity. He is especially sensitive to certain noises such as the school bell or the vacuum cleaner. Simply coping with the everyday noises generated in a school was a huge problem for him. He is also very disorganised, has poor short-term memory and is totally unco-ordinated.

However, because he looks 'normal', his teacher expected him to act normal. When he didn't, she considered him to be a very naughty boy. She made no allowances for his special needs, and in fact was quite harsh towards him, despite the involvement of the LEA outreach teachers who were trying to educate both her and the head teacher.

Robert spent most of his time outside the head's office, not knowing why he was there or what it was that he had done wrong. Within four months he was cutting his clothes and hair and was also beginning to pick his skin constantly whilst in school, to the extent that it was bleeding. He cried late into the night and was constantly tired through lack of sleep. It was clear to me that he was becoming severely depressed.

As you can imagine, it was very upsetting to witness my vulnerable little boy falling into such a distressed state. I had no alternative but to remove him from the school. I vowed then that I would never let him suffer like that again.

After a month or two at home, I transferred him to another school in an adjoining village. I had begun to consider whether it might be better if he were to be home educated. Although I did little more than make tentative enquiries at this stage, at least I knew there was another option if things didn't work out.

At the same time, I used our negative experiences in his first mainstream school as evidence for my appeal to the SEN tribunal on the grounds that his educational needs were not being met. It had the desired effect: the LEA promptly upped the hours of Robert's special support assistant from thirteen to twenty hours per week, with added specialist teacher support and speech and language therapy. Consequently there was no need for a hearing and I was able to withdraw the appeal.

For about two years we had a period of stability. Things started going downhill, however, when he entered year six at age ten. We discovered that the head teacher, Robert's class teacher and his special support assistant were all leaving in the near future—a lot of change for a little boy who does not cope well with change.

Robert began picking his arms again in school. By now he was much better at expressing himself and was able to tell me that he wasn't coping very well. He had been finding the work in school very difficult; much of what he was doing required imagination and abstract thought, which Robert simply did not possess.

Around this time I embarked on a tour of doctors, psychiatrists, psychologists and skin specialists in an effort to address the self-mutilation problem. Robert's arms were a mass of scabs and open wounds, which looked awful. The experts responded with an assortment of potions, bandages and advice, none of which seemed to resolve the problem.

I had no clear idea how often he picked his skin, because he only did it in school. It was not something he ever did at home. From what I can gather, he used to do this mainly in assembly times or when the class teacher was reading to them. I can only think it was triggered by a combination of stress and boredom.

He would certainly switch off in assembly for a number of reasons. Firstly, because of his eyesight difficulties, he couldn't see properly what was happening at the front of the hall. Secondly, the subject matter was of no interest to him. Thirdly, the hymn singing and acoustics had a terrible effect on his sound sensitivity. He must have found the twenty minutes of assembly each morning deeply distressing, but at the time I wasn't aware of this. I only saw the results: the raw, open sores that appeared on his arms day after day. At the time, knowing that it was happening but not knowing when or why compounded my feelings of helplessness.

By now the prospect of home educating had been looming in my mind, and in my heart I knew that it was only a matter of time before we took the plunge. I had already joined the UK home educators' support organisation Education Otherwise for advice and support. Since we had a computer at home, I also subscribed to UK-HOME-ED, an Internet e-mail support list where parents can discuss ideas and philosophies and generally provide a sympathetic ear. I acquired information about my legal responsibilities of educating otherwise, and I also gained confidence from others in similar situations.

After Christmas, the new class teacher started. I had hoped that Robert would see out the summer term of year six, after which he would not be a registered pupil anywhere and would simply be home educated. Unfortunately, Robert was not coping well at all.

His new teacher made no allowances for his sound sensitivity. She didn't recognise any signs of his distress and he was given no 'time out' to recover. At the same time, the other children could see his distress and yet they would taunt him and tease him, which only compounded his anxiety.

Every night after school he would collapse in a heap, crying and deeply distressed, unable to get the words out of his mouth. He suffered what can only be described as a complete melt-down. He had contained himself all day, keeping his thoughts, anger and anxieties bottled up inside. When the school day was over, it all came pouring out.

He often didn't make it to the car before the tears would roll down his cheeks and he would sob uncontrollably. On one occasion the head teacher saw this, and even though I explained that Robert was like this most days when he got out of school, the head teacher seemed unconcerned, remarking that he was 'fine in school' and that, really, 'there was no problem'.

During the short drive home from school, I would try to listen to him in between the sobs and try to make sense of what had happened to him, while at the same time his younger brother was excitedly telling me what sort of a day he had had, too. After we arrived home, Robert would sit in the car while I settled his younger brother to watch television, and then I would return to sit in the car with him. Often he would refuse to get out of the car, and I would leave him for half an hour or more, so that he could gather his thoughts.

By tea time he would have calmed down and relaxed, but then we might have to do some homework and he would begin to cry all over again. I would sit on the settee, cuddling him, wiping away his tears, and listen to him telling me about his day. Sometimes what he said was disjointed and didn't make sense; at other times he could clearly explain who had said and done what. As for homework, often we just had to abandon it.

Night after night, I would lie next to him in bed until the early hours talking to him, telling him everything would be all right, but deep down I knew it wouldn't and I wasn't sure how I was going to make it any better. I knew that if I didn't act fast, he could once again become severely depressed.

I had to consider whether I had time to educate the new class teacher on how Robert's special needs affected his learning and his ability to relate to his peers and to other adults. Was it worth painfully going over the same ground yet again with another teacher for the sake of another six months? And in the meantime, what effect would this have on my son's mental health? Would he be completely messed up?

As it happened, I took Robert out of school two weeks into the new term, after yet another incident in school. Initially, the official line was that Robert was away from school because of stress; however, I had no intention of returning him to school again—a fact I did not at the time openly divulge to those in authority, but would have done if pressed. As it was, Robert's special educational needs were being reassessed by the LEA; it was therefore obvious that at some future point the LEA would be making contact.

At the start I had no clear idea about what I was going to do or how I was going to do it. Robert's self-esteem and confidence were low, and he was suffering from anxiety. He worried constantly about having to go back to school, despite my constant reassurances that this would not happen. He had developed a deep mistrust of everyone and everything.

Robert's mental health was my first priority, but I also needed to address his education. I decided that I would need to acquire lots of National Curriculum materials and resources in order to cover the sort of things he would have been doing in school.

Having scrutinised his school timetable, we took a trip to the local W H Smith. I stocked up on age-appropriate workbooks, covering all the subjects he would have done in school. I armed myself with folders, paper, crayons, pens and pencils, filling the shopping basket with school supplies, so that we could do school at home. In retrospect, it was an act of pure impulse, but at least it made me feel better about the situation we were in, even though I parted with almost one hundred pounds on just one shopping expedition.

I wasn't quite sure how things would work out, but felt that if we had all the 'correct' resources and materials, we could easily do it. Of course, somewhere along the line we would need to be fairly flexible, as I still needed to work part time. Fortunately I had sympathetic employers who allowed me to take Robert into work. It was also lucky that my job allowed me to work outside office hours, when my husband could take over.

Initially I figured that we would do about four hours of school work a day. I based this figure roughly on his school timetable, after deducting time for assembly, lunch and breaks—not to mention all the lost time traipsing round from class to class.

In the early weeks of home education, Robert and I sat at the kitchen table and did National Curriculum maths for an hour followed by English, geography and history. Although he did the work, I could sense that he wasn't enjoying it; most of the questions had no bearing on his life. Yet he was enthralled by current events in Kosovo and talked incessantly about Iraq and Saddam Hussein. He read the daily newspaper from cover to cover, and his interest led us to buy several different papers, from comprehensive broadsheets like *The Times* to the tabloid press, making comparisons along the way.

Although he has exceptionally good reading and spelling ability, he does have some difficulty interpreting words and their meanings. This led to many questions that demanded immediate answers. After a while, I reminded him of the thesaurus and dictionary I had bought and he began looking up the answers for himself. This served two purposes: it eased some of his dependence on me and also provided him with useful research skills.

His enjoyment in reading newspapers has grown and he now reads them for the first hour of each morning, taking in current affairs and anything else which catches his attention. We spend much of our time discussing political and other current issues, and because he is genuinely interested, he is learning a lot. I have realised that it is pointless trying to make him learn something that doesn't interest him: he simply will not retain the knowledge.

Because Robert has poor imaginative skills, he is not interested in fiction, nor in child's play or children's programmes. However, he is very interested in documentaries and factual programmes. He is computer literate and adept at using the Internet, spending hours researching subjects and downloading material from web sites. He also enjoys typing up plays that he has written himself. Although they are lacking in imagination, it doesn't really matter; at least he is having a go and there is no negative feedback in our home.

Within a few weeks of buying all those books and resources, we seemed to be developing our own learning style. The National Curriculum books went into a huge resource box and are there if we feel the need to use them. We now spend a lot of time walking and talking, exchanging views and ideas, taking in nature as we do so.

We also have a number of projects up and running, based on things that interest Robert. As an example, one of our current projects is on Israel. We are able to consider and discuss everything about the country, from culture to politics. We are not bound by time limits or waiting for a bell to ring. We visit the library and access information in a wide variety of ways. Robert is also considering doing Spanish as a foreign language. We will probably invest in an interactive Spanish CD at some stage, but for now we have borrowed one from the library.

We visit a wide variety of interesting places: museums, parks and historical sites. We meet up with other home-educating families about once a week, often doing something that is educational, but more important, it gives us an opportunity to meet others socially. I now regard several home educators as personal friends, supportive and willing to share experiences on varying styles of home education.

With the time saved by not being constrained by the school day, we now have plenty of time and opportunities to work on social skills, self-help and independence.

Because we have been aware of Robert's difficulties since he was very young, I have been involved with several parent support groups over the years and have always been particularly interested in how adults with Asperger's syndrome have fared in the education system. What sort of employment prospects and independent living skills have they gained?

A few years ago I met a young man of twenty-two with Asperger's syndrome, called Gary. He is in some ways very similar to Robert, although he was not diagnosed until he was seventeen. He described his experience of secondary school as 'four years, nine months and two days of hell' in a place where he felt like 'an alien in a foreign country'.

He found the social aspects of school life particularly hard to deal with, because he could not understand when people were genuinely joking or being sarcastic. He desperately wanted to make friends, but lacked the necessary skills to do so and, in fact, had no friends at all throughout his secondary school years. He was often bullied, or physically and verbally abused—and not only by the other children. His experiences made a depressing story. However, he did manage to pass five GCSE exams with reasonable grades.

When I first met Gary, he was managing to hold down a full-time job in an office while living with his parents. Soon afterwards, his parents retired and moved away from the area. Before they left, they installed Gary in his own newly decorated, completely furnished modern flat.

I will never forget the first time that Robert and I visited him there. The whole place was completely festooned with old newspapers, piles of dirty clothes and money just scattered on the floor. Decaying rubbish was heaped up in a corner of the living room, with half-eaten food from a previous meal next to it. In another corner of the room was a pile of unopened Christmas presents, although it was midsummer. Gary had neglected to open them, as he had no one to share them with on Christmas day.

We were offered a cup of tea, but the only milk he had was long past being drinkable. In his fridge was a row of packaged sandwiches, one for each day of the coming week and labelled accordingly.

Gary himself appeared dishevelled; his clothes were creased and stained. He seemed oblivious of the mess and dirt. He was more concerned about what to do with a large pile of letters and unpaid bills which he had stacked on one side. It was obvious that he was not coping at all. Despite being equipped to work in an office, he had no idea how to take care of himself.

One thought that has often crossed my mind since that day is this: what is the point of enduring five miserably traumatic years in school to gain a so-called education, when at the end of it you are not even capable of basic self-help skills or living independently?

Gary was re-housed shortly after our visit and now lives in a unit with other men who have severe learning difficulties. His situation has often been at the back of my mind. His experiences have helped shape my own philosophy about the kind of education we want to provide for Robert.

Robert is very sensitive and also very much aware of his deficits. He wants to know how to hold conversations and 'read' what people are thinking, how to understand body language, how to know when people are being sarcastic or telling lies, how to deal with awkward situations, how to maintain eye contact with strangers and understand those messages that people can send to each other just by looking. He wants to know all the social rules, how to play and join in with others, and he needs the chance to practise and make mistakes in a safe environment, without fear of ridicule from others.

Robert needs to be helped to understand social behaviour that others learn automatically. Here I can draw on my own professional experience. In a previous occupation, I worked for a large organisation where I was responsible for creating training programmes. I researched, designed and implemented courses in interview techniques, including the use of body language, eye contact and responses to questions. These skills have come in handy recently. Robert and I spend a lot of time watching people in various situations, often making use of television programmes, and discussing the implications of what we observe. Since we began home educating, Robert has become more assertive and sociable, and has had plenty of opportunity to practise making eye contact.

We have only been home educating for two years and, of course, we are still developing. We began home education with a formal approach, but have now found something more comfortably informal that works best for us. We do not follow a timetable, because we have found it far too restrictive; we tend to do work for as long as it holds Robert's interest.

Robert does attend formal information technology lessons once a week at a local adult teaching centre. He passed his computer literacy and information technology (CLAIT) course in less than three months. He has also acquired certificates in business studies and Internet technology. I firmly believe Robert's future will be working in computers.

Our lives have changed completely. My career has changed, too. I completed a postgraduate certificate in education law and have worked as a legal assistant to a solicitor specialising in education law.

Over the years since Robert was born, I have advised hundreds of parents of children with special needs from all over England and Wales, helping them to understand the law regarding statements and appeals to the SEN tribunal. On two separate occasions, I successfully applied for grants from the National Lotteries Charities Board to fund a post for a developmental worker to provide independent and impartial advice and support to parents of children with special educational needs who are battling within the education system.

My other interests have blossomed as well. I have acquired a national certificate in horticulture from the Royal Horticultural Society—a subject I hope to pursue further.

Since leaving school, Robert's arms have healed completely and I am hoping the scars will fade in time. His depression has vanished. We have at last dispensed with all those NHS professionals because, after twelve years, we no longer need their services. Our only contacts with the professionals now are with the optician, for Robert's routine eye check, and with our family doctor—though only for normal childhood ailments.

I met once more with the LEA, not long after Robert was removed from school. They readily acknowledged that meeting Robert's special educational needs would be difficult, but they were not very forthcoming with a solution. They eventually suggested two possible school placements: a specialist residential school three hundred miles away, or a small independent school that was a seventy-two–mile round trip from home. This would have required Robert to travel for nearly three hours per day. We decided that neither of these options would be practical for us.

The choice seems to be either to return to school with some very expensive support services or to continue to 'do my own thing' and educate otherwise. I feel that sending my son back to school, even with full-time support, would not be in his best interests. Interestingly, the LEA are willing to provide expensive support for something that has no reasonable prospect of working and could even be damaging. The very system that is designed to help families like ours often does the complete opposite.

In an ideal world, I would like the LEA to provide me with a financial sum to purchase the provision I feel is necessary to meet my son's special needs—a sum significantly lower than the amount they are prepared to spend in supporting him in school.

After researching what was available on the open market, I decided to put together an educational package to be implemented mostly at home, consisting of a combination of distance learning courses and local computer courses. I presented this to the LEA for their consideration, with details of the costs. Initially they were very receptive, since the package clearly met Robert's needs and would be an efficient use of resources. It was, of course, much cheaper than any of the options they had offered us.

However, as time went on they became less enthusiastic. They indicated that they were reluctant to create a precedent by funding our home education programme. By the time they wanted to discuss it further, eighteen months later, we had moved on. I decided I now didn't want their interference. We politely informed them that we would make our own arrangements to meet Robert's special educational needs. They replied wishing us well in our endeavours and I have not heard from them since.

I continue to help many families who seek support for their children's needs in schools, but I no longer seek it for myself. In the course of helping my own child, I became an expert in education law, statements, tribunals and all the procedures involved in obtaining support for children with special needs. I've learned the details of the system, both legal and practical. Now that I know so well exactly what is available and possible within the school system, I no longer want it. I know that it can never provide our son with the education he deserves.

One day, about a year after leaving school, Robert and I went shopping together. As we were wandering round, I started thinking about how different things were at the same time the year before, how low his self-esteem was and how he would have preferred to sit in the car while I rushed round the shops. He hadn't the confidence to walk round the shops with me, just in case someone spoke to him. I remembered how I had to spend the last week of the school holidays getting him in the right frame of mind to return to school, and how facing and dealing with each and every day was filled with all kinds of unpredictable and unwelcome incidents for him.

As I was thinking all this he suddenly said, 'Thanks, Mum, for taking me out of school. I can honestly say I now enjoy living.' It was said right on cue as if he had known what I was thinking. I felt a lump appear in my throat, and my eyes feeling prickly. To look at him and talk to him, he was not the same boy as he was the year before; he had grown and was much more mature. I wondered briefly how things could have been so very different if we had carried on sending him to school. I am so very glad we didn't!

My whole philosophy on education has changed completely. Robert is now very receptive to learning and is, for the first time, thoroughly enjoying his life. He is happier, calmer and more inquisitive than he has ever been. Now that he is home educated, we will ensure that he achieves his full potential and is prepared for life in a modern civilised society, something I do not believe schools could ever do.

4

Home truths
Stephen's story

Elizabeth Pite

Imagine you are climbing up a steep hill with some friends. It is a hot summer's day and they are all lightly clad. However, you have a very heavy rucksack on. As they leap nimbly up the track, you toil along far behind, hot and sweaty. Nevertheless, with grim determination you get there in the end, even if long after the others.

This analogy for the difference between 'normal' people and those with Asperger's syndrome (AS for short) was used by a young man with AS on a television programme about five years ago. At the time, he was studying for a maths degree. I would love to know how he's getting on now, especially since his vivid and apt imagery has helped me to have insight and hope as I plod on with my son. We may be miles behind, but we are making progress and will get there in the end.

The analogy is helpful with respect to home education. From my reading and experience I would judge that it is more difficult and challenging to home educate a child with AS than most. Certainly my other two children have been easy in comparison, but that does not mean home education is not realistic for AS, as it may still be better than any of the alternatives. Carrying an unusually heavy rucksack is often painful: you fall down or even lurch backwards sometimes. It is easy to feel envious or despairing, but fortunately we do gradually make our way up the hill, and for every two steps backwards there are at least three forwards.

Where did we start? How did we get to where we are now? What does the view look like from here?

How we started

Ten years ago, when my son Stephen started school, schools were very different places from today. The first round of the National Curriculum had only just been introduced, and there were no invidious league tables or soul-destroying inspections. I was keen for him to start school, and excited about its possibilities for him. How my views have been changed by my bitter experience!

Stephen was always a lively and demanding child, with endless energy and determination, most of it coming my way. I find the incessant demands of young children a challenge anyway, and because he was my first I took longer to recognise that his unusual characteristics were sufficiently disabling for him to need a label. I assumed his problems were due either to bad parenting (this guilt feeling lessened when his sister turned out to be fine), to his obvious high intelligence or to his 'skewed' development (*i.e.*, that he would grow out of it).

Since he was not yet fully potty trained at playgroup age, I had to accompany him, which gave me the opportunity to observe his difference even at that young age. Whilst the others were rushing about on trikes and slide, he would be sitting alone in the book corner 'reading' the pictures! However, I am a bookworm too, so at the time it just seemed to reflect his interests.

He liked his year at nursery, especially as they did a project on dinosaurs, his interest at the time. Socially he was obviously immature compared to the others, but then he was the youngest. However, when I asked if he could stay there for another year, I was told that it was out of the question. So, despite my reservations, school was the only option.

Even if I had known then that home education was a viable alternative, I doubt I would have considered it. I desperately needed the respite that school offered, to give time to his little sister. His refusal to accept discipline or direction, his self-absorption and his explosive tantrums were already making home life difficult. I also hoped he would find school interesting and enjoyable.

I did try to persuade the school to let him stay part time, as at nursery, as I felt that was all he would manage. I am not very good at being assertive, and they were good at 'patting anxious parents on the head', so he duly went full time after a few weeks' induction. A fortnight later he lost his temper badly and attacked the teacher. I was soon in the head's office, being told that he was 'too young to exclude', as legally he did not have to be at school anyway! I burst into tears, and the crisis was resolved by Stephen's going part time for the rest of that year.

However, his very loud voice, constant fluent chattering and lack of social inhibition (shouting out in assembly!) had made him famous throughout the school in his first week. His 'crimes' when in a temper (scratching and biting) soon made him notorious, and having been labelled the 'bad boy', he ended up being blamed even when innocent. Parents were sometimes hostile, even saying to me, 'What that boy needs is a good hiding!', but some at least of the staff were sympathetic and we both made friends. Stephen made one particular friend, whom he still sees every Sunday, but some other children became adept at needling him until he exploded.

I once asked the head if Stephen could be referred to the educational psychologist, but was told budgets were tight and he was not a priority case. Other schools would probably have referred him; the head often admitted to being baffled by his behaviour, but didn't welcome outside help. Even once he was full time at school, lunchtimes were a problem and eventually he started coming home for lunch. Fortunately, we live near the school, but it was still disruptive, and he hated having to go back again so soon after a rushed lunch.

The situation really became serious once he started the first junior class. There is a huge jump in social expectations between infants and juniors, which most children manage to negotiate. Stephen's already marginal social position was exacerbated by being the youngest in the class and by having a very mild teacher, since he only understands very strong, clear directions and obvious penalties—otherwise he assumes he is in control. It finally became clear to us that there was something so different about Stephen that he would not catch up, but needed extra help.

We had joined the National Association for Gifted Children (NAGC) and, through them, obtained a private assessment from an educational psychologist. He confirmed Stephen's high ability and insisted that it could account for his social difficulties. When we fed this report back to the school, they did then take his ability seriously, which they had previously ignored, but had little extra to offer.

By then Stephen was completely antagonistic to school anyway and it was a struggle to get him there. The school tried a behaviour modification programme—that is, bribing him to behave—but after a few weeks Stephen asked to be taken off it. He could not explain why, but I now realise that he knew he could not manage the required effort, however tempting the bribes. The task was too difficult for him. He persisted in seeing his own needs and rights as paramount, and was unable to see another point of view or believe that he had hurt someone, since he himself had not felt the pain.

As Stephen became more difficult and aggressive, at both home and school, my relationship with him deteriorated. I tended to blame either him, or myself, or sometimes the school for our problems. He seemed so selfish and self-absorbed that it was difficult to relate to him. I became increasingly critical of his refusal to stop hurting other people.

However, gradually I started to see him differently, to be more sympathetic and to recognise that he had a genuine difficulty and lack of perception. There was one particularly revealing assembly, when his whole class stood up in front of the school to sing a song. The other children were all looking at the teacher and singing. Stephen was looking all over the place, and even picking his nose, seemingly unaware of where he was or what he was doing. It was like some of the more immature reception class children when they first started school, but he was nearly eight. He was like a baby compared to his classmates.

As the situation continued to hurtle towards catastrophe, I had two chance conversations that revolutionised my perceptions and turned me from victim to protagonist. I was talking to a very close friend and saying that I was so desperate that I might even take him out of school, although I didn't want to be seen as a crank, when she told me calmly that her brother was home educating his children, and there was an organisation called Education Otherwise that supported such people. Suddenly it was not just what religious fanatics or those obsessed with hot-housing their children did, but a perfectly sensible option chosen by ordinary people!

Even so, I still dithered for some months, terrified of criticism or of being a social outcast. When I finally took the plunge (after a particularly bad incident), I found most people neutral or supportive. Some even said things like, 'Good for you! I wish I had the time (or money, courage or ability) to do the same for my kids.'

The other chance conversation led to the knowledge that I did not have to wait for the school to refer my son for assessment, but could do so myself through our family doctor. It seems such a simple little piece of information, but it was hugely empowering. Without it, we might not have got a diagnosis at all.

When I first started home educating, more than six years ago, I was full of optimism and enthusiasm, imagining that, as his mother, I would succeed with time, patience and one-to-one help. I may have been overflowing with maternal love and care, but I was pretty quickly disillusioned.

Stephen resented any attempt to encourage him to do anything productive, educational or helpful. All he wanted was to be left alone to play with his Lego or to read about or draw horrible monsters. He was particularly reluctant to write anything (still true).

I was not always realistic about the appropriate level of work or attention span of a seven-year-old child. However, if I did not get the 'pitch' exactly right, he would react angrily and negatively. He refused to do any practice or consolidation work, and could not cope with making mistakes. He preferred only to try things he knew he could do, except that then he would say they were boringly easy.

This is a real dilemma. It is very hard to learn anything if you are not prepared to take risks and learn to cope with failure. I was inclined at the time to blame his difficulties on his bad school experiences, but now I see more of it as due to AS. Certainly, his attitude has proved intractable and still dogs us now, making it difficult for him to enjoy work.

After a few months at home, Stephen spent three months at the local child psychiatric unit being assessed. As before, our advice was ignored until their usual method of dealing with an outburst (restraint) failed, providing further negative experience for Stephen. After this they followed our advice, which was to remove him from the situation and get him on his own, preferably with a book, and then leave him to calm down. This always helps, so it is a pity that it is not always possible. It is also frustrating that, again and again, professionals ignore the advice and experience of parents, despite the fact that we know our child best.

At the end of Stephen's placement at the unit, when they gave us the diagnosis of Asperger's syndrome, they did so tentatively, as a 'best fit' model. I feel this is a good way of presenting such labels, as no two children are the same, and the classical description of Asperger's syndrome is unlikely to match any child exactly. However, it provides a basis: a useful starting point for trying to accept, understand and help a child who cannot cope with our complex and subtle society and its expectations.

We had never heard of Asperger's syndrome, and had only vague knowledge of autism. When we read the literature, we felt both anguish and relief. Anguish, that he had a lifelong handicap, so we could no longer fool ourselves that he might catch up. After eight years we had a bereavement to mourn, of the son who was going to have a normal happy life as we had done. Our relief was that it was a condition irrelevant to all our fumblings and mistakes. Perhaps we were 'good enough parents' after all! Also it gave us something to work on, some insight and possible strategies for helping Stephen with his social skills. Nevertheless, it took me a year fully to accept the diagnosis; even then, I kept hoping until comparatively recently that he would somehow progress enough to be able to integrate back into mainstream school.

The psychiatric unit's analysis made sense, and their recommendations of what he needed at school sounded reasonable; the problem came when we asked where a suitable school was, and it turned out not to exist. Since he was clearly too bright for any special school, all they could recommend was that he return to the school he had just left.

This was their only serious offer. Apparently continuity and a full-time state education were more important criteria than the fact that it had gone so disastrously wrong and that some of the other children either mocked or hated him. Also, the way he was going, with increasingly violent outbursts, he would soon have been excluded anyway.

I felt I had no alternative to home education. It was fortunate that our family circumstances made this possible, although I did have to give up my part-time job. I was currently at home with my new baby anyway. I do not know what we would or could have done if this had not been possible.

Thus we started on our first phase of home education.

First time at home: 8–10 years old

For three years (apart from the assessment at the unit) Stephen was at home full time. To begin with, I drew up over-ambitious timetables that we never used. It was soon clear that Stephen regarded the hours between 9:00 a.m. and 3:00 p.m. (school hours) as the only times in which I could influence what he did. Co-operation was patchy, but never failed to cease at the magic hour of 3:00 p.m.

In the beginning I was very concerned about the spectre of a home visit from the LEA. Our only correspondence from them had been fairly ferocious about needing a qualified teacher, *etc.* I am not naturally organised and systematic, but I tried very hard to keep a detailed record of everything we did, and even produced some work schemes and plans.

I used various methods of record keeping and providing structure. To begin with, I just wrote a diary each day of what we had done, usually a few numbered points of educational activity. A teacher friend initiated me into the trick of making everything look like intentional education! Here is a typical early example, when Stephen was nearly eight:

Wednesday, 8th June

1.   Wrote nonsense poem (English)

2.   Did some Heinemann maths (maths)

3.   Played with pirates (creative and imaginative play)

4.   Wrote gift list (English)

5.   Played with Anna (social skills practice)

6.   Listened to schools radio programmes (listening skills; also music, drama, *etc.)*

7.   Times tables: 3, 4, 8, 11 (maths)

8.   Beavers (socialisation)

Stephen and Beavers managed to stay together, but he parted company with the Cubs after only a few weeks. He was not ready for the higher degree of structure and conformity. Perhaps he only likes structure he has personally negotiated!

We kept this diary for about a year. Here is a late entry, from the following year:

Monday, 3rd July

1.   Mental arithmetic

2.   Story writing: 'Creeps of Death'

3.   Singing with *Music Workshop* on the radio

4.   Social activity: a barbecue

When the home visit finally came, the inspectors only stayed for an hour and barely glanced at all Stephen's work I had planned so carefully. I had gained Stephen's co-operation by pointing out that if the inspectors were not happy, it would mean going back to school, which was what he dreaded above all else. However, they mostly engaged me and my husband in general talk. Their only comment on his work was that it ought to have the date on it!

After the inspection we relaxed a bit, but I was concerned about the next one—never dreaming that they'd never be back!—and I occasionally read scare stories about hostile LEA attitudes in the Education Otherwise newsletter. So I continued to keep detailed records, and to try to structure a 'broad and balanced curriculum' that would be acceptable to them.

I read, and was intrigued by, ideas of autonomous education in the Education Otherwise newsletter and John Holt's books, but it did not seem applicable to us. A combination of Stephen's AS and his negative experience mean that, left to himself, he would achieve nothing. Also, I have seen how bored and grumpy he becomes if his life is not structured for him. He may resent, and constantly argue against, 'work', but he likes taking exams and having some success in his life—and so far his only successes have been academic.

Recently he has vindicated my approach by insisting that we have a timetable and stick to it more rigidly than in the past. He will now agree that he finds it helpful to have an imposed structure, but when he was younger he could not articulate his needs, so we had to try to guess, and of course frequently got it wrong. He likes the security and predictability of having his time mapped out—though I have realised that he also loves negotiating (well, haggling really) and getting away with doing less than he should! Certainly if we ever threaten to stop nagging him, as we are heartily sick of the constant battles and tension, he then immediately caves in and co-operates.

After the diagnosis, we decided that if he was to stay at home, we would like some outside help. We asked whether the psychiatric unit could provide a social skills group or help of some kind, but they had nothing to offer. I got very used to professionals expressing concern or dismay at our position without actually offering us any practical help. As our LEA inspector said, 'You are either in or out' (of the system). Having chosen home education, we were on our own.

We decided to employ a friend, who was a primary school teacher at home with her youngsters, to tutor him for one and a half hours a week. This not only gave me a break, but also some structure and ideas for the rest of the week. She encouraged him to do projects which we could then work on at other times. She was much better at motivating and inspiring him than I was, but, as she pointed out, it is easier to do so for a short time, and she had certainly had enough at the end of the ninety minutes! She also kept him in line with the school curriculum and suggested ideas for me to interest him with. Stephen always enjoyed going to her, and it was a real blow when she returned to teaching after a year.

One real advantage of being at home was that we could tackle Stephen's writing difficulties by responding to him individually. One key feature of his final refusal to co-operate at school was their insistence that he should use joined-up writing, despite the fact that he still found printing an effort and had been consistently late at all the pencil skills. He was much readier to co-operate with writing when I let him revert to printing.

The other incentive was to let him write his own highly imaginative fantasy stories instead of requiring him to write about 'my summer holiday' or any other such personal writing, all of which he found impossible. He could also make his stories as long as he liked, and his preference was to try to write a book, so they ended up pretty long at times. When his tutor felt that he was ready to try joined-up writing, and could provide suitable exercises for him, my one-to-one help was invaluable and led to mostly readable, if rather messy, handwriting.

Another area in which he desperately needed to go at his own pace was maths. He grasps concepts so easily that the only way to keep him from boredom (and hence refusal to do it) was to go faster than normal. Fortunately my husband and I are both maths graduates. The difficulty was in getting him to do enough practice to consolidate and remember new skills. Also, his concentration was (and is) very patchy, so that something he can do with ease one day will seem impossible the next. This does make him frustrating to teach, as it is difficult to tell how much has really been absorbed and retained.

We also found some of the BBC radio programmes helpful for structure and variety. *Drama Workshop* had some useful social skills input, too—only I'm not sure Stephen actually learnt much from it! Still, we enjoyed the suspense and story lines. Our other favourites were *Music Workshop, Ghost Writer, Together* and *Listen and Write*. We also sometimes went to a friend's house to watch some of the BBC education programmes on television (we do not have a television ourselves). This was structure, outing and treat all in one. *Landmarks* and *Zig Zag* were particularly good.

The friend and tutor previously mentioned encouraged us to use a more systematic and 'school friendly' system of record keeping. I would take a sheet of paper and write down the left-hand side the names of the National Curriculum core subjects. At that time this meant English, maths, science, technology, humanities, art, music, religious education (RE) and physical education (PE). I would then divide the rest of the page into blocks, one for each week. I could then write his activities in the relevant blocks during each week, and the whole sheet would last about a month. This was easy to fill in, ensured his curriculum was reasonably balanced, and looked impressive (for those inspectors who never came back!).

We used this system for about eighteen months, after which it gradually 'died the death'. After two and a half years' intense focus on Stephen's education, I felt drained and exhausted, unable to continue, and just waiting for when he could try school again.

Taking on the LEA

My exhaustion was exacerbated by a protracted tussle with the LEA. After Stephen had been out of school for a year, we approached some schools with a view to trying part-time attendance. We were clear that full-time attendance was unrealistic, but Stephen was having very little contact with his peers, and I needed more time for his baby sister.

When we first joined Education Otherwise, there were regular local meetings and we went along. However, Stephen not only did not make friends easily, he also upset some of the other families. We made one useful contact with a child he saw regularly for about a year, until the other boy returned to school, but the meetings soon ceased anyway, as the local co-ordinator stopped organising them.

Once we had talked to schools, it became clear that Stephen would need a statement of special educational needs (SEN) before we could get anywhere. This completely contradicted the view given by the educational psychologist after his diagnosis that a statement was unnecessary and irrelevant.

When we asked the LEA to assess him for statementing, they replied that they could only do so if he were already in school. Since we were not prepared to put him into school unsupported, we were in a 'catch-22' situation. We successfully appealed to the SEN tribunal, a process that took most of a year as well as endless time, paperwork and meetings.

The tribunal itself was a formality, since the LEA were acting illegally by not considering all the evidence before refusing to assess him. However, the subsequent process of assessment and finding a school took most of another year. It was difficult to be wholly committed to home education in the midst of such uncertain and protracted negotiations, especially as I kept hoping for a sharing of the burden. It was when I was most exhausted and in need of help that I also lacked the energy to try to find any support. I suspect this is a common dilemma.

School again: 10½ –12 years old

Stephen started school again almost exactly three years after he had left. This time he was in a middle school, only part time, and with a support worker. To begin with, it went very well, but as his hours increased, so did the problems, and he left again a year later.

There were fundamental difficulties in the way in which Stephen and the school viewed each other. Stephen did not learn from experience or exposure, and he lacked a sense of proportion or perspective. Having decided that he hated school, he persisted in this view even when there was evidence to the contrary. He might appear to be enjoying himself, but he would never admit it. He also could not recognise or express his emotional feelings, and was highly biased in his own favour when describing any incident. Thus we could not tell how things were going by talking to him, as one would normally expect to.

On the other hand, it is now clear (hindsight is a wonderful thing!) that the school viewed him with suspicion as a potential troublemaker, took him with reluctance, and focused on his difficulties rather than his considerable strengths.

For example, he arrived at the school just as they were doing the year six SAT exams, so he joined in and did extremely well—as I said before, he likes exams. When he got a level six in the maths exam, an exceptional result, instead of congratulating him, the teacher attributed it to his unfair advantage of having been at home and therefore having been taught extra topics. Whilst this was in one sense true, it was not making use of a success to help to build his self-esteem, which was still fragile. His life so far had been full of failure and disappointment.

In such a climate it was essential for us to have good communication with the auxiliary assistant, and for her to be sympathetic to Stephen, but unfortunately she was both badly matched (not tuned in to him at all) and also very defensive, taking our every remark as personal criticism. Our recommendations on how to handle him were ignored, and we were made to feel interfering and undermining of her authority when we tried to intervene.

Stephen was and is sometimes very difficult, but if we had been seen as partners rather than biased antagonists it would have helped. Generally, the school seemed to view parental involvement with suspicion. They were the 'experts'. Since we had kept Stephen at home, we were seen as over-anxious parents, biased about our son and ignorant of how he could best fit into school. By the time we had a showdown and insisted on being taken seriously, it was too late and the situation was irretrievable. If I had been more confident and assertive, I might have handled the situation better and avoided some of Stephen's worst experiences. On the other hand, the sharp deterioration prevented us staggering on longer, as we had at the previous school.

By this time we fully recognised the difficulty of finding a school to suit Stephen. If a school has an easygoing atmosphere, it may well be more accepting of Stephen, but he would not cope with a noisy or disruptive classroom, or the lack of clear rules and a predictable routine. A traditional quiet and orderly class suits Stephen much better; he says it is the only place he finds it easy to concentrate or work—hence his liking for exams; but a school in this mould is less tolerant of his behaviour and less willing to allow him any exceptions to their rigid rules, even if that is the only way he will be able to cope.

For example, the middle school had banned fountain pens, due to the silliness of some boys. Stephen has always had a lot of difficulty with writing, and he found any other kind of pen much harder to use, but they refused to make an exception. Instead they suggested that he should learn to use a laptop, which would have meant painfully acquiring new skills and also would have made it harder for him to write manually in the future. In general, the lack of flexibility meant the school expected him to do all the changing and fitting in, which was unrealistic and just setting him up for failure.

Despite our reservations, we decided to gamble on trying a third school. I was still desperately hoping that he would be able to reap all the positive benefits of school that I and my husband had appreciated, and that many children in our society still benefit from when their schooling goes well. I had also decided to home educate the two girls, one of them just for a year, and could not envisage coping with him, too, especially as he constantly got at, or even hurt, the sister who was just two years younger.

Stephen's stay at this school was by far the shortest (six weeks), but it had some positive outcomes. The school, which was private and academic, was positive about Stephen's high ability and wanted him to succeed—a welcome change from the negative focus of the other schools. Also, they treated us as experts on him, asking us to brief the staff and giving us full and serious attention.

For the first time, Stephen actually enjoyed being at school, found the lessons generally more interesting and even made friends. However, the effort of conforming was still a big strain, and he 'broke out' rather on Fridays. Also, the school had no mechanism for special needs or behavioural problems, and the deteriorating situation with other boys was not sufficiently monitored (breaks were unsupervised in the classroom) until it was too late and other parents started to complain. Nothing serious had happened, but the school took fright and decided Stephen should leave rather than take any chances with him. They did say that he could return if things improved sufficiently, but that is difficult to measure in abstract, and so he has not returned.

Both Stephen and I were desperately disappointed. I was still being too optimistic and unrealistic about his difficulties. I suppose I was still trying to get him onto the 'conveyor belt' which would lead to self-confidence, qualifications and a career. Stephen finds self-motivation so difficult that he will need the structure of a job if he is to achieve fulfilment and self-sufficiency. This is much easier with academic qualifications, which are simpler to obtain through a school or college, especially for practical subjects and coursework. Stephen also finds the structure and expectations of an institution helpful.

It was at this point, when the last and best chance had failed, that I fully accepted and recognised Stephen's AS as a genuine and lifelong handicap. Stephen was very upset and angry, then depressed. For the first time, he had actually wanted to stay at school, but not been allowed to. Previously he had been more than happy to say 'goodbye' to schools and clubs where it hadn't worked, a bit like Coriolanus's 'I banish you.' He liked this school, especially for teaching him a card trading game called *Magic: the Gathering*, which rapidly became the obsession to end all obsessions. Indeed his obsession with it hastened his exit from the school, for it was when he was upset at a game going badly that his anger spilt over into lesson times.

Unlike the other children, he had no instinct for when it was 'safe' to play up (*i.e.*, out of sight of authority). Schools always treat visible crimes more seriously, and this unwritten rule, well understood by other children, always causes problems for those with AS. Indeed, it was a major cause of his problems at all three schools, as there were plenty of children who behaved badly, but took care to do it out of the sight of teachers.

It was in many ways easier not to be in school. Despite the stress of having Stephen full time, we avoided the debilitating effort of endless meetings and negotiations, not to mention the constant anxiety of waiting for the telephone to ring with another bad tale of what Stephen had done.

Home again—this time to stay

We started full time at home again over two years ago, when Stephen was twelve. This time we had vague hopes of a return to the last school in a year or two's time, depending on progress. We decided we must have tutors for some subjects, especially as I had the girls too, and the school offered to help us find some. In particular, they came up with a French tutor, and also lent us some textbooks. The tutors not only took some of my load, but also encouraged some independence in Stephen.

The subjects we targeted for tutoring were those we would find difficult to cover, which he had some interest in, or which we could find tutors for. This led to French, Latin and chemistry. After a few months, we also decided to enrol him on a distance learning course for GCSE English with Open Learning Centre International, to try to help structure and motivate his study.

We also decided to try the GCSE exam in maths, which we tutored, to try to give him a positive focus to work for. This was not always easy, and the administration required to enter as an independent candidate is not trivial, but we managed in the end. We chose the IGCSE, which has no coursework requirement. Stephen was pleased to be trying a GCSE exam so young; it boosted his self-confidence to have something positive to talk to people about and he liked impressing them! We still had to give him lots of encouragement, as maths is just something he is good at, not one of his real interests, but he enjoyed the exam and ended up with an 'A' grade.

This success not only encouraged us all, it also gave us an entry point into a local further education (FE) college. They were sympathetic to our position, and because Stephen had demonstrated that he could handle GCSE-level material, they decided to let him attend the physics GCSE class, although they had never had someone so young before. They also encouraged us to go on a trial basis, and were happy for me to accompany him. No one minded or teased, as he was so much younger than they were anyway. It was soon clear that he would be fine and that I was not needed, so I used to have a peaceful couple of hours in the library instead. By dint of encouragement, and careful coaching about when to get off the bus, eventually Stephen was able to travel there on his own sometimes, and now goes by bus to Latin as well.

His independence skills have come gradually and with endless encouragement. The key is for him to have sufficient incentive. When first out of school, he shadowed me everywhere. I managed to get him to go a few yards to the newspaper shop, but the real breakthrough came one day when he was desperate for chips (his food obsession), and I also had an exhausted toddler who was desperate to get home. In this dilemma he managed to force himself to go fifty yards down the road to the chip shop whilst I waited for him. From this success we gradually progressed to reasons why he would have to go alone from home to get them.

The first time he went to college alone was when I had to stay with his little sister, who was ill, so the choice was to go on his own or miss the class (he prided himself on his 100% attendance). Similarly, he can now go to town alone, because he gets his new *Magic* cards or computer game faster that way. What we need now are some incentives for him to learn to cook or wash himself regularly!

During the past academic year, his timetable (which he insisted I stuck to even when he didn't) included an outing virtually every day, whether to French, Latin, chemistry or physics lessons. He was always more grumpy and unco-operative on the days when there was not a fixed external point for him to focus on. This summer, at age fourteen, he passed physics GCSE with a 'B' and English GCSE with an 'A', and got a 'B' in one module of a maths 'A' level.

The English exam really highlighted some of the problems AS can cause. Stephen's command of English is excellent, with a large fluent vocabulary. He hates written work (one of the biggest causes of tension at school was the emphasis on neat handwriting and pointless copying out), but when he is inspired, his imaginative writing is good enough to have won prizes in local competitions. However, he has great difficulty with anything personal or emotional, as required by many of the exercises beloved of English courses.

Nevertheless, the course was going pretty well, so we decided to enter for the exam. I was proud of the way he knuckled down to the coursework, even taking care with presentation, but when we saw the exam papers, we nearly despaired.

To begin with, there were questions he refused even to attempt, and all of the questions were compulsory. In a panic, we contacted his distance learning tutor, a friendly Welsh lady. She did not really understand the problem; after all, most people like to write about themselves, or their favourite celebrity, or whatever! However, she gave him a pep talk and suggested we should arrange for him to have some extra time, which we duly did on the strength of his statement (about all the use it's been!). In the end, he didn't use the extra time, but it gave him some breathing space to react to unfortunate questions if necessary.

For the past eighteen months, we have actually had a sympathetic professional (a speech therapist) on our side. She has taken time to get to know Stephen, included him in some social skills classes at a local special school and come to meetings with me when appropriate. She has also arranged for him to have a social worker and hence a support worker at a local club, which worked for a while.

It has made such a difference to have support from within the system, and I feel less isolated and beleaguered. The speech therapist also encouraged us to pursue the LEA over funding. As a result, they have agreed this year to fund Stephen from home. That is, they have accepted their legal responsibility, and acknowledged that what we do is not from choice, but from lack of appropriate provision. Therefore they pay not only for his tutors, *etc.*, but also towards some of my time costs!

Emboldened by our successes last year, Stephen is taking four more GCSEs at the college this year. So far he is coping with being there for between two and five hours a day, and doing all the travelling on his own. He loves being treated in such an adult way, and has never seemed so happy. He is even starting to chat to some students, although others find him irritating. It helps that he is large for fourteen and his voice is already broken, and that the other students have grown out of the worst habits of his own age group. Anyway he has a few other friends of his age, especially another boy with AS whom he sees often.

The college seems to offer a useful compromise, a 'third way' that is neither home nor school. Since lots of people there attend part time or have special needs or both, and since there is a huge age range, he actually sticks out less than anywhere else he has been. It is a measure of their flexibility that last year, if my alternative arrangements for his little sister fell through, there was no problem with her sitting with me in the coffee bar or library, although she was only six! In any case, he is now so 'out of line' with school (ahead in some subjects, behind in others), there is no point our even considering it!

A typical day

Like many adolescents, Stephen hates getting up in the mornings! I was pleased when a recent article in *New Scientist* reinforced my belief that regular hours are better for you, so I generally try to get him out of bed by 8:30 a.m. or so. He then has his dry cereal (never with milk—he has some food phobias) and perhaps toast before he disappears to his room again.

He is supposed to start work at 9:00 a.m., but almost never does—he loves getting away with things. Also, these days he is often going out to college at 9:00 a.m. or before. We had a good patch when he did some of the exercises from Madeleine Portwood's book *Developmental Dyspraxia*, and this went quite well until he got bored with them. Otherwise he might manage a bit of homework or a maths question or two, but usually reluctantly.

The focus is always on break time. This means rushing up to his room to slump hunched on his bed with a book or magazine. If he has been out most of the morning, then he will still insist on his statutory break when he returns. A stroll through the park on his way home from college or a browse in the second-hand shops on his way home from Latin does not count as a break in his eyes. This break often slides into lunchtime, which is also a rigidly defined break with an unalterable minimum of ninety minutes and an unlimited maximum.

In general, Stephen sees all work as an evil to be negotiated away or absentmindedly forgotten in order to increase his breaks. Sometimes I think that he sees it all as a game, and that he enjoys all the arguing and negotiating that I find so stressful and debilitating. For if I suggest that I stop trying to structure his time, he is very clear that he wants me to do it, even if he always kicks against it. Nowadays, as an adolescent, he seems particularly to enjoy pitting his wits against mine, especially when he wins. Perhaps he will end up as a barrister or politician!

Once it gets to about three o'clock, Stephen finds himself unable to work until late in the evening. However, he also likes to have a set time for his favourite activity, computer games. He gets very agitated if this is late or missed for any reason, although it is fine for it to be 'accidentally' extended!

For a few months, he had a fixed computer time between four and five o'clock. Next we tried a later time, for several reasons. Computer games are his current obsession and, as Tony Attwood says, we feel it is important to try to manage or contain his obsessions, as otherwise they dominate the whole of his and the family's life. Our current notional limit of an hour is frequently exceeded, but his acceptance of it means that, at least sometimes, we can insist on keeping to it without too much strife.

However, he got so used to the four o'clock time for computer games that it was becoming a restriction on days out. He is never ever keen to go out of the house (he accepts routine visits to tutors, but anything else is resented), but usually will relax and enjoy the outing once it is a *fait accompli*. For a while, though, he became very agitated if we got to the magic hour of four o'clock and he was not back at home zapping monsters. A trip he was actually happy with would suddenly become a disaster to be bitterly rued (from his viewpoint, not ours).

To resolve this conflict, we tried moving the statutory hour to later in the evening. This had the advantage that earlier computing time could be offered as a bonus rather than a right, but the drawback that the games left him in an overexcited state in the late evening, which kept him awake longer in bed. Also, he resented the change. Recently, he has reverted to an earlier time without its being so fixed, which we hope will keep everyone happy.

Although a lot of the effect of the computer on him is negative, it has also enabled some important breakthroughs. I think this is what Tony Attwood means by 'managing obsessions': they can be used as an opportunity for growth. Computer games are a common interest for boys of his age, so have been a means of Stephen's making one or two new, if sporadic, friends. Secondly, the advent of a new computer with some of the latest games has helped him to maintain his long-standing friendship with another 'eccentric'. Thirdly, he is learning some group co-operation and turn taking from the multi-player game *Worms*. He has even 'managed' a game of this involving four or five players, without any serious disagreements!

Slowly and painfully, he is learning not to shout all the time, nor to give a constant running commentary like a sports commentator, nor to get too upset if they win and he loses. He still gets very upset when his games go wrong, but is gradually recovering faster and raging less violently. Recently we have even managed to interest him in writing his own games. It has taken a lot of time and patience from his father to get him interested, but he is now very self-motivated and keen to work on it.

After tea there is the usual battle over homework, which he always refuses to do any earlier in the day. What generally happens is that he insists it will take hours and he's too tired, *etc.* After a long drawn-out argument, perhaps half an hour, he will finally settle to it, often after 9:00 p.m. He then dashes it off, often sloppily, in about fifteen minutes. He seems unable to remember this, and the next day we go through the same rigmarole all over again.

It is as if he cannot remember the many good experiences, when the homework was easy, but focuses on the rare bad time, when he had to struggle a bit, and then assumes it will always be like that. Recently, the college structure has also helped him to get homework done more positively, and we are getting fewer and shorter arguments. He is finally starting to take some responsibility for managing his own time and learning to cope with bad experiences—perhaps because he has fewer of them.

Until recently, our lives were dominated by the way in which one bad experience could put him off permanently. Whether it was a food, a game or an outing, only one hundred per cent consistency was acceptable. The ninety-nine good times were irrelevant if once we slipped up. We may have been having a successful and enjoyable day out, but let one thing go wrong (such as not being back for computer time at 4:00 p.m.) and immediately the whole day was a failure in his eyes.

This negative approach seemed intractable. It led him to a restricted and predictable diet and a preference for staying indoors, either in his room or on the computer. When we wished to take him out, we had to insist on his coming, and then put up with the inevitable grumbles even when he was patently enjoying himself. However, he is gradually coming to accept the inevitable and to acquire a sense of proportion when things go wrong. Recently he has been heard to say that it has been a good day, despite not everything being perfect.

Bedtime is notionally 10:00 p.m., but again, this is a rule just waiting to be undermined. At least the light is usually off by 10:30 p.m., and then peace reigns until the next morning. When he was younger, he did have some sleep problems, including night terrors, but perhaps because my sleep is so essential to me, bed is one battle we managed to win when he was a toddler, and he now prefers just to lie quietly if he can't sleep.

Reflections on Stephen's label

There are both advantages and disadvantages for Stephen in his label of Asperger's syndrome. The drawback is that people can pigeonhole him: they may assume that he has a standard set of characteristics or that his behaviour is inevitably 'skewed'. There is also a danger that providing a label is seen as some kind of solution to a problem child, meaning that the professional can stop thinking about him, rather than an inadequate model which is just a starting point for finding appropriate provision, always open to refinement and revision. Psychiatry is inevitably an inexact and provisional science, because people are endlessly complex and variable, always capable of surprising or astounding us and defying any label which seeks to restrict their potential.

The diagnosis also gave me a huge shock, like that of bereavement. I had painfully to discard much of my rosy-tinted view of my child, and learn all over again how to love him and relate to him. The advantage was that I started to have more realistic expectations and to make more appropriate allowances for him. I also had the gigantic relief of no longer feeling consumed with guilt for being a useless or failing mother. Just as it was not all my fault, so nor was it all Stephen's fault either. We had to move away from a culture of blame and see the problem as external, and one on which we could work together constructively.

Because autism is a spectrum which shades into normality, it is important to be clear why a label is needed. My experience has led me to the criterion that a person needs a diagnosis if life is a mess without it, and if the label is one which will help to make sense of and sort out that mess. However, 'if it ain't broke, don't fix it.'

I reckon I know a number of people who would fit the criteria for Asperger's syndrome, but I can see no useful purpose in pursuing the issue, since they have found an acceptable *modus vivendi* without any such label. Others may see them as eccentric or odd, but humanity needs the richness and variety they provide—and who is normal anyway?

I would even argue that it was easier in the past for such individuals to survive without special attention, as life was more ordered and predictable, and social rules generally more consistent and explicit. Also, I believe that less was expected of young children socially, in terms of relating well to their peers. There are other conditions, such as attention deficit disorder (ADD), that have also suddenly become more common and I do think we need to ask why we suddenly have such a mass of labels applied to so many children. Are we being unrealistic about what children are naturally like?

When we look at our family characteristics, it is quite easy to see Stephen's difficulties as an unfortunate combination of inherited tendencies. Whatever the cause, the fact is that in his critical early years

Stephen did not have the usual basic social instincts, and we did not recognise that he needed explicit extra help with them. If he had had a diagnosis earlier and some appropriate help, then maybe our lives would have been different. Before the diagnosis, we found his inability to learn endlessly frustrating, and we wasted energy and stress in futile attempts to change him.

I now think, ironically, that it is fortunate that Stephen's autism protected him from the full effect of his negative experiences at school. His insensitivity to others and his natural resilience may be infuriating, but they have helped him to survive in intolerable situations.

Yes, he hated school, but mostly because the work seemed boring and irrelevant and he was not able to choose how he spent his time. We still suffer from the legacy of that burning resentment. However, he never really felt or understood his effect on others, nor showed any shame or embarrassment. When things went wrong, in his mind it was always the fault of his 'enemies'. His self-centredness and lack of remorse may have perpetuated the bad situation, but they also stopped him from being depressed by it.

We have consistently been told by professionals that we are depriving our child of his best chance to learn normal social skills by keeping him out of school. Our experience has been the opposite.

Stephen first started to notice and react to other people's feelings when he first came out of school, as he then began to notice when his baby sister was crying and rush to tell me. Her obvious and simply expressed needs impinged on him as no one else had done, and helped him to develop important social skills. For the first time, he started to differentiate in his approach to people. He spoke to her in a simple way, held her gently and played simple games to amuse her. This was a marked contrast to the uniform way in which he treated everyone else, from toddlers to headmasters!

By contrast, the social skills he was acquiring at school were mostly negative, to do with teasing, bullying and isolation. A school playground can be the loneliest place in the world for the child who has no friends. We do have to learn how to get on with people we don't like, but schools are not necessarily good at this. For a child like Stephen, who generally relates better to those who are older or younger rather than his peers, it is easier to acquire social confidence and skills in the more natural community at home than in the very artificial community of school, where you are forced to be with your age group all the time.

Some general reflections on our experience

As parents we constantly make choices for our children. Whether to home educate is perhaps one of the more important ones, but every day has little decisions in it and some of those are hard, too. As W H Vanstone writes, in his book *Love's Endeavour, Love's Expense*:

> Love proceeds by no assured programme. In the care of children a parent is peculiarly aware that each step of love is a step of risk; and that each step taken generates the need for another and equally precarious step. In each word of encouragement lies the danger of creating over-confidence; in each restraint the danger of destroying confidence.

If my son had not had Asperger's syndrome, I might have been spared much stress, anguish and failure. However, I would also have avoided many valuable and maturing experiences which have changed me for the better. It is because parenting Stephen involves walking such a difficult tightrope between encouragement and restraint, where failure is frequent and costly, that I identify so closely with what Vanstone says. Later in the same passage, he writes:

> A happy family life is neither a static situation nor a smooth and direct progression: it is an angular progress, the endless improvisation of love to correct that which it has itself created. [...] The care of children teaches us that the resolute and unfailing will of love becomes active in improvised and ever-precarious endeavour.

He wrote this out of his experience as a parent and, like him, it is only when I have been pushed to the very edge of existence, feeling that I can no longer cope or go on, that I have been able to grasp the most fundamental truths about the nature of love, its precariousness and its colossal demands of faith and hope. As Vanstone also says, 'Truth is grasped in the boundary situation.' Deciding to home educate has often made me feel marginalised, but this has given me a clearer understanding of society and how it works.

Whether I see our experience in a positive or a negative way depends very much on how I am feeling and whether we have hit a crisis. The same glass can be viewed as half full or half empty. In the past, I have found it too easy to view Stephen's AS with bitterness or despair. However, during the past two months he has made massive progress, and at the moment life is wonderful—like a rebirth! I now find it easier to think spontaneously of Stephen's many good qualities and advantages.

His honesty and straightforwardness are very likable, as are his sense of humour and youthful enthusiasm. Increasingly, he is a companion and 'good company'. We can enjoy a shared joke or a mild tease, when his eyes will catch mine meaningfully, and sometimes we have genuine conversations. We delight in his real progress in self-restraint and his increasing demonstrations of concern for other people, especially when they are in tears. His self-esteem has obviously increased, and he now wants to 'fit in' and be seen as normal by other people.

On balance, Stephen is now no more 'difficult' than many teenagers. For many parents it can come as a shock to find that their delightful child has metamorphosed overnight into a sullen stranger, whereas for us it is a delight and relief to have a son who now tends to argue only as much as many boys of his age, rather than about everything incessantly!

Overall I am convinced that, whatever other mistakes we may have made as parents, our decision to home educate was definitely not one of them. I certainly regret sending him to school at the tender age of four, and our subsequent attempts to integrate him into the school system. I may regret or resent the sacrifices I have had to make in order for Stephen to stay at home, but I am in no doubt that it has been in his best interests, given the alternatives currently on offer.

I may have a utopian vision of a school based on open, flexible learning like the FE college model, but that may not be realistic for most children either. After all, most children enjoy and even thrive on the current system. What is needed is a recognition that school is actually harmful to some children, that they deserve better, and that, at least for some families, home is currently the best way to provide it.

5

Is this normal?
Kevin's story

Jackie Stout

Kevin was twisting his head about, unable to satisfy himself or go to sleep. It was nine o'clock in the evening and I was near tears after nursing him continuously since morning. I was desperate for rest, and no amount of singing, rocking, or nursing was taking me in that direction. I called my La Leche League leader and asked her, 'Is this normal?' She explained that Kevin was breastfeeding overtime to build my milk supply for a typical three-week growth spurt. What she said next made a lasting impression on me. Her words became my mantra and the life-long basis of my child-rearing and educational philosophy. She advised, 'Whatever Kevin does is normal for Kevin.'

Through the years, I held on to the belief that Kevin's unique and puzzling blend of characteristics was 'normal for Kevin'. When he was younger, I had seen the term Asperger's syndrome (AS), but dismissed the diagnosis after reading the word 'autism'. My son was not autistic. He was normal. Then one day, almost five years after I had begun homeschooling Kevin, I was scanning Internet web sites and clicked on OASIS, the acronym for 'Online Asperger's Syndrome Information and Support', a web site (www.aspergersyndrome.org) owned by Barbara Kirby.

I read the history of Hans Asperger and then the modern-day description of AS. My heart skipped beats as I recognized all of the characteristic AS traits. Kevin was fifteen years old. I had always instinctively modified his world to provide whatever he wanted or needed. I had rejected mainstream advice, well-meaning relatives, medical opinion, school authority, and anyone or anything that interfered with my unwavering belief in him. I viewed him as not merely normal, but spectacular. I was the expert on Kevin. No one understood him or cared for him as I did. Now, with one stroke on the keyboard, I learned that my son had Asperger's syndrome. My mind drifted back to the many times when Rick and I had thought Kevin was different from our other children, to the times when we briefly allowed ourselves to wonder if maybe something might be wrong with him.

'Sis boom ba!' Rick would smile and shake Kevin's belly as he surprised him with nonsensical sounds. At only three weeks old, Kevin would giggle and laugh like a much older baby. Yet, when I bundled him next to my chest in a Snuggly sack and tried to vacuum, Kevin screamed, not fearfully, but as if in horrible pain. This happened so consistently, we began to vacuum only when one of us took Kevin out of the house.

I now know that Kevin has hyperacusis, one of the many sensitivities common to children with Asperger's syndrome. While Kevin loves certain sounds, others cause him pain. Complex guitar and drum patterns, especially those with odd time signatures, are pleasant to his ear and appeal to his kinesthetic senses. Others, like the whirring of a blender or static on the car radio, are excruciating to him.

From infancy, Kevin enjoyed my singing and reading aloud. I was sure that I had fostered his love of reading from time *in utero* when I read him my college literature assignments. So what if he preferred *Pudgy* books? By the time Kevin was three, it was clear that he possessed an unusual vocabulary, even though his speech was difficult to understand. Many of our neighbors called him 'the little professor'. He often asked complex questions about power and electricity, and once led me through the steps to making an electromagnet from a fork, copper wire and a battery. It worked! Kevin loved to read the Roma Gans *I Can Read and Find Out* science series while still a pre-schooler. I picked up the book *Does This Mean My Child is a Genius?* by Linda Perigo Moore and wondered....

Some of Kevin's interests seemed a little odd to us. At age two, he asked for a rubber chicken and a whoopee cushion. By age five he had memorized the Swiss Colony cheese catalog and asked for *petit fours* and an executive gift basket for Christmas (he got the *petit fours*). The same year, Kevin found *A Bartender's Guide* and committed the entire book to memory. He is still looking forward to being twenty-one so he can try a White Russian. His precocious verbal abilities, unusual interests, and excellent memory are classic AS traits.

Kevin's homeschooling experience began almost before he was born. For the first eighteen months of his life, he had his dad and me all to himself for reading, taking long walks, and playing. Our home turned into non-stop activity and fun with the addition of his sister Laryn, and soon after, his brother Ben. Our house was a wall-to-wall Toyland, with experiments in progress and stacks of books covering the counters and tables. Paint, feathers, paste and macaroni were staples in our cupboards. On rainy days, we danced for hours around our living room, and in the winter we built elaborate snowmen and decorated cookies. In the middle of the kitchen floor, my children made wonderfully messy casseroles of eggs, flour, cereal, coffee, and assorted ingredients, while I marveled at their creativity. My father-in-law, an elementary school principal, prophesied, 'They're not going to want to go to school. They're having too much fun at home.'

Kevin was nearly five when we began thinking about preparing him for school. We selected a three-days-per-week program at our local YMCA. We had an inkling that Kevin's motor development was not like other children's his age, since he couldn't use scissors, was less adept than Laryn with crafts, couldn't catch a ball, ran a little 'funny', and sounded different from other children when he spoke. We thought pre-school would round him out for Kindergarten.

Kevin refused to color or complete worksheets in pre-school, but since I thought they were a waste of time and creativity, I was unconcerned. I was sure such things were boring and patronizing to him. Near the end of the second session, it was time for the children to learn to swim, but Kevin refused to enter the pool. I came to the YMCA and got in the water with him. Kevin clung to me, absolutely petrified. Years later, he explained that he was given a picture of an octopus in a swimming pool to color on the day before entering the water. Kevin assumed he would be swimming with an octopus and deduced that this was an unsafe venture.

At the end of the pre-school program, I met with the teachers to discuss his progress. I refused to believe them when they told me they thought Kevin was an abnormal five-year-old. They said he seemed unaware of other children and didn't care about others. That's because he's so intelligent, I countered, feeling they just didn't understand that Kevin was on a higher plane. Furthermore, they said he couldn't write his name, was deficient in motor skills, and needed to be evaluated for speech.

This information was coming from two women whom I regarded as arts and crafts teachers, certainly not people as well read as I about individual developmental differences and advanced intellectual abilities. I walked away upset that my son had been misjudged. I know now that the teachers were responding to behaviors typical of young AS children: literal thinking, poor motor skills, and oftentimes what appears to be little empathy or concern for others (which is, in fact, an inability to read facial expressions or intuit what others are thinking or feeling).

That summer I took Kevin to a speech pathologist, who found omissions of some letter sounds and a rate and rhythm disorder. She predicted his speech would improve in diction and pronunciation, but would retain a distinctive quality, comparing him to the American sportscaster Howard Cosell. Mrs. Addy told me there was something odd about Kevin, besides the fact that he kept breaking his pencils and falling off his chair.

One day, as I pulled into her driveway, Mrs. Addy ran out to the car shouting, 'I know what's different about Kevin!' At the age of five and a half, he had scored at a sixteen-year-old level on a Peabody Visual Word Recognition test for vocabulary. This was the highest score Mrs. Addy had ever seen in a child this young. Many years later, we would recognize his speech distinction and unusual vocabulary as being a hallmark feature of AS known as pedantic speech.

As Kindergarten edged closer, Rick and I became concerned that Kevin's delayed motor skills might prevent school success. We consulted an orthopedist, who reassured us that Kevin was on the low end of normal in motor skills. He suggested a psychoeducational evaluation to rule out other problems.

Rick and I took Kevin to a group of experts who came highly recommended. After two days of testing, the doctors announced their findings: Kevin had oppositional defiant disorder (ODD), attention deficit disorder (ADD), and was at least two years behind in motor skills. They recommended Ritalin, occupational and behavioral therapy, and predicted poor school success.

Rick felt torn between what his own medical training was telling him to believe, his deep worries for his first-born son, and his need for denial. I flatly refused to trust assertions that were in direct contradiction to what I saw in my everyday life with Kevin. I told the doctors they were wrong about my son.

We went home and I began teaching Kevin how to write his name. We traced the letters in rice and sand, shaped each one from home-made play dough, and laid out our bodies and brooms on the floor to spell K-E-V-I-N. Using a chunky pencil with a special grip and large sheets of paper, he connected dot-to-dot images of each letter. Eventually, Kevin was able to scrawl the letters of his name on a single sheet of paper by imprisoning them in little cages with bars.

Ignoring medical advice, and without providing any medical history, I enrolled Kevin in public school. His Kindergarten teacher was nurturing and developmentally oriented, and agreed that Kevin was on his own timeline. I was satisfied that I had done the right thing.

First grade was fairly uneventful for Kevin, except for difficulty with increased writing demands and little social interaction. Kevin's second-grade teacher had done her master's thesis on attention deficit disorder and was certain that Kevin had ADD. Rick and I conferred with the teacher, principal, an occupational therapist, the speech therapist, and school counselor about Kevin's inability to finish his work at school, his lack of friendships, and his unflinching verbal candor.

The school officials pronounced Kevin to be lazy, unmotivated, and probably poorly disciplined at home. I defended him, noting his accelerated reading ability, and comparing him to his younger sister Laryn, who was in first grade down the hall from Kevin. They had the same home life, I pointed out. She was performing academically and behaviorally at a level higher than any other child in her class.

Rick and I believed these rural school people to be lazy and unmotivated themselves, but we were feeling insecure in the face of so many negative voices. Once again we took Kevin to another reputable group of specialists. This time he was diagnosed with ADD, and proclaimed learning disabled (LD) and gifted and talented (GT). Their findings, based on tests that I now realize were not designed for children with AS (especially the WISC-III, which presumes a knowledge of social nuances and is timed), included symptoms of nonverbal learning disabilities. We were told this was consistent with right hemispheric brain dysfunction. They recommended Ritalin. We were cautioned that denying Kevin this medication would be like keeping insulin from a diabetic or nitroglycerin tablets from a chest pain victim. We tried it. After an initial positive response, Ritalin was largely ineffective, an experience common to many AS children who have been misdiagnosed with ADD.

Our neighborhood became a lonely and unfriendly place for Kevin. Children quit inviting him to birthday parties. They didn't understand his ideas or vocabulary, and some made fun of him. He reacted strongly to teasing that other kids took in stride, and the neighbors began to think Kevin was different from their own children. An acquaintance stopped at our driveway one day to chat. When Kevin approached, the man good-naturedly said, 'Hi, buddy,' and threw a few air punches at him. Kevin, believing himself to be attacked, flew at the man with a garden rake.

It became increasingly difficult to relate to other parents. Like any mother, I looked to other mothers for support, but instead I received awkward silences and looks of reproach when I told them stories about

Kevin. They thought we were indulgent, and Kevin strange. Rick and I decided to begin afresh in another community and school district, so I researched school districts for a high-quality gifted education program and an understanding of learning differences, and we moved.

I shared parts of Kevin's second psychoeducational evaluation with the new school. The doctor had suggested some accommodations such as shorter written assignments and multiple-choice testing. The teaching staff and principal were fairly receptive to Kevin's GT/LD/ADD label. The third-grade teacher was accustomed to disorganized kids. Shockingly, many of her students, mostly boys, were taking Ritalin. She patiently structured Kevin's school life and allowed him academic shortcuts like answering essay questions orally and forgoing study guides.

Mrs. Russell liked Kevin, and although she thought him cheeky at times for correcting her, appreciated his quirky humor and great vocabulary. In the middle of third grade, she recommended him for the gifted and talented language arts program. With some trepidation, the GT teacher accepted Kevin; she was concerned that Kevin might have trouble with the performance aspects of her class.

In fourth grade, his teacher saw that, although Kevin had extreme difficulty memorizing simple math facts, he understood many advanced concepts. Again, he attended the daily GT language arts program, and, intermittently, support services for handwriting remediation (ultimately, a futile exercise). Difficulty with rote memorization of math facts and dysgraphia (handwriting difficulty) are both often seen in children with AS.

Those two years at the end of his public education were the most trying for Kevin and our family. In the classroom, Kevin was scoring 100% on multiple-choice tests, and learning concepts with ease. He knew more obscure and general facts than any of his classmates, yet he was not able to tie his shoes or keep up with the writing demands of his GT classes. Every night, Kevin dictated his assignments, and I diligently wrote his words. Every task was a struggle to complete, oftentimes requiring me to pull responses out of Kevin. Even though his speaking was littered with extended metaphors and brilliant associations common to natural writers, he couldn't put together even the simplest writing assignment without my outlining his ideas and leading him through the process.

I was called to the school frequently for ridiculous, non-academic complaints from teachers. Once, Kevin's music teacher complimented him in class for correctly answering a question about Mozart, and he told her, 'Quit staring at me, you look like Scruffy the Puppy.' He reacted like most children with AS who are singled out: he uttered the first idea that popped into his head, unable to fathom why the truth shouldn't be told. Needless to say, his music teacher thought he was being intentionally disrespectful.

I was aware of the academic and behavioral stresses of school, but had no real idea of the scope of the emotional torture Kevin was subjected to until later. Initially, he was happier socially at his new school. He hung out on the playground and ate lunch with two other atypical and intelligent boys. They walked around talking about googolplexes and finding odds and ends on the playground, while most children played kickball and tag. Still, there were boys who homed in on Kevin's vulnerabilities, harassing him almost daily with taunts of 'fag' and 'retard'.

School stresses accumulated, causing problems at home. Rick and I had conflicts over Kevin's performance, behaviors, and needs. I was changing from a fun-loving, patient mother into a joyless homework sergeant who didn't have time for her other children. Worst of all, Kevin was becoming depressed. He held it together while he was away from home, but ranted and cried in his room each day after school.

One day, I was invited to attend a school celebration. Kevin's class was sitting on the curb, the children laughing and poking each other playfully, watching a band marching by. Kevin sat hunched over, talking to no one, with his eyes half closed and his mouth hanging open. At age ten, he looked old and sad and tired. I realized that enough was enough.

My son needed rescuing. I consulted Dr. Linda Silverman from the Center for Gifted Development in Denver, Colorado, who studied asynchronous learners—highly gifted children with areas of extreme weakness and unusual sensitivities. I believed this description might be a fit for Kevin. She suggested to me that I homeschool Kevin, and scoffed at my question, 'But what about socialization?' After reading several books, including *Homeschooling For Excellence*, by David and Micki Colfax, I felt sure we had found the right path for Kevin. Rick and Kevin weren't too sure about doing something so unconventional, so radical, but I pushed forward, knowing that Kevin could not survive any more public education.

Initially, I loosely followed the school's curriculum, thinking that we might homeschool for only a year, and that Kevin would be prepared academically to return to public school if the experiment didn't work. We began in our basement with a large desk, bookshelves filled, and a computer by our side, spending three to four hours each morning on 'school work'. The afternoons belonged to Kevin.

Those first few months were ones of discovery. By pre-testing Kevin orally before we read the material, I discovered that he already knew everything in the fifth-grade science text, most of the sixth, and scattered information from much higher levels. I found Kevin to have a great knowledge and love of history, and that he didn't need to be in a chair or looking at me to be completely aware of everything he heard. He could more easily interact and learn if he was untwisting paper clips or chewing on paper bits.

Allotting scheduled times for each subject wasn't optimal for Kevin, because we frequently ended up spending all of our time on one or two topics, and because Kevin's desire to know and discuss didn't end when 'class' was over. He spent his free time playing computer games like *Sim City*, effortlessly absorbing details of city government, civil engineering, and economics. Other times, he ran errands with me, talking a mile a minute about an infinite variety of topics.

Projects in school had been a disaster, but at home Kevin was free to follow through on his own ideas. His first project was to shape and bake a chess set from blocks of black and white Sculpey (polymer clay). Kevin was enjoying learning, smiling and laughing again, and quickly returned to his generally charming self. One-on-one teaching and guiding was just the ticket for him. Kevin could be 'normal' at home.

Writing independently was Kevin's weakest area, so I devised ways to encourage composition and organization of his thoughts, including signing Kevin up for private keyboarding and computer lessons. Over a two-year period, he became a very capable keyboarder. I used techniques from books on learning disabilities to encourage Kevin to think of ideas, like story starters—cards with odd pictures. He made headlines from unusual newspaper articles, dictated bizarre little stories to me, and wrote character descriptions.

Writing caused Kevin great anxiety, so we worked in smaller chunks for shorter periods. It was vital that whatever we did together was fun and attractive to him. Often, he would reject and avoid various attempts I made to encourage writing, either by becoming upset or distracting me by delivering completely off-the-subject information. Still, Kevin enjoyed talking and was happy to have personal attention from someone who was hanging on his every word.

Eventually, he became interested in composing dialogue to go along with claymation films he created with Laryn, Ben, and his friend Oliver (who Kevin says does not have AS, but is definitely not neurotypical). One day, Kevin was dictating a script and became quite aggravated by my lack of typing speed. He pushed me aside, and has been composing and typing his own work ever since. He has written extensively, including a dark comedy series of irreverent, strange, and decidedly adolescent stories about a character named Gerbert. Like most people with AS, Kevin needs to have a large sense of control over any endeavor, in order to maintain a sense of internal control and ability to focus.

Math was another anxiety producer for Kevin. In school, much emphasis had been placed on the rote memorization of multiplication facts and, at first, I continued the attempt to get this essential information ingrained. Kevin became math phobic. To turn this around, I gave him a calculator and told him that calculation was merely the mechanics; concepts were the important part of math.

We disregarded pre-set, external expectations of age-appropriate performance and worked side by side, skimming through *Saxon Math 6/5*, doing only the odd-numbered problems and passing over concepts he knew. Kevin liked *Saxon Math* because the books didn't have distracting pictures or extraneous information. The ongoing review style of presentation cemented the concepts and bolstered his confidence. By the time he was fifteen, he was ready to begin Algebra I.

On rare occasions Kevin would request Ritalin to take just during math, but the results were so inconsistent and the intermittent side-effects of fatigue and fogginess so unpleasant, we both realized it was not a good choice. It was during this period that my doubts about Kevin's having ADD grew stronger. Whatever made focusing often difficult and unpredictable was unclear. I continued to explore many theories and diagnoses, but nothing seemed to fit. There was no other choice but to continue doing what worked for Kevin, and change the plan as often as necessary, sometimes daily. With homeschooling we had that option, and Kevin had the benefit of having his needs recognized and responded to promptly.

Like many people with Asperger's syndrome, Kevin has never particularly liked fiction literature. Looking back, I can see how the complexities of identifying with emotionally-motivated character relationships were quite irritating to him. At the time, I assumed his impatience with fiction was related to his intelligence, not the mind blindness associated with AS. 'He just can't be bothered with such trivia,' I thought, and concentrated on making sure he understood literary terms, symbolism, and genres.

Kevin read non-fiction avidly as his vocabulary, base of knowledge, and ability to make wildly unusual associations exploded. Over the years, he was occasionally drawn to fiction, and read *Dune*, *Jurassic Park*, the Orson Scott Card *Ender* series, and *Candide* by Voltaire. He has had a sporadic interest in science fiction.

Primarily, Kevin has gleaned information from television programs, magazines, and books on statistics and trivia. Instead of reading the newspaper, he prefers watching television news and following Internet news sites. He regularly reads many magazines, including *Discover*, *Popular Science*, *Time*, *Psychology Today*, and *Guitar Weekly*. Kevin is able to read difficult medical and scientific articles and recall them almost in their entirety. He usually talks with us about topics long before they appear in the popular media. To this day, he keeps abreast of current events, discoveries, and research with daily visits to his favorite Internet sites.

The freedom of home education has inspired Kevin's inherent, unquenchable, and unstoppable thirst to learn about the world. For example, during his early homeschooling years, he spent close to two years collecting and reading, researching and cross-referencing, memorizing and extemporizing on books relating to the game *Advanced Dungeons and Dragons*. Each detail he learned led to another question or interest, from myths to maps to world history and beyond. He utilized his favorite tool, the computer, for hours on end and often into the night, reading, learning, and thinking. Being a homeschooler gave him the time and resources to explore intensively and widely whatever he was interested in, whenever his personal level of coherence and energy allowed.

Kevin typifies a person with AS. He does not relate well to peers, due to his inability to understand nonverbal communication (which makes up seventy percent of communication). He has an aversion to peer involvement, stemming from many negative experiences with teens.

One day, I took Kevin and Oliver to the high school bookstore to purchase a biology book. Just as we arrived at the bookstore, the lunch bell rang. In an instant, the quiet hall roared to life with hundreds of teenagers. Kevin wanted to leave, but I coaxed him to wait. Almost immediately, two boys came up to Kevin and one said, 'He wants to date you.' Kevin was furious, anxious, and confused. He had barely captured my attention before a vice-principal approached, clamped his hand on Kevin's shoulder, and boomed out, 'You don't go to this school do you?' Oliver mumbled 'no' for Kevin, who was clenching and unclenching his fists. 'I knew that, because if you did, you wouldn't be wearing a hat,' the man snarled in Kevin's face. 'We don't wear hats in school! What are you doing here?' I removed Kevin's hat and explained our presence. We barely made it out of the building before Kevin exploded. It took two days to calm him, and we had only been visiting.

Kevin rarely participates in group activities outside of homeschooling. Although he is handsome and stands at six feet two inches tall, he has not gone through the usual teenage phases, such as caring in the slightest about clothing fads or using slang. He is concerned about attracting any kind of public attention. He refuses to attend a movie alone, for fear that his worst nightmare will come true: he might have to interact with teenagers.

During his adolescence, Kevin became more aware of being different from his peers. He isolated himself more from the few friends he had, preferring instead to spend hours alone in his room on his computer or watching his favorite television shows. The verbal expansiveness of Kevin's younger years turned into agonizing perseverations —repetitive, escalating monologues about personal concerns—as he became older. His anxieties multiplied as he began worrying endlessly. Kevin would ask me, 'What's wrong with me?' and pleaded, 'Please fix me.'

Although I was intensely concerned, I rationalized that Kevin was a worry-wart like his father and grandmother, was dramatic, and would grow out of this stage. I decided that he needed a skill to boost his confidence. Kevin was quite focused on rock 'n' roll, reading music lore encyclopedias, and watching MTV with his Dad, so I bought him an electric guitar and amplifier and insisted he take one lesson. He loved it! Despite his history of fine and gross motor deficits, Kevin learned to play the guitar, bass guitar, and the drums. He takes lessons weekly from musicians who have become mentors to him, and has become immersed in his musical interests. He is a self-styled expert on musicians and all varieties of guitars.

Kevin's life for the last four years has revolved around music. With his almost eidetic memory, he enjoys speaking at length about endless details of music minutiae. He also has spent some time composing complex drum patterns and guitar riffs. Having an intense, focused interest (or series of interests) is a distinctive feature of AS.

As Kevin became increasingly anxious, isolated, and unmotivated, we asked our pediatrician to prescribe Prozac. Kevin bounced back with interest in taking more music lessons and a little more energy. He continued, mostly unschooling, learning at a rapid rate. We attempted Algebra I, but Kevin became more anxious in direct relation to the number of variables in math problems, regardless of the texts or approaches we used.

He was fifteen years old, fretting about his future. Could he ever live on his own? Would he be a bum with pizza boxes and empty beer bottles strewn about his one-room apartment? Would he be able to get into a good college? He was intermittently unhappy and then energetically lecturing us on trivial information ranging from the difference between a stove-pipe hat and a top hat, through detailed mechanical descriptions of obscure guitars no longer manufactured, to vitriolic diatribes against environmentalists or whether right-wing fundamentalists were taking over the United States.

Oliver would come for visits from Chicago and they would spend the weekend entertained, spouting loud and loose teenage associations. We knew very well by this time that Kevin was not like other teenagers, but still believed that he would eventually grow out of what we thought of as immaturity.

I continued scanning web sites for glimpses of other children like Kevin, but I never found anyone remotely like him until the night I happened upon OASIS. Finally, we had an explanation. Kevin had Asperger's syndrome.

As luck would have it, a Most Able Autistic Persons (MAAP) conference was being held in Indianapolis the next month. Rick and I attended, and on the final day we brought Kevin for a few hours. As we walked around the hotel filled with parents, professionals, and people with AS, I was deeply moved to hear teenagers who sounded like Kevin, talking about subjects I thought only Kevin talked about. Tony Attwood gave the keynote speech. Temple Grandin spoke about her life. Every speaker gave information pertinent to Kevin and our family. Kevin was less receptive, as he sat playing air guitar and invisible drums and said, 'I've never seen so many pathetic people together in one place in my life.' He was offended that we saw any connection between them and him.

At the meeting, we ran into the psychologist who had evaluated Kevin in the past. He agreed that Kevin probably had Asperger's syndrome. He was sorry that the AS diagnosis had not been available to him at the time, and he wanted another chance to help our son. Kevin was tested yet again.

After two hours of mostly the WISC-III, and two fifteen-minute meetings with Kevin, the doctor reported his professional medical opinion to Rick and me. According to him, Kevin's IQ had dropped sharply because we had taken him out of school, he had regressed socially, and he was exhibiting almost psychotic thinking. Kevin had been quite amused with himself for making up what he considered to be clever stories about serial killers and lion tamers, instead of giving serious interpretations on picture-conclusion tests. The psychologist, like many who believe themselves to be knowledgeable about Asperger's syndrome, used these stories as evidence of Kevin's mental instability, instead of signs of his social immaturity.

I had learned enough about AS in the previous two months to know that his findings were wrong. Rick and I disagreed with the psychologist's recommendation to send Kevin back to high school, where teachers could encourage Kevin to retain his footing in reality, or worse, take him to Tri-County, an out-patient mental health facility. Once again, we were failed by medical experts who were supposed to know more than we did.

Vacation plans were already in place, so we went away battered and worn. We begged our pediatrician for a prescription for Buspar, but the drug did nothing to stem Kevin's anxiety. We spent three weeks in England, France, and Spain listening to Kevin perseverate on how Frenchmen hatched from croissants, and Spaniards were communists for not letting him buy an extra slice of cheese for his burger at McDonald's. London was the only city Kevin enjoyed, primarily because he understood the language and he could buy candies and cookies with different labels at the tiny stores outside our hotel. Public transportation with strangers speaking different languages and being forced to subsist on foods with foreign textures and spices were especially unpleasant to Kevin. Despite his disdain for sightseeing, and despite his spending some time alone in the hotel while the rest of us went out, Kevin still learned a tremendous amount about Europe (especially European television).

When we returned stateside, I read voraciously about Asperger's syndrome and autism, and looked for another doctor. I was determined to prove that Kevin didn't have a low IQ or a psychiatric disorder. I wanted to understand the parameters of Kevin's autism, to find out how we could help him. I never lost my conviction that 'whatever Kevin did was normal for Kevin', but I was very worried. Rick was willing to have Kevin tested, but after being beaten over the head for years with what was wrong with our son, he was not optimistic about the outcome. We grieved over lost expectations and feared for Kevin's future. Our homeschooling and family life in general was at a low ebb.

I became actively involved with Asperger's sites on the Internet, sifting through and assimilating complicated and often disheartening information. Through word of mouth, I found Robin Murphy, Ph.D., a psychologist with an intimate link to AS. Her uncommon understanding of Asperger's syndrome was reflected in her testing and counseling methods. She evaluated Kevin over a four-month period, testing him for three to four hours at a time on numerous occasions. With few exceptions, Kevin was tested untimed and allowed to use a calculator.

Most psychometrists discontinue testing after the subject fails to answer a specific number of questions correctly. Dr. Murphy recognized that many people with AS are not comfortable answering questions if they are not one hundred percent sure, even though they often do know the right answer, so she encouraged Kevin with phrases like 'You know this one,' and 'This one is a little tricky. Look carefully,' and 'Take a guess. You guessed right on the last one.' She was able to continue testing far beyond the limits of his previous testing.

She also knew that an accurate diagnosis, behavior management and planning, and predictors of success were dependent on testing as many facets as possible, including social and language pragmatics, non-verbal testing, IQ, autism scales, and others. Dr. Murphy requested that I stay in the room during all testing, in part because AS individuals are more relaxed when a trusted person is present, and also so that I could see which tests were being used and how they were administered. I was able to observe her methods of interacting with AS clients.

We met with Dr. Murphy to review her final written report. Kevin demonstrated classic Asperger's syndrome characteristics. Testing revealed no signs of right hemispheric brain dysfunction, with similar strength in verbal and performance areas. He had performed at a superior level academically and intellectually, placing him fifty IQ points higher than previous testing, at a college graduate level and post-graduate level in all subjects except math, where he tested at high school level. Kevin's testing revealed extreme social immaturity, little ability to read facial expressions, self-centered and unrealistic thinking, and weak central coherence (responsible for his organizational difficulties and ADD-like symptoms).

Dr. Murphy believed our decision to homeschool saved Kevin from academic and performance failure, and especially from severe social and emotional harassment and influences which might have resulted in depression or even delinquent behavior. We discussed his current homeschooling life and his general discontent and concluded that we needed to find an alternative plan for integrating Kevin into adult life. She helped us to understand that Kevin would need individual guidance, concrete information, and hands-on support to help him make good educational and life decisions.

We finally comprehended that Kevin would probably take many more years than the average teenager to reach a maturity level where he would be able to live independently. Dr. Murphy pointed out that his intellectual strengths would be the key to future success, but his social immaturity could be a major factor holding him back.

From the time Kevin first learned about AS, he has cycled through feelings of disbelief, anger, relief, acceptance, and pride. I left Tony Attwood's book, *Asperger's Syndrome*, lying on the kitchen table and he read bits and pieces of it, coming to me with questions. Eventually, he read the entire book and some of Francesca Happé's book *Autism: an introduction to psychological theory*. Kevin began to understand himself better and, to a limited extent, others. Medications prescribed by his neuropsychiatrist, Dr. Christopher McDougle of Riley Children's Hospital in Indianapolis, have also proved beneficial for decreasing anxiety and increasing central coherence.

At sixteen years old, Kevin needed a new challenge which might ease him past some of his fears and self-doubt, and at the same time stimulate him intellectually. I believed that a positive college experience would fit his autodidactic learning style. With a documented diagnosis of AS in hand, Kevin applied to Ivy Tech State University through the Special Services department. The English portion of the entrance exam was waived, because he had previously achieved a very high score on the verbal SAT (a standard pre-college exam). He was permitted to take the math portion of the exam untimed and with a calculator, which he passed, allowing him to sign up for freshman courses.

Kevin selected Psychology 101. We met with his professor before the first class meeting and explained a little about AS: that Kevin might appear not to be listening, would not make eye contact often, and would most likely not participate in class discussion or be able to take class notes. Mr. Balsley was very receptive to his personality and needs.

Even though Kevin professed that psychology was not a 'real science', he enthusiastically enjoyed the class. He wrote seven papers during the course and scored 100% on every one of them. He had been granted the option of taking exams untimed and in a private room, but that became unnecessary after he achieved a perfect score on his first multiple-choice exam in only eleven minutes. Soon he was able to find his way in and out of the building alone and, in time, Kevin relaxed into his once-a-week foray into college, fairly comfortable in a community where the average student was twenty-five to thirty-five years old and cared little about individual physical appearance and personality differences.

From the initial meetings with his counselor, whose office Kevin declared 'reeked sickeningly of Chinese take-out', through college enrollment chores, to listening to his classmates talk about subjects inane to him, Kevin persevered. Initially, he required a lot of support. Sometimes, Rick and I would come up with three or four ideas for a paper. Only when Kevin accepted one as his own would he head off to his computer and come back, hours later, with a nearly flawless completed assignment.

At the beginning of the semester, I read each psychology chapter aloud to Kevin and methodically helped him study for exams. By the middle of the term, Kevin had taken over completely. His confidence in his intellectual abilities and his hopes for the future grew. During the next two semesters, he successfully completed two college-level algebra classes.

Kevin will continue to need help as he gradually increases his number of college hours. Instead of attending high school, Kevin has found what he needs by skipping an impossible adolescent period and moving on to college, somewhere he can be himself and be intellectually challenged at the same time.

Taking psychology was an impetus for a great deal of personal growth in Kevin, as well. He was able to generalize huge amounts of information he learned, in an academic setting, to his own life and personality development. This class gave him a logical format for reasoning and explaining human behavior. At seventeen, Kevin's goals for the next few years include progressing further musically and continuing his college studies in math, music theory and composition, writing, and Latin. Another goal he set himself was acquiring a driver's license—a goal he has now achieved.

Homeschooling was a life-saving choice for Kevin. Like all parents who homeschool, we have had periods of doubt about our choices. I have learned from struggling through those doubts. Parenting Kevin has led me to embrace the philosophy that with a good environment and available resources, a child will seek out and learn what he needs, when there is a purpose or a curiosity to know. I have learned to reject ways of living and growing that run counter to the survival, success, and happiness of my son, because 'whatever Kevin does is normal for Kevin', and because he deserves a rich and rewarding life comparable to any other person's normal life.

6

But will he ever speak to me?
Greg's story

Alan Phillips

'But... will he ever speak to me?' I asked the professor of psychology at the specialist diagnostic centre. I was desperate to know. It had become the most important thing in the world to me. I just wanted the chance to ask my son if he was happy—to hope that maybe, someday, I would hear him call me 'Dad'. The professor answered that it was very unlikely, as Greg, then six years old, was completely non-verbal and profoundly autistic.

It's funny the things you remember, like the time I offered the nursery nurse in charge of Greg the biggest box of chocolates if she could get him to say that one word—'Dad'. Alas, she was never able to collect her prize.

The prognosis for our son was very poor and we could not be given much hope. Some developmental psychologists and speech therapists claim that children who do not speak by the age of six years are unlikely ever to develop speech. Call it stubborn parental optimism, but despite everything, we knew that one day we would find a way to help him.

My thoughts went back to the sunny September morning when Greg was born. I counted his fingers and toes, and I remember the feeling of relief and gratitude that our son was born perfect. He started to develop normally for the first eighteen months of his life, even developing language. Members of our family had commented that Greg seemed exceptionally clever, especially in the way he used to remember and say his nursery rhymes. Lee, Greg's older brother by two years, was very forward, so we had someone to compare him to.

Of course, this period of normal development, followed by a plateau or regression that seems to kick in around eighteen months, is typical of autism and may be familiar to many parents with an autistic child. Without that knowledge, however, it was completely baffling and frightening.

Every journey has its beginning, and we had already climbed a very difficult and slippery slope to get to the diagnostic centre. For most of the earlier years of Greg's life, we felt alone and unsupported. This whole period of trying to obtain a diagnosis and the correct education for our son represented the most awful, stressful period of our lives. It is hard to convey how disappointed we felt and the magnitude of the difficulties we had faced. It is something that has scarred us forever.

Following on from the struggle to gain a diagnosis, we found ourselves on a second slippery slope—even more difficult to negotiate—with the education authority. Greg was not receiving an education or help appropriate to autism at the local school for children with severe learning difficulties. Like a 'good' father, I trusted what both medical and educational professionals had told me. My wife, Helen, on the other hand, used her motherly intuition to sense that all was not right. I still regret having persuaded Helen to stifle her doubts and go along with those who I felt were better qualified to help us.

When Greg started school, we were very optimistic and positive and wanted to be supportive, but after eighteen months of patient waiting we were becoming increasingly concerned about his lack of development, especially in his language, which had by now virtually dried up. It was a dilemma. On the one hand, we wanted to keep favour with his teachers and the school so that they would do their best for Greg. We were afraid to upset them, because we felt we needed them. On the other hand, our concern was so great that we just had to find the courage to bite the bullet and ask questions.

Our daring to question not only caused friction, it culminated in alienation between the school and our family. Outwardly the school tried to maintain a professional approach, but inwardly they took it personally, and at times it rebounded on Greg. A quite unnecessary atmosphere was developing. It was soul destroying.

From both the medical and educational perspective, I felt as if my son was like a seedling that we were continually digging up in order to examine whether or not his roots were developing; then he would be re-planted, only for the process to be repeated. I knew it would be difficult for any plant to survive and flourish under these circumstances, and so it must have been for Greg.

Everything was so much out of our control! It seemed that most of our energies were needed to protect what help we had already won. It didn't make any sense to keep upsetting ourselves in fighting the system, and we knew in our hearts that it would be far better to redirect our energy.

In a single stroke, just by removing ourselves from the educational system and the negativity attached to it, we saw an immediate difference. As a family we found inner peace, but home education transformed our son. How I wish that Greg's old educational psychologist, who claimed that our son would not benefit from individual attention at school because his concentration span was only seconds long, could see Greg now, at age eighteen, as he concentrates on a project for over an hour at a time.

I would like to say that we got into home education for some ideal vision and with a clearly identified goal as to how to help our son—but I can't. The truth is that we were so fed up, disheartened, disillusioned and, in the end, worn down by the politics and negativism of the educational system that we considered we had little to lose by trying something different.

We had put up with the shortfalls of the school system, grateful that they took responsibility for Greg's education, but ultimately we found that there exists a cut-off point when it becomes not simply an argument about securing the best possible education for your child, but something far more important: it is about seeing your child's future and his survival in our world going down the pan.

Many parents who dare to challenge the educational system eventually ask the same question that we had to face: is it better to bang your head against the stubborn walls of authorities as you battle for the help your child needs, or to redirect your energies into something more positive? Personally, it is a tremendous relief to be off that merry-go-round.

'I'll give them three weeks and they will be back,' the school said of us when we took Greg out. Well, it was eleven years ago and we never did look back. I do not have any regrets about taking Greg out of school; my only regret is that I should have taken him out of school much earlier. Actually, with hindsight, I say it would have been better not to have sent him to school at all. If I could have my time again, I would have home educated from the beginning.

There can be no greater challenge than bringing up an autistic child. The final straw is to handle the pressure of dealing with education authorities, experienced in delaying tactics and ambiguity, when your child has allowed you two hours sleep a night for the last three consecutive nights. It can often feel as if the entire world is against you.

I am sure many readers will recognise the frustration and helplessness one feels when children are at an age when they are unable to use language or to show when they need help. Most of us can think back to how we felt holding a screaming baby in our arms, and how we longed for the day when our child could talk and tell us what was wrong so we could comfort or help him. Living with a non-verbal child means one can be in this state perpetually, sometimes becoming overwhelmed with feelings of powerlessness.

Our disillusionment with the way the education and medical authorities had treated us, plus our concern with Greg's deterioration at school, would have been enough reason to take him out of school, but our association with the Option Institute in the USA clarified for us other important factors that must always have been in the back of our minds. We had a desire that Greg should be educated in a loving, accepting and non-judgmental environment, and that the people with him should really understand his difficulties and be supportive of his individuality. It was clear to us that these objectives could not be catered for at school, where there was an agenda to push Greg to conform to the norm.

Our first venture into home education was part time. Having secured a nursery nurse for each morning at school, we still felt the unstructured afternoon sessions were threatening and not helping Greg, so Helen decided to teach him herself each afternoon at home.

We had, in all but name, introduced and directed the teaching programmes used with Greg in school. We had learned it all from books, attending seminars and speaking with other parents, so our movement into home education was a natural progression and something we were familiar and relatively confident about.

To be honest, I think I would have found the prospect of home educating too daunting at the beginning. It was probably best to have broken ourselves in gradually as we gained our knowledge and practical experience.

The principal methods we were using at that early stage were programmes like the Geoffrey Waldon approach and TEACCH (Treatment and Education of Autistic and related Communication handicapped CHildren) and also music and movement therapy. We were actually one of the first of a handful of parents to use TEACCH in the UK when it was introduced from the USA. 'Holding therapy' was in vogue at that time and we even tried that for a while.

We have seen many fashions of different methods and approaches come and go. Some were effective; others I would choose to forget. The methods used then bear little resemblance to what we do now. We have found that different families find programmes or methods that suit and appeal to their individuality and that of their child. As a general rule, I would say that if the parents really believe in the approach, then it is likely that this will serve them best.

Helen was proving to be a natural teacher for Greg. It is probably true that every mother, if she could but trust herself, is potentially the best teacher any child could have. It is as if, when a child comes of school age, the mother's teaching skills are placed on hold or no longer valued, and she feels compelled to step aside to let teachers take over.

We know that Greg had made the best progress in his life before he went to school. We believe that sending him to school without the correct provision and understanding did untold damage, and we are all still living with the consequences of that to this day.

It certainly is true that home education is a big decision, but why would we not trust in our own proven abilities as natural teachers? We would not even think to question this in the pre-school years. We realised that in order to move forward we needed to go back and reclaim the full-time responsibility for Greg's education and therefore his future.

Families sometimes ask our opinion about whether or not they should take their child out of school, or whether they should home educate from the start. We would not want to influence anyone, as such decisions are very personal and have to take into account the dynamics of the whole family and a myriad of other questions. I truly believe that every parent could do it.

Parents do, in any case, teach their children far more than they might give themselves credit for. But do all parents have the motivation, determination or even the inclination to do this full time after a child reaches school age? The reality is, it would drive some parents crazy even to consider the idea of home education.

Without the desire, it is unlikely to work or be sustainable. We are very mindful that home education, particularly for a special child, is a huge commitment. If parents feel trapped, and are only choosing a home education programme because they do not like the alternative, it is unlikely that their adventure will last or be as successful as it could be.

I believe this to be particularly true if you have a child with an autistic spectrum disorder, because such children are so acutely sensitive to their total environment and the attitudes of people in their life. Trading one hostile environment for another would not appeal to me as a basis for helping my son deal with his autism; he is unlikely to reach out and be attracted to our world if he perceives it as unfriendly. However, if it is in your heart to try home education and you feel it is something you are compelled to do, you will be able to do it.

We reside in a normal semi-detached house and live on a modest income, so we would not call ourselves privileged. We had no prior experience as teachers, and we had our other son to consider. It is inconceivable that we would ever have contemplated home education if there had been a school that could have offered Greg appropriate help. For the most part, however, we have found teaching Greg at home a very stimulating, enjoyable and rewarding adventure.

Our confidence was given an enormous boost by our understanding of how a school might create a developmental programme for such a severely autistic child. It really is a much simpler task than parents first think. We tracked down developmental checklists, which are fairly easy to obtain. These are basically lists of things that children do at various stages of development. We would work down the list, ticking the particular activity that Greg could do and then introducing the next item as the target activity.

We didn't need to 'reinvent the wheel': with the checklists, we had a ready-made guide to activities which could be introduced methodically, at the appropriate time and in the correct order. Since the checklists were broken down into categories like fine motor skills, gross motor skills, language development, pre-writing skills and so on, it was also relatively easy to ensure that Greg was receiving an appropriate education that covered all bases.

Once you have a system in place, it becomes far less daunting a prospect to believe you can offer your child an effective home education. It also seems to reassure educational psychologists and any other people you might work with from your education department that you are organised. What parents might lack in actual paper qualifications to do the job is more than made up for by their having determination, enthusiasm, love, a desire to do the best for their child and a sense of making things fun—for us, the main factor in helping Greg to learn and grow.

Because our house was so small, we constructed a chalet-type building in the garden, which was to be Greg's classroom. Actually it is quite sophisticated and, aided by some fund raising that we did in the early years, we were able to equip it with a one-way mirror and sound system, so that we can unobtrusively observe, show and teach the people we have working in our programme.

Although this teaching environment would not be essential if circumstances and space did not allow it, it did provide Greg with a safe, distraction-free environment where it was much easier to attract and hold his attention. We kept the decor fairly simple and neutral. Even the lighting was addressed: no fluorescent lights, since many autistic children can hear the buzzing and detect the strobe-like pulses they emit.

As Greg was a child who would not willingly interact and had only seconds of concentration, we considered this attention to detail quite important. I am talking about creating the optimum environment, but even if you are only able to change or arrange a few things, just think of it as one less thing that your child will have to deal with.

Keep in mind that it did take us some time to get things sorted out. When we first started, we taught Greg in our dining room, then a converted bedroom and finally in his custom-designed chalet classroom.

It may be useful to think of the room as a filter, removing every external distraction that we could identify in our attempt to make things more accessible and digestible to our son and less of a sensory overload. It was also a safe environment where one could relax: no expensive ornaments, no potentially dangerous substances and so on; the room was essentially 'childproof' and an environment that would encourage free exploration. We know Greg has great difficulty with his creativity and imagination, and it is his lack of inquisitiveness and interest in exploring objects, environments and people that contributes towards his difficulty in learning.

Only one person at a time went into the room to work with Greg. We always knew that people were a major difficulty for him, so we considered it unreasonable to insist that, as the world was full of people, Greg would just have to get used to it. Having sent Greg to school, we knew that just placing him in a so-called sociable environment did not make him sociable or any more tolerant of people, nor did it make him talk. It made sense to us that if we could reduce Greg's exposure to what he found difficult to handle, it might give him sufficient respite to enable him to rebuild his confidence.

Once Greg showed increased interest in people, we gradually increased his exposure to other social settings, but it was always structured. For example, if we were to take him shopping, we would deliberately take him when it was very quiet, carefully giving him ample time to assimilate new situations before moving on to more challenging ones. Slow but sure wins the race.

Having spoken with hundreds of parents over the years, we realise how important socialisation is to us all, especially to parents of a child with severe autism who typically spends most of his time isolated in a world of his own making. Indeed, educationists often focus on the socialisation aspect as a criticism of home-based education programmes. We realise that what we have done with Greg is basically the opposite of the traditional school experience and thinking. In order to help Greg to become more sociable, we initially 'isolated' him—except, in truth, his autism actually did that, and we simply created an environment that he could handle.

Our approach has been to construct for Greg a solid foundation on which his ability to handle more challenging situations can be built. In creating this island in a sea of confusion, we had a definite intention of stripping out all possible distractions and overwhelming experiences, but this was only the first stage in a greater plan. As and when Greg has demonstrated that he is more comfortable, we have re-introduced situations that represent more of a challenge to him, at the same time offering a strategy to show him how to cope with them.

We have trodden on many eggshells with Greg, but experience has been a good teacher. We have had to find ways to help him with his behaviour rather than be controlled by it. Recently, we were in the camper van, meandering through the beautiful Welsh mountains, on our journey home after a weekend break. We stopped the van for a rest and a bite to eat at a beautiful picnic spot, but Greg was enjoying the ride so much that he didn't want us to stop, and showed his disapproval by banging the sides of his head with great energy. It was difficult to deal with, especially as he was by now trying to take a chunk out of my arm.

I helped him to calm, and then gently explained to him that I realised how much he enjoyed the drive, but I could not let his behaviour control us: right now we were tired and needed a break. I also explained that I wanted him to understand it was in his interest to try to control his behaviour. We all enjoyed these outings, but his explosions were so intense I felt that they could jeopardise one of the few things that we could all do together as a family. Greg and I had to work through this, so I told him that later on I would stop several times on the way home. I wasn't angry with him; I just wanted him to have opportunities to be able to practise his self-control.

After the break, we set off and, true to my word, at the very first lay-by I pulled in. As one could have predicted, Greg once again began to shout and shake with agitation, and once again I asked him to calm himself down, which he did eventually manage to do. The next time I stopped, it looked like he was going to shout and become intense again, but this time he stopped himself and smiled. I cheered his control. I stopped several more times on the way back, but he didn't shout again and mostly laughed. I think both Greg and I learned a lot about each other that day. I was proud of him and, I guess, a little bit of myself!

The teaching programme that we use was originally based on the philosophy of the Option Institute, now called 'Son-Rise'. There are in fact several other proponents who suggest a broadly similar approach: 'Gentle Teaching' and Stanley Greenspan, to mention a couple. Option, like Lovaas, TEACCH, Higashi, *etc.*, is really an approach and a guiding philosophy. We have added to it a curriculum, which makes it an educational programme.

There are actually elements of several different teaching ideas and programmes contained within our approach. All of this is overridden by an element of common sense. Whilst many of these curricula and teaching guides offer a source of useful ideas presented in a logical, progressive manner, we have learned to trust our judgment and free ourselves to choose priorities that will better serve Greg and his individual circumstances.

To give you an example: yes, we would like to teach Greg to identify his colours, but it is more important that he can ask for the toilet when he needs to. I guess that we try to position ourselves to see the world from his perspective, thinking, 'If I were Greg, what would help me the most?' and letting that take precedence over any arbitrary educational goal. Trusting that Greg will show us where he needs help and what style seems to help him most has been a very successful guide in constructing his programme. You just need to create space to observe.

Greg has difficulties in language and communication, social interaction and creative thinking. We want to deal with these core areas consistently, and this takes precedence over a specific teaching goal. Taking the example once more of teaching him his colours: if he is looking at me and we are interacting, we would tend to celebrate and promote the social aspect of this; if he speaks or attempts to communicate, this is celebrated and encouraged; any spontaneity or creativity is applauded to help Greg towards flexible thinking and therefore to be less reliant on his repetitive and ritualistic behaviours.

I hope this clearly demonstrates where our priorities are; yet we do include specific teaching activities as well, because we also have a goal of wanting to exercise Greg's brain in order to help him grow as a person. In the school system, all too often the teaching activity is seen as the most important part, whereas in Greg's home programme we believe celebrating language and interaction is the most effective way to help our son.

We have used another Option concept of allowing the child to become the teacher, so we reverse our rôles and allow Greg to show us what he is interested in, following his lead and doing what he is naturally motivated to do. Our part is to foster and gently develop any interest he expresses, but we are also going with the flow of who Greg is, showing our acceptance of his choices and our respect for his value as a person.

In my session with Greg yesterday, he danced up and down the room shouting 'play—guitar—fast—Dad!' At one stage he beat on the bodhran and shook the maracas—and we were together, we were a band! Smiles, laughter and music filled the room. The atmosphere changed when I asked Greg to come sit at the table and do some simple reading. He looked bored and there was a growing tension between us. When he asked me for a rice cake, I used this opportunity to stop and think, 'Why am I doing this?'

I realised I had temporarily lost my way. I had become a 'teacher' trying to impose my agenda—but Greg was getting nothing out of it, so why do it? I returned, not just with the rice cake but, tapping into his enthusiasm for food, I also brought the portable cooker, a wok and an assortment of washed vegetables. Greg enthusiastically chopped the vegetables. They were not at all even, but he did do it all by himself.

At one stage, he tried to cut with the knife, but he was holding it upside down and it was hard work. I wanted to help him, but I held back and watched his cogs turn. Holding back was the hardest part. Greg paused and corrected himself, turning the knife to its correct position. Then he looked up and gave me a beautiful smile. At that moment, he knew how proud of him I was—and he of himself. He burnt the onion and garlic a little and added a bit too much soy sauce for my taste, but he had prepared himself a stir-fry. He continued to smile all the way through, finally wanting to sit on my lap. A beautiful calmness and peace again filled the room—and now I felt a better teacher.

We do actually flip the rôles and take the lead by guiding Greg and introducing concepts, but we lean very much towards enthusiastic invitations as opposed to demands. Keeping the balance of showing Greg a very loving, accepting and supportive attitude whilst simultaneously offering him opportunities that stretch him and allow him to grow has always been our Holy Grail. The times we have been most effective are when we have managed to achieve this balance.

We want Greg to know that he is really loved as he is—including his autism. Whereas most programmes seek to stop repetitive, ritualistic behaviours, we do the opposite and not only allow Greg to be autistic, we give ourselves permission to let go, have fun and join him in his world on his terms. Please note that 'join' is very different from 'copy'!

Greg's current repetitive, ritualistic behaviour is to tap in a very precise pattern on a plastic building brick. We may spend five minutes on that, tapping on his brick together, before he spends perhaps twenty minutes at the table practising his writing. I am a willing participant in Greg's world and he in mine, but wherever we are, we are there together.

In the beginning there was little bond between us, but this has changed completely. If you have a particularly withdrawn and isolated child, the concept of joining him in his space with warmth and sincerity may provide a platform to build a very beautiful relationship between the two of you.

If you are willing to consider this approach, I would add that it only seems to work if you are sincere. If you 'join' your child as a tactic, thinking, 'I will do this behaviour with him so I can get him to the table to do some real and useful learning'—well, good luck to you! I have tried that and it has never worked for me.

The mind set that I felt helped me was to appreciate that things were incredibly difficult for Greg and, although I knew he was different, it was his way of taking care of himself in our alien world. So, for me, every time I tapped on his brick with him, it was as if I was telling my son that I loved him very much. It is an exercise in suspending, if not letting go, all fears for his future and allowing myself to be truly present with my son on a moment-to-moment basis as his friend.

As Greg has developed more concentration, language, understanding and interaction, the balance has changed. We are now able to spend more time developing his skills and introducing more traditional subjects like geography, nature, science, reading, writing, craft projects and so on. We have also introduced Greg to the computer. We never forced or pressured Greg to come to the table to do work, but he is now a very willing, interested student who can often enjoy these activities, so they seem much more relevant and appropriate.

Language development is a very strong feature in our home programme and is obviously of paramount importance to a child in Greg's situation. One thing that we found very successful in promoting language was to have high shelves in his playroom, so if he wanted that piece of apple or a certain toy, he had to find a way to let us know. I am not suggesting a strict rule such as 'if you do not ask, then you do not get', but rather first creating a space where communication can begin. We were looking for any form of communication.

In the beginning, if he simply looked up at an object, we would note that as a communicative intention, first celebrating and then trying to expand it. With great excitement we might say, 'I saw you looking up at the shelf, Greg. Do you want the apple or drink? Tell me clearly.' We started by picking out relevant key words, choosing something we thought really interested Greg and towards which he therefore had some motivation. We also gave him a clear and simple single word for each item or object, keeping our sentences very short and easy to understand, and we spoke with great enthusiasm, fun and passion.

At school, I remember their trying to teach Greg 'please' and 'thank you', but these are abstract words you cannot see or touch, so we deliberately chose concrete words, mostly nouns, so we could show him the object as we spoke the word. The niceties and politeness in our language would follow later on.

Taking as an example the word 'drink', Greg eventually started to approximate the sound 'dwi' after our many attempts at modelling the word clearly for him and encouraging his response. It is important to be very supportive and to acknowledge the slightest attempt at co-operation. It did not matter that the word was not that clear. Later this became a pretty clear 'drink' and has graduated to 'Greg wants a drink of water, Dad.'

You may be wondering how much it costs to run a home-based programme. That depends on what you want for your child and whether you want—or can afford to buy in—services from outside experts. Although home education can be very inexpensive, running a programme like Son-Rise or an Applied Behaviour Analysis (ABA) programme can cost quite a bit, especially if you use the organisations' training, consultation, feedback and assessment facilities. We were one of the first families in the UK to obtain funding from our local education authority (LEA), and I have to say that we eventually enjoyed good support from them. Our budget allows us to buy in expert advice, to pay for people to work with Greg and to buy teaching materials.

Asking education authorities to fund home-based programmes is becoming more popular. We had a stressful two-year battle, so I cannot pretend it was easy, but things have moved on and precedents have now been set. A tight, well-presented case may prove successful. Your case is stronger if you are able to prove that local provision would not meet your child's needs, as the LEA has a responsibility to provide a suitable education. It is worth bearing in mind the potential savings to the education authority, which might otherwise have to pay astronomical fees for a residential placement at a specialist school. We know parents who have been allowed extremely generous amounts to fund their programmes.

So how do you fit in family life? You don't really! Having a child like Greg inevitably changes your life—but a different life need not necessarily mean a lesser one. Most of the parents we know who have children with autism do not get out much and, as time goes by, they seem to develop friendships mainly with other families in the same situation. To have a 'normal' family life, you would have to consider sending your child away to a residential unit. We could not conceive of sending Greg away.

When Greg was at school we didn't seem to go out much more than we do now, so I don't think home education really affects us much socially; however, Greg's autism certainly does. His behaviour, and the quite challenging phases we still go through, mean we have to be very selective about the people with whom we can leave Greg. We have now found a middle ground: we can organise our lives to fit in things that Helen and I would like to do together. I think this is both healthy and important for all of us. For a long time, we had to count solely on the wonderful support of my parents, but recently we have been able to get additional support from our Social Services department.

We have also found time for family life by recruiting people to be involved in our programme for Greg, first as volunteers and later as paid participants. Although we have spent a lot of time in training our people, and have had to develop some managerial skills so that things run smoothly, it has created some space for us to do our own thing and fit in family chores.

I have asked my other son, Lee, if he feels he has missed out on anything, as I do have a sense that pretty well everything seems to revolve around Greg in our house. I asked him to be totally honest. Had he felt left out? Had I been unfair? Lee's reply surprised me. He says he does not feel as if he has 'missed out', and he regards our intensive involvement with Greg as no different from our having full-time jobs, like his friends' parents.

Lee is very independent now and has his life beautifully organised. He is never at a loose end, leads a very packed life, has plenty of friends and has found himself a good job that he enjoys. I think our involvement with Greg has actually helped him in many ways; the training we have received has generally made us better and more accepting parents.

We have not always found things plain sailing. There have been periods when we felt lost and despondent, and we have made many mistakes. Whilst we still have much to learn, I think I am beginning to understand why Greg, our special child, was born to us. I realise that he is perfect in himself and doesn't have to change; we were the ones that needed to change. We are very proud of him and glad that he is our son.

No matter how severe your child's autism is, Greg's achievements are proof that there can be hope for those who used to be considered 'hopeless'—and, yes, I have my wish! Greg calls me 'Dad' most days and he tells me he is happy: 'Yes, good,' he says. The experts were wrong. Greg was eight and a half years old when he started to talk. Never let anyone extinguish your hope and dreams for your child's future.

Postscript

We are now entering a new phase in Greg's education. Having just turned eighteen, our son is in transition into adulthood and will soon leave the education system; however, we do not see our rôle ending, as there is still much to do. Greg shows flexibility, willingness and a capacity to allow us to guide him in new and exciting directions. It is much easier to teach him things now than at any other point in his life.

Currently, we are negotiating with our Social Services department to gain their financial support for our work to continue under Direct Payments and Independent Living Fund (ILF). These benefits are designed to enable people to continue living at home by allowing them to buy in the help and support they need. In Greg's case, there is no appropriate provision available to support him within our borough, so the only alternative would be to offer him a residential placement out of the area, which would be very expensive—probably more than four times the amount that we are likely to be offered. Home-based support therefore provides a solution for all parties involved.

Now that Greg is an adult, we have been looking for more mature activities for him to enjoy. Most significantly, I approached an employer to see if I could secure suitable employment for Greg. What we have arranged so far is that Greg works voluntarily at a local wildlife and animal sanctuary. He works for a couple of hours each week at the moment, performing such duties as grooming the donkey, clearing overgrowth from paths and—his favourite job of all—litter collection (he is as adept as anyone at operating his litter picker).

Greg seems to get a great deal of satisfaction out of his job, and I remind him that even if he can only do a little, he improves the environment for all. He appears to be well liked by the people and, in his own unique style, is starting to form friendships with his workmates.

Maybe it took Greg a couple of minutes to work out that it was better to pull the wheelbarrow over the kerb rather than push it, as he delivered his load of hedge clippings to the bonfire, but I gave him the time to learn by experimentation. He looked pleased at working it all out by himself, and each subsequent time he did this task he automatically did it the easier way. I was so proud of my son. I am so excited that he is now able to use his thinking skills in these practical and flexible ways to solve problems for himself.

After he had finished, he sat on the wall to rest with another member of the staff. When I looked later at the photograph I had taken, I noticed the beautiful smile he was giving to the young lady sitting next to him. In one hand he held his bricks and bag, so he still has one foot in his world of autism, but all of the time he demonstrates movement and increasing ability to share in our world—and enjoy it!

You are warmly invited to contact Alan Phillips by visiting his web site at www.autism.pwp.blueyonder.co.uk.

7

In the real world, it's OK
to be different
Alex's story

Grace Carpenter

About us

Our family consists of me, aged forty-six, and my two sons: James, aged fifteen, and Alex, aged thirteen. I should also mention the boys' father, John. Although he died of cancer when the boys were six and four, he is obviously also an important part of our family story. Both the boys have a home-based education.

My main rôle at present is that of mother and co-ordinator of my children's education. James's main interests are countryside conservation work, gardening, camping, walking and photography. Alex's main interests are maths, physics, computing and reading. Alex has Asperger's syndrome.

Why we decided to home educate

My husband and I were interested in the idea of home education even before our first child was born. I felt my 'good' grammar school education had been very shallow and narrow and had left me ill-equipped for adult life. John, on the other hand, had very little formal education, but found his own means of obtaining a good general education in early adulthood, going on later to obtain formal qualifications. Between us we were sceptical as to the necessity or efficacy of schooling as the main means of educating children. We were fortunate in having met a home-educating family who told us about the home educators' support organisation Education Otherwise, so we knew it was a realistic option if we could juggle the demands of work and money.

If I am honest with myself, I think we would nevertheless have gone along with the crowd and sent James to school if we had thought that he would be reasonably happy with it. However, he turned out to be the sort of person who was much happier with small than with large groups of people. We tried playgroup, but he soon told me, 'I don't ever want to go to playgroup again, Mummy, not even when I'm a big grown-up man!' and I knew he meant it.

It was clear to me that he was getting little from playgroup that he couldn't get in other ways. There were no activities on offer that we didn't do at home, and he spent less time interacting with other children in that setting than he did in more intimate settings. We had such good fun playing at home, going to the woods and visiting friends and family that I could see no point in making him miserable by sending him to playgroup. A little while later, we joined Education Otherwise. Getting to know other home-educating families stopped us feeling pressurised by conventional wisdom.

James had some difficulties in his early years that would now be described as attention deficit disorder (ADD) or attention deficit hyper-activity disorder (ADHD). It was clear that he and school would not take to each other, so we carried on as we were, letting his fifth birthday come and go. Many of our early decisions about home education were made specifically in relation to James's temperament and needs, long before Alex's diagnosis of Asperger's syndrome.

By the time Alex was approaching school age, my husband was already terminally ill. We felt strongly that we needed to enjoy our time together as a family, rather than thinking about school. We had lots of outings, we went on holiday and we had a big family party a few weeks before John died. Because we did so many things together, the boys have lots of really good memories of their dad, even though they were so young. This was far, far more valuable to them than sitting in a class-room or being in a playground.

I reconsidered the school issue after John died. I was struggling to adjust to our new life, and I needed to earn some money; however, I knew that James would still be very unhappy in a school environment. My main reservation about sending Alex to school was the fact that I was sure he would be terribly bored. He had taught himself to read at an early age, and he was clearly also very able with numbers and shapes. I decided to work part time while the boys were minded by another home-educating parent, and we settled down to the life of a home-edu-cating family.

Our long path to diagnosis

Alex was a very happy, placid baby and toddler. For a long time I thought he was intellectually slow, because he was very passive and was a late talker, but it didn't worry me: the most important thing was that he was a happy little person.

The first indication that he was not slow came when he was around two and started doing jigsaw puzzles designed for older children. He started reading at three and a half. At around the same time, I realised that when he was apparently amusing himself by sounding out random letters, he was actually making requests to me by spelling out whole sentences phonetically. For example, 'kan i hav a jrink ov joos?' His speech was still unclear, and our health visitor thought he might be deaf, but full tests showed that he had no hearing impairment.

What I now realise is that, in those early years, Alex had a lifestyle that suited him very well. He was looked after by only a very limited number of people, life was reasonably predictable and not too many demands were made upon him to interact with others, because he had a very active and chatty older brother. It is only in retrospect that I can see he had traits indicative of Asperger's syndrome.

When my husband became ill, and later died, the symptoms of Asperger's became more overt. However, at the time, and for several years afterwards, I thought Alex's difficulties were a result of the emotional trauma of losing his father. It was only after he was diagnosed that I realised why he had found it so extraordinarily difficult to cope with that loss and those changes: it was because of his Asperger's.

The main symptoms were emotional and social withdrawal and the development of obsessional behaviour and rituals. He found it particularly hard to cope with anyone's touching him or his possessions and he developed elaborate blowing and rubbing rituals. When I asked him why he did it, he told me, 'I'm rubbing off their feelings.' (He recently explained to me that he meant he was rubbing off the feeling of having been physically touched.) He pushed and hit out at any small children who intruded into his personal space.

As emotional trauma seemed to be an adequate explanation for Alex's behaviour, the appropriate response seemed to be lots of tender loving care, backed up with explanations about what had happened to his dad, and opportunities for him to explore his feelings about his loss. (I now understand why he was never actually able to take up these opportunities.) Of course this was an appropriate response: he gradually recovered some joy in life, he became less withdrawn and less obsessional, but tender loving care was clearly not sufficient: his 'recovery' was much, much slower than I thought it should be.

When Alex was just nine, we moved house and I decided, after lots of discussion with the boys, that we would try school. I chose their schools very carefully: in fact, the location of our new house was determined by the location of the school I felt would be best for Alex. Both his head teacher and class teacher were sympathetic and constructive when I explained his problems.

Alex seemed to feel reasonably positive about trying school, but putting him in a classroom was like putting a magnifying glass on everything he found hard to deal with. He was bored and frustrated by the lessons; he hated having to spend all day with other children, for many of whom he consequently expressed little other than contempt; he was teased and bullied in the playground. The school thought he probably had either dyspraxia or Asperger's syndrome, or that he was just finding the situation hard to deal with because he was very able and accustomed to having the freedom to work in his own way and at his own pace. However, they really were at quite a loss as to how to respond to him, and were very reluctant to 'treat him differently from the other children'.

I guess things might have been better if we had already had a diagnosis and the school had had access to more support and advice. It was at this stage that I asked our family doctor to refer Alex to the Paediatric Assessment Centre. I also started reading up about Asperger's syndrome. In due course it was confirmed that he had 'difficulties compatible with Asperger's syndrome'. He was just three months away from his tenth birthday.

Some thoughts about diagnosis

Some people are opposed to the whole idea of diagnosis, because of the negative effects of labelling. I think I would feel a dilemma if Alex were in school. I would know, on the one hand, that a diagnosis was necessary in order to access appropriate provision for him. On the other hand, I might be worried about its possible stigmatising effect.

However, understanding that Alex has Asperger's syndrome has transformed our lives in a very positive way. It has enabled me to learn how his mind works and to get to know him in a way that was not previously possible for me. I have also been able to help him to start to understand how the 'typical' mind works, so that he can learn how to communicate more effectively. Although he still thinks many of the standard ways of communicating are 'mad', he now understands that he has to use them if he wants to get through to 'mad', typical people.

I explain to other people that Alex has Asperger's syndrome, and what that is, to enable them to communicate more effectively with him. I also explain the positive aspects of Asperger's, such as his amazing memory, his logical mind and his mathematical and computing skills. Thus I see the term 'Asperger's syndrome' not as a *label* of a problem, but as a *description* of a set of characteristics: a description that is useful in helping 'typical' and Asperger's people to learn how to communicate with one another.

No more school

The boys went to school for two terms in total. It was a very unhappy experience for Alex. James had settled quite quickly into the school routine and was achieving well; however, he was clear that, on balance, he preferred to be home educated.

I felt our whole life lacked a depth and quality that had previously been present. I resented the time spent on things like ironing school uniforms and doing time-filling homework. I was very unhappy with things such as the way in which Alex was expected to accept whole-class punishments on occasions when he had done really well in managing to conform to what had been requested of him personally, and by how James's physical education teacher repeatedly swore at the children.

These were 'good' schools with good reputations, but, for me, they could not measure up to what home education could offer. So, just before Alex was officially diagnosed, I withdrew them from school. I resolved that, unless they made a firm request to return, they would never go to school again. Any niggling doubts I had had previously about whether they were missing out by not going to school were now dispensed with. I knew that, for us, home education was right.

Why I believe home education is right for Alex

I believe that home education offers advantages to most children, in terms of their academic, emotional and social well-being and development. The reasons I see home education as being particularly useful for children with Asperger's syndrome are essentially the same, but there are specific ways in which it provides my son with a positive environment.

People who have Asperger's syndrome are very prone to anxiety, and the more anxious they are feeling, the more autistic will be their behaviour. My approach is therefore to aim for a relatively stress-free life for Alex, so that he is as free as possible from the restrictions that his Asperger's syndrome could impose upon him. (In reality I frequently fall far short of this aim, but I try to hold on to it as a guiding principle.)

Some may argue that it is artificial to guard him from stress, but I believe this gives him the best possible chance of developing his social skills. When he is exposed to more stress than he can handle, he becomes so inflexible and obsessive that he cannot bear to be with other children and, if forced to be, alienates himself from them and is unable to join in with normal social interaction. On the other hand, when I succeed in shielding him from excessive stress, he is able to participate in a more normal way. In this way he is freed up to develop the skills used in social interaction, to make friendships and, above all, to enjoy himself.

Everything I have read about Asperger's syndrome, every conference and parent group I have attended, suggests to me that school is probably the most stressful situation in these children's lives. I am therefore convinced that, by excluding school from Alex's life, I am giving him the best possible chance of developing his social skills and a good friendship network.

I am assuming that, as an adult, he will not choose a job or lifestyle that will require him to spend long stretches of time in close proximity to thirty-plus other people, so I don't think the school experience *per se* is necessary in preparing him for adult life. I understand that young people with Asperger's syndrome are usually very relieved when the time comes to leave school, but that, on the other hand, it can be a very difficult adjustment for them to make. Their teachers and helpers have spent twelve or more years helping them to develop strategies for coping with the school institution, and suddenly they need an almost entirely different set of strategies for dealing with adult life. With home education there can be a much more gradual evolution from childhood into adulthood, as home-educated children become accustomed to taking their place in the 'real world' at a much earlier age.

The way in which home education is structured allows a lot of this 'shielding from stress' to be done away from public view. Thus Alex can usually manage to participate in social situations without any obvious special provision having to be made. In this way it is possible to avoid making a big deal about the 'special needs' label.

From my point of view, it can be a bit like the proverbial duck gliding smoothly along the water whilst paddling furiously underneath the surface. I have often done a lot of background work to enable Alex to participate in a social activity, such as making telephone calls in advance to find out the proposed content and structure of the activity; explaining Asperger's syndrome to the organiser if it is someone we don't know; explaining to Alex what will happen and what will be expected of him; and trying to give him a relaxed and stress-free time in advance of the activity (usually by letting him have plenty of time entirely on his own). When I've succeeded in all of these, he usually has a really good time and copes very well. It may sound like a big effort to have to do all this, but it becomes second nature. And of course, being human, I don't always succeed. However, by using this strategy, I find I am able to expose him to more and more social situations, with increasing success.

One bonus of the home-educating lifestyle's being so varied and flexible is that it does not give Alex the opportunity to become fixed in rigid routines. I don't deny that it can make him anxious and cross when, for example, plans are changed or activities start late. However, I am able to give him regular reminders that plans may need to be changed, start and finish times for activities are often approximate, people get held up in traffic. Because I know how his mind works, I usually have a good idea of when he needs these reminders (his agitation becomes obvious) and he is gradually, if grudgingly, learning to accept these things as inevitable irritations.

Most children with Asperger's syndrome have very specific interests. They need to learn that not everyone necessarily shares their interests and therefore does not necessarily want to hear a great deal about them. For our part, as parents, we must learn to value and respect their special interests, and we do well to remember that it is quite likely that their future career will lie within that area. Home education enables children to have the time and freedom to explore and develop areas in which they are particularly interested and have special skills. When it comes to competing for employment in future years, it may well be that their superior degree of skill and knowledge will help to compensate for whatever deficits they have in the area of social skills. It is also worth noting that, because so many home-educating parents encourage their children to spend a lot of time pursuing their own particular interests and talents, it is not regarded as 'odd' to have specific, passionate interests.

In the areas in which children with Asperger's syndrome are likely to struggle at school (subjects like literature, physical education or religious studies), they can develop at their own pace. When children are set challenges far ahead of their abilities and level of development and do not understand what is required of them, they gain nothing but unhappiness, frustration and damage to their self-esteem. In a home-educating environment they don't have to study these subjects in a formal way, but can be helped to develop them in the course of everyday life.

Just to take the example of physical education, Alex could never be described as a physical person and he finds it hard to participate in team sports. However, he enjoys cycling and swimming (he has taught himself to dive), sometimes enjoys a game of table tennis or golf or goes roller-blading, and has recently started sailing. There is no pressure on him to participate in these activities; he does them because he enjoys them.

How we home educate

Every family must find its own way of going about home education. My approaches to James's and Alex's education have been entirely different, because they have completely different interests, completely different personalities and temperaments, and completely different ways of learning. I guess their different positions in the family probably also have an impact.

I often say that I have had very little to do with Alex's academic education. What I actually mean by this is that he has always taken so much initiative in pursuing his interests that my rôle has mainly been to encourage, support, provide resources and assist when requested, rather than to lead or initiate.

When he was tiny, he happily occupied himself for long periods of time with puzzles, drawing, cutting out, playing with his toy farmyard and similar activities. It was years later that a friend—who knows nothing about autism—remarked upon how he used to love lining up all the animals and vehicles in his toy farmyard. I wouldn't have noticed this piece of 'autistic' behaviour, because I was not aware of its significance at the time.

When he was three, he noticed me teaching his older brother to read. Unusually for Alex, he came and involved himself when he saw this going on and made it clear that he wanted to join in as well. I taught him a little bit, really just so he would not feel left out, but he very quickly started developing his own reading independently. For a long time I was puzzled as to how he was able to learn to read words with complex letter patterns without my having taught them to him, but he later explained to me that he always looked at the writing when I was reading stories to him. I had not realised he was doing this.

By the time Alex had got to the age when one might be feeling one should start giving him some slightly structured programme of education, there was really very little room for me to interfere in his day. Sometimes I might have a bright idea for some fun 'educational' activity I might do with him. However, when I went to him I would invariably find him doing something like reading a book, playing with Lego, making a cardboard model or playing with Polydrons. I could never see any point in interrupting the activity he had chosen for himself in favour of my idea.

One of my rôles was in providing him with resources. He probably started using arithmetic workbooks (bought from W H Smith) when he was about four. Again, I bought these for him so he did not feel left out when his brother had them. Later on, he also had science and English workbooks. However, whilst his brother tended to work fairly systematically through these books, Alex jumped from one page to another, doing half a section here and half a section there. I remember, at the time, trying to encourage him to be more systematic, but he would not accept my suggestions. I now realise that he has his own very individual learning style and that he likes to dip into a wide variety of sources (books, magazines, CD-ROMs, the Internet, *etc.*) in order to build up his own understanding of a subject.

A few months ago Alex accepted that the discipline of following a fixed course of study is sometimes necessary. This was because he wanted to take his maths GCSE and understood that he needed to be thorough and to practise in order to attain a high level of accuracy in the exercises. He managed this for quite a long time, but, having come to a section he finds somewhat challenging, he has now got fed up with maths for the moment and is spending more time on other interests.

Obviously there is absolutely no hurry for him to take any GCSE exams; neither is there any need to make him spend time on maths at the moment—he is already well ahead of what he would be doing in school. I look positively on the fact that he has been able to be disciplined and systematic in an area of study for a period of time, and hope he will be able to develop that further in the future.

Someone who ran a parent group I attended for a while frequently reminded us that people with Asperger's syndrome often want to know, 'What is the point?' Alex could see no point in structured programmes of study when he was younger, because they did not fit his personal learning style. When he chose the goal of obtaining a good GCSE pass, he could see the point of following the syllabus. Although he has abandoned the goal, he still accepts the principle.

Another resource I provided when he was younger was videotaped schools' programmes. I would tape about seven or eight programmes each week, trying to cover a wide range of subjects over the course of the year. These programmes served to reassure me that we were covering all the subjects usually covered in school, and Alex enjoyed watching most of them.

We have always had lots of outings. Outings are one of the joys of the freedom to use one's time as one chooses with home education. Thinking back to Alex's early years, they were often simple things like going to the playground, or to the park to feed the ducks. But we also did things like visiting the Science Museum and art galleries, and went out sightseeing in London. As far as I can remember, his response to these outings was usually somewhere on the scale between contentment and enjoyment.

As Alex got older, he became more reluctant to go on outings and, in my most guilt-ridden moments, I feel he spent several years being dragged around places that his older brother and I wanted to visit. In my more positive moments, I speculate (or rationalise?) that perhaps it was good for him to be taken out and about rather than being allowed to become more withdrawn. It is very tempting to use the Asperger's to explain away any difficulty I have had with bringing up Alex, but of course we all have to learn how to be parents 'on the job', making lots of mistakes along the way. Added to that is the fact that every child is different, so just when you think you are beginning to get it sussed with one, along comes the next one who needs a completely different approach.

On the most simple level, I could say that I had got into a pattern of life that suited me and my first child, and had not really yet noticed that it didn't altogether suit Alex's interests and temperament; however, there were definitely also some 'Asperger's factors'. I remember, for example, when Alex was very small, being aware that I just didn't know him as well as I had known his brother at the same age, and I really found it hard to say what he enjoyed. James had chatted and asked questions endlessly from a very early age: by the time he was two, I felt I knew exactly what was going on inside his head. I found Alex's slow speech development very frustrating, because I longed to know him better.

Obviously, I now realise that it was not just the absence of speech *per se* that was preventing me from getting inside his head. When he subsequently became extremely articulate, I discovered that the things about which we enjoy communicating tend to be very different and that he did not use speech to articulate his emotions. Over the years, I've learned to respect his difference, and have also learned from him as he talks to me about his scientific and philosophical speculations.

I've also learned that I need to explain to him, in very concrete terms, that it is important to try to communicate with people about what he is thinking and feeling if he wants them to be able to meet his needs.

For example, it took me a couple of years to realise that the reason he always hung round me saying 'I'm bored' when we visited certain families was that he knew they had a games computer and he wanted to play on it. We used to offer him all sorts of toys and amusements, but to no avail. Once I realised that 'I'm bored' meant 'I want to play with their games computer', I was able to start helping him to learn to express his desire explicitly.

Another factor that made Alex more reluctant to go on outings was his difficulty with walking. I now realise that this is most probably part of his Asperger's. I frequently used his buggy until he was nearly five, but I suppose I felt he was too old for it by then. I already realised that he was not particularly well co-ordinated, but didn't realise quite how tiring he found walking. We now know that he also has hyper-mobile foot joints, and this also makes walking quite uncomfortable for him. So Alex is, understandably, reluctant to go on outings that require very much walking, unless it is one in which he is extremely interested.

As I have got to know Alex and his needs better, I have been able to introduce outings in which he is more interested, and try to find ways to reduce the amount of walking involved, for example by cycling. I have also learned to take books and story tapes with us when we go out, because he may suddenly decide he has had enough and is extremely bored.

Over the years, these issues have got much easier to deal with, particularly now that James is old enough to want to spend time at home alone and is developing his own independent social life. This means I can take Alex out on his own to places that are of particular interest to him. If he suddenly decides he has had enough, we can just go home if necessary, without having to cut short anyone else's enjoyment.

The most frequently asked question about home education is 'What about socialisation?' All I can say, from our own experience, is that this really is not a problem: Alex has a good and varied social life through the Education Otherwise (EO) activities we attend and the friendships we have built up. He has participated in a huge variety of activities through EO, including art and craft activities, drama, African drumming, canoeing, climbing, archery, go-karting, swimming, skating, survival skills, theatre trips, workshops in museums and art galleries, visits to National Trust and English Heritage properties, camping and much more. Our involvement with EO has provided a very significant part of Alex's education and social life.

Alex has a network of acquaintances spreading right across South London and Kent, and is part of a close-knit group of a dozen or so boys and girls ranging in age from ten to sixteen. I really couldn't ask for a better environment to develop his social and communication skills. Because EO friendship networks are based upon whole families getting to know each other, there is a high level of investment in disagreements and upsets being resolved constructively rather than allowing patterns of bullying and victimisation to develop. (Obviously we don't always succeed, but I would say we do quite well.) The fact that friendship groups are mixed-age is very helpful, eliminating most of the destructive elements of peer pressure.

Friendships between the children also tend to be maintained over many years, leading to their being able to recognise and respect each other's strengths and weaknesses. I see Alex's friends both supporting and protecting him from situations that he finds difficult, and also challenging him in constructive ways: they often seem to know, better than adults, just how far he can be pushed. He, like all the others, is valued for the skills he brings.

Obviously, becoming this integrated into the EO network has required a commitment from me, and is something that has evolved over many years, but I am confident that it will stand Alex in good stead into his adult life. All the fourteen-pluses in his immediate friendship circle are now attending adult or further education classes part time, but still remain active members of Education Otherwise, so there is no sudden loss of these older friends as they move on to new stages of their lives.

Finally, home-educated children naturally have access to all the same community facilities available to children who go to school. Over the years, Alex has attended numerous Saturday and holiday workshops run by the local library, the local authority's Sports Partnership, the Youth Service, and by our Quaker Meeting. One of the advantages of not going to school is that he has enough energy available to go to these things. This kind of session usually involves fairly small groups of children and is organised so as to be experienced by the children as fun.

What about the future?

I like the saying that 'Paths are made by walking.' We all have our own unique contribution to make to the world, and this applies equally (perhaps especially?) to people with Asperger's syndrome.

Even when my children were much younger, people used to ask me things like 'Will they take GCSEs?' I supposed that they probably would, but how could I know? They had not yet reached that part of their life journey. It is only when they get to that point that they (with my advice and support) can choose whether to follow the well-trodden path, or whether to decide that a different route suits them better.

It seems to me that one of the central issues for a person with Asperger's syndrome is to find his own niche in life, where he will feel comfortable and from which he can most easily make his own contribution to society. If that is honestly my aim, then I think I must be open to allowing and helping Alex to find the best path to that place. Paradoxically, he sees his future as lying along a very conventional academic route: GCSEs, 'A' levels and university.

I am not quite sure what it is that people fear can go so drastically wrong if they follow their instincts about what is right for their children today. How can I do what I believe is wrong for him today (*i.e.*, send him to school) because of some vague worry that, at some future date, it *may* prove not to have been the right thing to do? Surely if it is the right thing to do *now*, then it is the right thing to do?

To be honest, I think I would be more fearful for his future if he were in school. In today's world of work, people need to be able to invent their own paths, so it is better to prepare them for that from childhood. There are now many different routes of entry to all levels of education and various careers, because of the widespread recognition that many people are not ready to apply themselves to serious study or work until after their school days. There are also plenty of young people within the EO network now who have never, or hardly ever, been to school; they act as ample rôle models.

The problems of home education

Any problems and drawbacks are going to vary from family to family. For me, finance has been something of an issue. Home educating is not, of itself, expensive, but it has meant I have not been able to do much paid work and have had to be fairly creative in finding appropriate child care arrangements when I have worked.

The downside to being a single home-educating parent is that all the responsibility is ultimately mine. For some people, though, having a partner may make it more difficult: for example, if the partner is not happy about home education.

I think I would have found it hard to have one child in school and one home educated, because, to me, that would be like trying to live two different lifestyles. However, someone else may find that is the easiest way of giving individual attention to the child who has Asperger's syndrome.

The issues are going to be different in each family. I can only speak for myself when I say that, although I sometimes find it hard to know how to provide for the next stage of Alex's education, and although we sometimes get on each other's nerves, by and large I find the home-educating lifestyle a real joy and feel that, as a package, it is providing my son with a good education in the broadest sense.

And finally...

I never try to persuade people to home educate, because I know it is not right for everyone, but I am tempted to advise that if you think it might be the right path for you, do it as early as possible. If school is not working, don't slog on with it year after year, allowing your child's self-esteem to sink lower and lower.

Of course, it is still worth switching to home education at a later stage: older children can still recover their self-confidence and become integrated into home education groups. However, if your child becomes part of the home education network from an early age, he will have the opportunity to form long-lasting relationships and to have his individual needs catered for without having to carry the 'special needs' label.

8

An inspiration to us all
Matthew's story

Karen Marsh

Matthew was five years old when he was diagnosed with Asperger's syndrome. He managed fairly well at a mainstream primary school with a special educational needs teacher throughout his first school years. He was twelve years old when we first started out in home education. The reasons for our decision to embark upon this were wide and varied, and had come about after two unsuccessful attempts at different private schools at secondary level.

Matthew had found the transition from primary to secondary school very difficult. In order to minimise his stress levels, we had chosen private secondary schools, because they were smaller in building size and numbers of pupils attending. However, he was extremely unhappy with both schools, due to bullying and his inability to fit in with his peers. It therefore seemed appropriate to look for an alternative way of education, as it soon became apparent that he was learning very little, if anything, due to his constant stress.

The decision to educate Matthew at home was not taken lightly. It was a joint decision among all members of our family: my husband, who is Matthew's step-father; my daughter, Natalie; my step-son, Ben and, of course, Matthew himself. I felt this was important, as we would all have to make some sacrifices in some ways. We needed to decide as a family that we could make this commitment.

One of the main sacrifices we were to make as a family was financial. I was giving up a good, thriving business as a driving instructor, which would have financial implications for the rest of the family. My husband, John, who is employed as a health scientist, would have to work more to try to make up some of this shortfall. He would also have some input and influence in Matthew's science lessons. With Natalie and Ben, we were careful to emphasise that Matthew was not having more attention than they were, and that we needed their help both in understanding and in other small but just as valuable ways.

Matthew was also to make a personal commitment to understand that he was still 'at school', even though he was at home, and that his 'school' days would be structured accordingly. Also, as he would not be having much contact with other children in a learning environment, he had to make up for this in other ways, such as joining clubs that he could go to in the evenings or weekends. This was particularly important so that he would still have contact with other children his age on a daily basis.

In return for Matthew's commitments to education and socialisation, we promised to give him planned, structured lessons on all areas of a broad curriculum, in which he could work at his own pace and level according to ability. Also, if at any time Matthew wanted to return to full-time education at a school, we would accommodate his wishes and find the most suitable place for him.

After our family discussion, and having been satisfied that we were all ready and able to make this important commitment, I contacted our local education authority (LEA) for information and advice. I must admit I was nervous or wary at first; I had expected that they would oppose or try to talk me out of my intentions. On the contrary, they were very helpful and supportive. We were given an information pack, which outlined the requirements of the education service in an advisory capacity, and a questionnaire, which we were to complete.

The purpose of the questionnaire was to ensure that we had thoroughly thought about the responsibility we were undertaking. Some examples of the questions were what arrangements there were for group work, how we were planning to monitor and assess progress and how we were providing provision for special needs. I believe these are good questions to ask prospective home educators, and if you have considered this project carefully and planned accordingly, you should not have any difficulty answering them.

The initial planning stage prior to commencing Matthew's education took approximately six to eight weeks. This involved intensive research, communication with the LEA, who very kindly put us in touch with other home educators, and discussions with the special needs unit and an educational psychologist. When it came to completing the questionnaire, we had no problems completing anything, because we had been so meticulous and thorough in our planning.

We were aware that, as home educators, we were not obliged to follow the National Curriculum for Matthew's lessons. However, we decided that it would be a good idea to follow it, for a few reasons. For one thing, it meant that getting hold of resources such as textbooks and educational CD-ROMs was much easier. Another reason was that if Matthew decided in the future that he wanted to return to school, he would already be familiar with the curriculum and its requirements. Also, the National Curriculum does provide an excellent framework for structuring lessons. It makes it easier to define your aims and objectives for the whole of your school year, and if you want to link any of your lessons with television programmes for schools, or even with other schools in your area, it is so much better.

And so it began. One of the most satisfying and rewarding periods of my life began the day Matthew came out of the school environment and I began teaching him at home. It is a decision I have never regretted, and both Matthew and I enjoyed the time tremendously.

Prior to the commencement of each new term, I would set out our objectives for that term for each subject. The main aims were that Matthew's learning was to be effective, that he would develop social skills and that he would continue to grow in both these areas. Of course, it goes without saying that Matthew had to learn at his own pace, and there was never any pressure to achieve targets. I set realistically attainable goals for him, because I felt it was important to have something to aim for. However, I found that he went beyond these in all subjects each term. Setting goals also helps to keep you focused with each subject, rather than drifting aimlessly. Matthew thrived on this kind of structured programme.

The textbooks that I used were what would typically be used in a school. I contacted various educational publishers and asked them to send me catalogues and price lists for their books, along with sample material where possible. I also informed them of my rôle as a home educator. All the publishers were very helpful and prompt in responding to requests, and through them I was able to buy the 'best value for money' books available for schools.

In addition to these, I purchased a copy of the National Curriculum guide, which proved a valuable aid to choosing the books that would cover subject syllabi best. Again, although it is not a requirement for home educators to follow the National Curriculum, I found it an excellent guide to each subject, giving me ideas for areas of study.

Having a clear framework of aims and objectives and planning the content of all lessons proved to be a major key to success. Furthermore, when educational advisors came to visit, as they did at least once a year, there were accurate records to show what we had achieved and what we wanted to achieve that year. This meant that relations with the LEA were excellent and, to be honest, I actually valued them, because it provided an opportunity for me to enquire whether I was being effective as Matthew's teacher.

A typical 'home school' day began at 9:15 a.m., after I had taken my other two children to their primary school. We had a set, structured timetable, just as Matthew would have had anywhere else. This timetable stayed the same each week, with only occasional minor changes if we were going on any trips, *etc.* We had three hours of lessons each morning, with a mid-morning break of fifteen minutes. There was an hour for lunch, and then two hours and fifteen minutes of lessons in the afternoon, with a fifteen-minute break between the two lessons.

This suited Matthew perfectly, as he likes structure to his day and an established routine. It also suited me, as I could take and collect the other two children from school. The lessons included English, maths, science, art, technology, physical education, cookery and religious education. We also had one lesson a week on personal and social education (PSE), to cover subjects such as drug and alcohol abuse and other issues.

In addition to our lessons, we would watch the news on television while we had our lunch. This was an extremely valuable resource, which provided us with topics for discussion in PSE and helped Matthew to develop a keen interest in world current affairs. It also helped to stimulate and establish a perspective on issues highlighted on the news that Matthew had previously had no interest in, or indeed had no access to while he was at school.

Matthew also had some voluntary work 'built in' to his curriculum. I felt this was important to establish and maintain a link with the community and to be of help to other people in some way. We visited the local volunteers bureau to find a suitable placement for him that he would be interested in. There was plenty of choice, and he eventually decided on an administrative rôle within a group called the Bully Free Zone, which is an organisation set up to combat the effects of bullying on school-age children. Matthew felt he could identify with this group.

His rôle was to assist in the office with filing and computer tasks. He did this once a week for a couple of hours, and enjoyed this work very much. It was an opportunity to learn new office skills, be part of a team and do something worthwhile for other people who valued his input. This was an important lesson for him socially, and was also effective in building his self-esteem.

To add extra interest and reinforce learning, we tried to have at least one educational visit for each theme in a particular subject. For example, when we were studying weather patterns in geography, I arranged a visit to the Meteorological Office in Manchester. When we were studying the water cycle, we had two visits to Northwest Water, and so on. These visits provide extra resources and learning packs, which are usually free. I found the educational advisor in all establishments exceptionally helpful if you explain that you are a home educator.

Some visits can also be arranged with other home educators. As we live in the Manchester area, I contacted the Museum of Science and Industry, and they informed me of activity days specifically for home-educated children. This is an excellent way of providing a group learning environment for your child.

One of the problems that we could have encountered with home education was in providing practical science lessons. Within a typical school, science is usually a mixture of theory and practical throughout, regardless of level of ability and age. However, to get around this, we searched the library for books on home experiments, which did provide practical ideas and opportunities covering most aspects of science. We purchased a second-hand clinical microscope to assist with biology, and also a home chemistry set. As John, my husband, is employed as a scientist, he chose and adapted some experiments for Matthew.

Occasionally Matthew had homework for some lessons, which he was to complete that night in preparation for a lesson the next day. This did not happen every day, as we were particularly keen for Matthew to develop his social skills in the evening by attending various clubs. We also encouraged him to maintain a friendship with a friend that he had in his previous school, and with another friend who has Asperger's.

The clubs that Matthew decided to join were Scouts, a local football team and a ju-jitsu class. I was very pleased that Matthew had chosen these groups to join, as they would help to develop social skills, and the football and ju-jitsu were sports which would help to increase his physical fitness and co-ordination. They all certainly had the desired effect.

Matthew is a keen Bolton Wanderers fan, so joining the Bolton Wanderers Junior Whites club gave him plenty of scope for conversation with the other children in the group, which proved to be an excellent confidence booster. The ju-jitsu developed his fine motor skills and helped to give him confidence with others of his age, as it is a contact sport. We were very fortunate with the Scouts club, as Matthew was attending a fairly small group, again with children of a similar age. Here, he learned new skills with these children and after a while he went on his first camping weekend with them to learn dry stone walling. This was a huge leap forward in Matthew's social development.

The factor that made these clubs a success was that Matthew's stress levels were much less. The groups were not too large and Matthew was sharing a common interest with others, but, more important, everyone was in these groups because they wanted to be there. For these reasons, I think there is less likelihood of children's feeling excluded from these activities, and these environments can be more conducive to forming friendships.

I can imagine that by now you are thinking, 'Where on earth did this woman find the time to do all this?' or 'How much did all this cost, and was it expensive?'

The answer to the first question is that I was a big believer in thorough planning. This saves so much time later on, and underpins all the lessons by keeping the focus on achieving desirable outcomes. The goal is effective learning, which is measured by progress, no matter how large or small.

The answer to the second question is that it can be as expensive as you want it to be. I bought books by negotiating where possible with publishers or making good use of libraries. I used free resources by contacting relevant establishments either in writing or by telephone. I recorded various educational television programmes for use at appropriate times. Incidentally, it is worth contacting television broadcasters such as the BBC for a free copy of their programmes for schools. They provide a wealth of information that supports their programmes.

The most expensive resource we purchased was a computer. There are, of course, endless possibilities for computers: you can use them for Internet access or use interactive software on CD-ROMs for most subjects these days. Although the purchase of the computer was expensive, we looked at the value the whole family would obtain from it, rather than just seeing it as a home education tool.

One of our best contacts for free resources was British Trades Alphabet (BTA) publications. I obtained the information about them from an Education Otherwise booklet. They produce 'studycards' that schools and home educators can use for projects on various subjects, along with details on how to obtain further information for more in-depth study. They can be tailored to suit any age and ability, and they really are an excellent resource. In addition, the projects can be submitted to the annual studycard competition, which is open to all children of school age.

Matthew entered the competition on two occasions. He first submitted a project on healthy eating, which was based on a studycard sponsored by the World Cancer Research Fund. One of the advantages of this project was that it was cross-curricular in theme: here was a learning opportunity involving science, English, maths and technology. It also helped Matthew's organising skills, something that he does need to practise.

Four months after we submitted the project, I received a telephone call to say that Matthew had won first prize in the Challenge Award section, out of all entries submitted nationally through schools or home educators. What an absolutely astounding achievement for Matthew! The prizes were cash to the school or teacher, and cash for the student who had submitted the entry. In addition, we both had an all-expenses-paid trip to London so Matthew could receive his certificate from the World Cancer Research Fund. This was, without doubt, one of the proudest days of my life and also one of the most memorable for Matthew. He had enjoyed doing the project, he learned much from it and it boosted his confidence, abilities and self-esteem immeasurably.

Matthew continued to take part in the BTA awards studycards projects over subsequent years of home education, submitting work of a consistently high standard, each time on a different theme. His efforts were recognised and rewarded with certificates of participation, which take as much pride of place as his first-prize certificate for his first entry.

Throughout the years of home education, Matthew always worked through his various subjects at his own pace, rather than that dictated by a school. This meant that he worked exceptionally quickly through subjects that he was particularly good at or interested in.

Matthew is quite talented with history. He can recall facts, figures and dates with the most amazing accuracy and he finds this very easy. For this reason, he really enjoys history and welcomes any opportunity to discuss or learn anything new to do with this subject. Within the first eighteen months of home educating, we found that Matthew had covered the three years of Key Stage 3 (the National Curriculum for children aged 11 to 14) in general history. I decided to contact the various GCSE exam boards to look at their syllabi and past exam papers for this subject. The staff of the exam boards were very helpful with any enquiries and points that I wanted to discuss for clarification, and some boards offered an extra information booklet as a guide for private candidates who might not be familiar with exam requirements.

After we had considered all the information received from the various boards and discussed the options with Matthew, he decided he would like to study history at GCSE level. We followed the syllabus for 'British Social and Economic History from 1750 to the present day', with the aim of sitting the exam the following June, at which time Matthew would be fourteen years old. In addition, Matthew and I decided it might also be a good idea to attempt the General Studies exam in this year, as Matthew is also quite talented in general knowledge, and there would also be the benefits of exam practice. We continued with all the other lessons as normal, just working through them at his own pace, still achieving the aims and objectives for each term.

One of the reasons we chose the exam board that we did was because they appeared to be fairly flexible with private candidates in the subjects they offered. With history, for example, there were alternative syllabi that covered the same topics, but allowed the candidate to sit an extra exam paper in place of the coursework elements. It was the same for general studies and indeed quite a few other subjects as well. I found this quite a strong influence in choosing this particular board and syllabus, as straight away there were no concerns about trying to get any coursework validated. Also, the exam board was very helpful in supplying us with details of where Matthew could take the exams in a local centre. Again, this was a very important issue.

Matthew worked extremely hard studying for these two GCSEs. We submitted his request for entry for these exams as a private candidate at Liverpool in January, well on schedule. One of the problems we did encounter was that Matthew would require extra time for the exams, as although his recollection of information is excellent, he does find it very difficult to be selective with what he wants to write and therefore he writes much more than he needs to, still answering the questions accurately and getting the relevant points in, but giving more information than necessary. Also, if he is using a pen rather than a computer keyboard, his writing can be very slow in an effort to present neat work, a factor which is extremely important to Matthew.

In order to get the extra time for these exams, we had to have a report from either an educational psychologist or a doctor. I therefore asked Matthew's consultant paediatrician for a report, which she very kindly wrote and we sent to the board. However, the extra time they offered was not enough in my opinion, and after speaking with the special needs officer at the exam board and going back to the consultant for a further report, we were eventually able to negotiate an extra twenty minutes per hour for each exam paper. As some papers were two hours or longer, it was sufficient time for Matthew to try to complete the questions.

In the months leading up to the GCSE exams, Matthew decided he would like to try to return to a school environment after his exams were finished, perhaps at the start of the following term in September. He was aware himself of how far he had come since we had first started out in home education, both academically and socially, and he was extremely proud of himself and what he had achieved. He felt that he had not only caught up academically with other children of his age, but in many ways had surpassed them.

This was a great leap forward from the days when some teachers had 'written him off' as a child of low ability educationally and socially. Also, as his confidence had grown with his socialisation skills, he felt able to try to return to school. We decided to respect his wishes and look for a suitable environment in which he could continue to grow and progress.

Over the years of educating Matthew at home, we had compiled a 'record of achievement', or portfolio of developments and successes. To this we added information on what Asperger's syndrome is and, in particular, how it affects Matthew. I also gave a statement on the 'subtleties' of his difficulties, and how they manifest themselves educationally.

For example, whilst in the rôle of Matthew's teacher, I had discovered that the very simple tasks can prove very difficult, whilst the difficult areas in some subjects can sometimes be very easy for him, and he can absorb highly technical information, facts and dates with no difficulty after explanation. Also, his inflexibility of thinking or approach to tasks can cause difficulties. When Matthew had taken a computer exam recently, he needed support for the actual exam to ensure he followed the instructions in the correct order, as the format required the ability to manipulate text in a particular way. Without the support, he would not have realised that this was a requirement, and he would have missed out some questions or skill tests, simply because he had not interpreted the question in the correct way, yet he could do all the skills with such ease and efficiency. He therefore had a 'reader' for the exam to get around this problem, and he passed the exam first time.

Within this portfolio there was also a written piece by Matthew, which outlined his interests and what he expected from the school if he attended. I also enclosed statements about his social development, and that although he had made great progress in this area, it would be very easy to inhibit his continued development.

I made a few copies of this record of achievement so I could take them to particular schools and leave the document with them for their perusal, to be returned to me shortly afterwards. We then visited the schools on a 'formal interview' basis, and then toured the building.

After visiting numerous schools, Matthew decided that he preferred the local high school that my daughter attends. We both felt that this school would best meet his needs, and they understood the difficulties of Asperger's syndrome, as they were already familiar with it. The special needs teacher had read Matthew's record of achievement and understood Matthew's particular areas of difficulty. This was a great relief, as at times much effort can be spent trying to educate other people on this condition. Matthew was also relieved that he felt she 'understood him', although he was keen to stress that he 'didn't want a special needs teacher with him all the time'. Matthew was assured that she accepted this, but that she would be accessible for him if he had any problems, and would be there as a link to ensure that the other teachers understood his difficulties and how they might manifest themselves in the school environment.

The school was aware that Matthew was taking two GCSE exams in June. They suggested that he attend the school for occasional days after his exams had finished, so he could settle in before the beginning of the next school year. Matthew felt this was a good idea and looked forward to visiting the school in this way.

June came, and Matthew sat the two GCSE exams at Liverpool. He had worked extremely hard in preparation and he had plenty of practice with past exam papers, so he was familiar with the layout and structure the exam would take. I was so nervous for him, in many ways. For one, I realised that I had the responsibility of interpreting the exam syllabus correctly, and I certainly hoped that I had done so. I also hoped that there would be enough time for him to complete the papers, as I knew that this would be a source of concern and frustration for him. I knew he had the knowledge, but would it be there on the day?

After the exams, Matthew started school for occasional days as arranged. He really enjoyed it and settled in extremely well. I was so pleased that he enjoyed attending school and he soon became an accepted member of an established class. He was particularly keen to take part in sports or games lessons, as this provided him with the 'common ground' of his peers in that he was very interested in sport, both active and passive. Academically, I was right in that he had caught up with other children, and in some subjects he was way ahead, which again gave him much confidence.

In August, Matthew received his exam results in the post for his two GCSEs. He was so nervous opening the envelope, as all the family were in waiting. He had passed! He achieved a grade C in history, and grade E in general studies. These results were the icing on the cake for Matthew and me, in recognition of all the hard work we had put in. These results would have been a great achievement for a child of sixteen or above, but to have them at fourteen with special needs is absolutely astounding.

Matthew is now fifteen years old and continues to progress and develop at school. There have been occasional hiccups, as expected, with misinterpreting homework requirements or cookery assignments, but nothing that either the school or Matthew has not been able to cope with. He has also had two weeks' work experience in a library, which he did very well. As his mother and former 'teacher', I have every confidence in his approach to all he attempts in school. He is, indeed, an inspiration to us all.

9

Once a homeschooler, always a homeschooler
John's story

Lise Pyles

When traditional school fell apart for my son, who was later diagnosed with Asperger's syndrome, we took that first tenuous step into the world of homeschooling. I didn't know that the decision would mean embarking on a one-way street. I had thought it would be a temporary move, a stopgap measure. Homeschooling was a scary undertaking for us, as it is for most folks, but we took comfort in the fact that if it didn't work out, we could go back to the regular school system at any time and just pick up where we left off. But could we really?

Although to most people's eyes we only homeschooled for a little over three of my son's primary school years, from age eight to eleven, much later (John is now seventeen), we are all still feeling the effects of the experience and still feel like homeschoolers. I realize now that when we began this educational path, we took a fork in the road. Even though we eventually met back up on the highway that is the public school system, we experienced a different landscape during those three years, and it has permanently adjusted our view of things. I dare say schools have a different view of us, too.

Luckily, most of the lasting effects from homeschooling have been good, but there have been surprises. We've encountered bumps in the road during all phases of our journey: as we got into homeschooling, as we lived and breathed it for more than three years, and then as we got out again. In many ways, though, we have never gotten out.

Getting into homeschooling

Historically, home education used to be chosen mostly for religious reasons. If you talk with parents of children with Asperger's syndrome, however, you soon learn that most of them never planned to homeschool, for religious or any other reason. More likely, this decision grew from desperation and a lack of other viable options.

Desperation certainly dictated our choice. My son John was diagnosed with a mixed bag of labels when he was three and four years old. 'Attention deficit disorder with autistic features' was what the pediatric neurologist said. (At that time, there was no such thing as a diagnosis of Asperger's syndrome.) John was prescribed Ritalin, which did help in some ways, but also had nasty side effects.

John was also found to have difficulties with gross and fine motor skills, language pragmatics, and sensory integration, all of which we regarded as separate problems at the time, but which we now know are typically part and parcel of Asperger's syndrome. He was assessed by the school as having borderline mental retardation, too, but that turned out to be wrong. It's hard to test a child with problems of focusing, language, and sensory overload. At the time, we did not appreciate the magnitude of his challenges, but I did feel that our child was bright, if we could only get to him.

All of this was hellish to deal with. My husband and I argued over what was wrong and over what to do about it. If there was any bright side during this time period, it was that he qualified for entrance into a publicly funded pre-school for 'at risk' kids. And, naïve parents that we were, we figured that a couple of years in this quiet and intensive pre-school would put him back on track with his peers, and everything would be fine.

But of course that did not happen. At the age of five, after two years of pre-school, John was still not connecting, and was still acting in odd and antisocial ways. The next year, Kindergarten found John being bussed to another school, to participate in a self-contained classroom for the behaviorally or emotionally delayed. This was not the appropriate label or placement, but it was the best the district had to offer.

Unfortunately, the best was not good enough. I say this in spite of loving the special education teachers and feeling that they had the best intentions. It just didn't work. My son rarely interacted with the group. Transitions between activities frustrated him completely. The noisy school bathroom panicked him, and the playground was too chaotic. Even cafeteria smells overwhelmed him. The overstimulation of working in a group, even a small one of five children, brought out behaviors ranging from biting and swearing to throwing chairs and ripping artwork off the walls.

Some good came out of it. The teachers worked with him on eye contact, motor skills, turn taking, and some academic subjects. However, little progress was seen for all the time spent, and he fell further and further behind. Every time John made a milestone, I would look up to discover that his peers had made three more. It was hard even to celebrate his small successes.

In the first and second grade, he continued in the same intensive class, but news wasn't getting better. He still could not handle a full day at school, still could not make the transition into a regular classroom, even with an aide. The teachers pushed it for months, and then one day, when John was seven, they wrote us a short note, saying that they had decided to stop trying. Now what?

We just hung on, living our day-to-day nightmare. Behavior charts ruled our moods, as we hoped that John would earn more smiley faces than frowns. After school each afternoon there was a guaranteed Ritalin-induced emotional downswing, full of tears, headaches, and anger. He was kicked out of his fourth after-school daycare about this time, and my husband and I decided that something had to give.

I had worked full time, but now quit my job to avoid at least the daycare trauma. That helped some, but didn't solve the school problem. John continued to get up and go to school with the grim resolve of a soldier braving the enemy, doggedly stepping onto that special school bus each morning. It broke my heart the day he came home and asked us what a 'retard' was, because someone had told him he was riding the 'retard bus'.

If we were anxious for another answer, John was positively obsessed with it. He hated school with an energy that consumed his evenings, weekends, and every conversation. And then he discovered that some little girls up the street homeschooled. What was homeschooling, he wanted to know? Why can't we do it?

Although homeschooling is more common now, ten years ago it was a foreign concept to most folks, and certainly to me. I hadn't even known it was legal. But John would not let the subject drop. Day after day he asked me about this, in that rigid persistent way that is such a hallmark of Asperger's syndrome.

And then, one day, John's teacher telephoned with the news that her class was being enlarged and she feared it was not going to work for John (as if it had been working?). She also told me that there was no other place in the district for him to go. I now know that this is not an answer that parents have to accept unchallenged, but as a young and naïve parent, I accepted it at face value. My son fit nowhere. I suddenly tuned in to what John had been intoning for weeks. What was this about homeschooling?

It started to make sense. I figured that it couldn't be any worse than our present situation. Also, we suspected that we would be moving out of Colorado within a year or two. The idea of starting at square one with a new school (new tests, new placement, new trauma for John) was more than I could stand. At least homeschooling was portable.

I contacted the school district for a copy of the regulations. Homeschooling is relatively easy in Colorado, but I saw one big problem. At that time, homeschooled children had to be tested every other year. If they scored too low, they could be forced back into public schools. This bothered me, given John's track record with test taking.

My solution to this problem was to sign up with a private 'umbrella school' for homeschoolers. For a fee, they helped us get organized, filed our attendance records and work samples, and were on hand to verify that our child was in private school (even though the school campus was our home and John the only pupil). Some regard it as only a legal loophole, but my response is: thank heavens for legal loopholes! We jumped into that hole and found a whole new world.

Homeschooling: the day-to-day regime

Homeschooling was wonderful. That first week, I kept expecting a truant officer to bang down my door, but after the initial anxiety wore off, what a breath of fresh air it was! No more telephone calls from the school, no more bad reports at the end of the day, no more assessments, meetings, conferences, or feelings of failure.

I had decided to pattern my son's education according to the writings of John Holt, generally regarded as the father of 'unschooling'. He regarded the young child as a natural scientist. To his way of thinking, our best actions as parents are not so much to teach as to facilitate, by providing access to what the child wants to learn.

And so it was that I decided to follow my son's lead, and let him steer our path. The problem was that my son expected to follow *my* lead! On our first morning of homeschooling, he sat down at the kitchen table and awaited directions. When I only started asking him questions about what he'd like to learn, he told me I wasn't doing it right.

I then brought out some workbooks in math and phonics, much to his relief. Although it altered my notion of what unschooling would be, I was in fact following his lead. He was telling me that he needed the comfort of predictability. Fine. It was a place to start. And if I had heard of Asperger's syndrome at this point and had been able to read about it, his need for structure and predictability would all have made sense.

As time went on, he became less rigid. He was able to relax and focus, so that within a month we discontinued Ritalin. Our mornings fell into a rhythm that was structured, but also loose. Our first activity was one that John enjoyed: a deck of quiz cards. If it was a rough morning, I avoided tough questions, and on the days when he seemed more 'on', I challenged him.

The day's work went best if he knew exactly what was in store, but also if he had a hand in its planning, so we took turns choosing tasks.

John's favorites were science and math, or sometimes geography or art. I would fill in with my choices of language arts of some kind (reading, spelling, handwriting, writing). He soon relaxed about his need for worksheets, and began to prefer some of the more adventurous activities.

Our methods became eclectic. Besides workbooks, we used computer games and board games. Yahtzee, Racko, and Monopoly are all great for math skills, Math Bingo came from a teacher supply store, and I invented more games as needed. An ice cube tray and varying numbers of raisins or pennies made fractions easy, for example. John's dad became an excellent resource for evening sessions in such topics as music, astronomy, and politics, and they often abandoned normal bedtime in favor of discussing politics or even just to play a game of chess. John discovered that learning could be fun, and I discovered that, when we stripped away all the distractions and sensory overload of the classroom, John was excellent at learning!

We were able to make rapid progress. We discovered unit studies, a technique of studying a subject in depth and from many angles, which can be great for children with Asperger's syndrome. These children often have such intense interests that it is hard to get them away from their subject. Learning goes more smoothly if lessons incorporate those intense interests. In this way, we studied Japan, weather, and other topics.

We joined a homeschoolers' group, too, which helped in slowly easing John into group situations. We moved cautiously, and only stayed as long as John was successful with it. Watching him interact (or not interact) allowed me to see what social skills were lacking and to coach him. Going so slowly and carefully, he learned to feel a sense of safety in group activities that I think he had never felt before.

I'm a big fan of Abraham Maslow's 'hierarchy of needs' theory. A cornerstone of that theory is that basic physiological and safety needs must be satisfied before moving on to learning. Our Asperger's kids are clothed and fed, but how many really feel safe? This is why, in my opinion, learning at home is such a tremendous option for our kids.

I wanted to try 'unschooling' again, but to avoid John's uneasiness that we were 'doing it wrong', I simply told him that he was working well in the mornings, so we could take afternoons and all day on Fridays off from school. During those times, he could do anything he liked except TV and Nintendo. My job during this time was simply to record all the things John did, and to log them in educational terms. What I mean is, I didn't just say, 'John made a tray of biscuits.' Instead, I wrote, 'Home economics and math: made biscuits, practicing using measuring cups and rolling pin.'

Of course, John did more than just make biscuits. With time of his own, he blossomed. He learned electronics from a kit, built forts, made Lego structures, opened a 'museum' in our spare bedroom, filmed a video, wrote complaint letters, conducted science experiments, and more. I'm confident that more learning happened during unschooling afternoons than during traditional school mornings. More important, he came to believe that learning is pleasurable and a natural part of everyday life, which is a primary goal for unschooling.

In our second year of homeschooling, when John was nine, we moved to England. Since we were affiliated with a military base, we were not affected by the local education authority, and continued as before. We had new terrain to explore, and happily visited museums, tradesmen, town markets, *etc.* Bolstered by the successful group experiences he'd had in the States, John cautiously joined a British Cub Scout troop, took swimming lessons, and joined a bowling league. I was still on hand to monitor and coach these situations, and while not everything was successful, progress was undeniable.

Then, three years into homeschooling, when John was eleven years old, we stopped.

Getting out of homeschooling

What led us out of homeschooling was a combination of my own insecurity and what I thought was a great opportunity. Even though homeschooling had been a lifesaver for us, it had gotten tough. I've read that 'burn-out' drives many homeschooling families to stop at around the three-year mark, and maybe we had a case of that. I just know that it was getting harder to instill excitement into our daily schedule.

We did not have the support or resources that we'd enjoyed stateside. Although I had access to the Internet (in fact, it was at about that time that I first read about Asperger's syndrome on the Internet, and felt that instant chill of recognition: that's John!), the Internet had not yet become the wonderful resource for homeschoolers that it is today. We were doing all right, but the spark I'd felt between us was dimming. Possibly it was doused by too many days of fog and rain, and the depressing atmosphere that came with it. We tired of feeling trapped indoors every day, we tired of the same old materials, and I felt that John was tired of the very sound of my voice. I know that I was!

The heaviest casualty at this time, though, was my confidence. John was so smart! His questions were getting more analytical, while my answers were getting more vague. I had always been comfortable admitting when I didn't know an answer, but it seemed there must be a limit to how hard I could lean on that old stand-by, 'Let's look it up together.' John seemed to need more academically than I could give him (how the tables had turned!), and I began to believe that, at some point, we would have to make a decision about the future. If we were going to continue to homeschool, we needed a new approach: tutors or correspondence courses, perhaps (again, not as prevalent as they are today). And if we were ever going to try public schools again, when should that occur?

As it happened, the school on the military base appeared to be the perfect test bed for seeing how John would cope in a classroom. The school was American (familiar to us), well funded, and small. Only about 120 students attended the entire school, and there were only eighteen in the sixth grade. I could imagine no safer place to let John have a try.

Of course we wondered whether John would fit into sixth grade at all. We'd been working in a near vacuum for more than three years, and he'd been horribly behind academically from the beginning. What if I had failed him as a teacher and he was still behind? I absolutely did not want to set him up for failure. Our first hurdle, then, was that I did not want to enroll John in the school until I knew how he tested, but the school would not test him unless he was enrolled.

Luckily, the school's special education teacher solved the 'catch-22'. She offered to test John during the summer on her own time (and unbeknownst to the principal). John tested at grade level in all subjects except math. In that, he was three years ahead. So much for worrying about our inadequacies at teaching!

It was a good sign, but John's feelings about going back to school were mixed. School was the horse he had fallen off of, in his mind. He yearned to be around other kids and craved access to teachers, but he was afraid. I really felt that he'd mastered enough social and academic skills that he could surprise himself and succeed this time. So, fingers crossed, we enrolled him and he bravely went to face his fears.

John later called that year 'the year I found my brain'. The boy who'd once been judged mentally slow and unable ever to sit among his peers walked into the sixth grade at age eleven and stayed. He coped with a middle school atmosphere of changing classrooms, changing teachers, and school lockers. He made mostly 'Bs' and 'Cs'. I have to say I was completely impressed with him! More important, the payoff in his own self-confidence was worth all of his hard work.

There were bumps in the road, however. He had trouble navigating halls, coping with crowds, and remembering to hand in homework. He thought of himself as separate from the group, so when a teacher said, 'Class, turn to page forty-one,' it did not occur to him that she was also talking to him. We discovered his mild 'face blindness' when he couldn't tell many of the kids apart.

Some of those kids were bullies. As far as John had come, he still came across as 'different'. His vocabulary was too big, his range of conversational topics too small. Body language was a mystery to him, and he had no idea how to make a friend, or even who was a danger. When it comes to bullies, Asperger's children have targets on their chests.

Meanwhile, the school did some subtle bullying, too. I felt we had one strike against us for being homeschoolers (I think we are often treated with suspicion), and another for John's being different. The school could have coped if he'd needed academic help, but they didn't understand a need for social help. As long as he behaved well for the teacher, nothing else mattered. His English teacher saw things the way I did and helped immensely, but nobody else did. In spite of several conferences, and in spite of my bringing handouts about Asperger's syndrome that the staff agreed described John perfectly, the school counselor put in writing what I am sure his co-workers were thinking. His view was that many of John's problems with social skills were probably due to homeschooling!

Parents need to heed this warning. No matter what strides have been made during years of successful learning at home, if any deficits still remain on the day your child re-enters the classroom, homeschooling will be blamed. For us, this was terribly frustrating, not just because it was wrong and unfair, but also because it weakened our arguments for getting special help. They did not believe John had a disability, only rotten parents.

If we had stayed longer, I would have fought this, but we moved at the end of that year, when John was twelve. Stateside I enrolled him in a much larger city middle school, a bad decision that I rectified a month later by pulling him out again. Very soon after, however, my husband got a job opportunity that took us to Australia.

John's appetite for the classroom was still strong, so we found a local private school, and were thrilled to find an American special education teacher working there who had not only heard of Asperger's syndrome, but also had experience with it. Who would have thought? I worked closely with her to ensure that teachers understood John before he entered their classroom.

John has been in that school ever since, doing better each year. At age fourteen, he asked to skip the ninth grade entirely, and now, at seventeen, he is doing well in the twelfth grade. He still has difficulties making friends, but he is making progress. He still has to deal with the occasional bully, but he now feels that they are the ones with the problem, not him. I agree!

John still benefits from those early years of home education. Because of the way it respected his nature, he retains a joy of learning and a seriousness of purpose that few school children have. He studies ahead because he's interested. He catches teachers in the hallway to ask just one more question. It may not socially be the norm to do this, and it startles some teachers, but most enjoy having John in their classes. One said, 'I wish all my students were like John. He is the only student in my class who knows why he is here.' I'm sure John wishes all the other students were like him, too. Imagine a class of kids who think as John does: where logic rules, life is predictable, and social pecking orders have no place.

As for me, I still consider myself a homeschooler. I may have let John join the herd, but it is not with a herd mentality. He is there consciously, not automatically.

Homeschooling has given me an education in the subject of education, too. I have read a great deal about learning and education, and no longer question my own instincts about my children and the way they learn. I listen to the education experts, but with clearer vision and healthy skepticism. Whereas I grew up in an age when no one ever questioned a teacher, I do question things. I offer suggestions and sometimes even argue. Teachers have lost their god-like proportions in my eyes, a change that makes for better teacher-parent teamwork, I think.

Once in a while I come across a teacher who is defensive about her methods and resists my suggestions, but not often. Teachers are there not just to teach, but to have kids learn, and good teachers will adjust to make that happen. For the most part—because John does so well, probably—they accept that I know my child and can give them useful advice when the odd problem arises.

It's a good thing they do. I can't go back to my pre-homeschooling silence and self-doubts, any more than Dorothy in *The Wizard of Oz* could pretend she hadn't seen behind the wizard's curtain. Oliver Wendell Holmes is credited with the quote, 'Man's mind, once stretched by a new idea, never regains its original dimensions.' Homeschooling seems to be a most mind-expanding proof of that adage, for both child and parent. There is no doubt that we are changed permanently.

Do I have regrets about getting into, and then out of, homeschooling? No. We got into homeschooling for great reasons, we thrived there, we got out for compelling reasons, and life is still good. Everyone must make his own choice. Our path was not without difficulties and trade-offs, but we have made it there and back, and have lived to tell about it.

To tell the truth, I miss day-to-day homeschooling. In my mind, however, once a homeschooler, always a homeschooler.

You can read more about Lise's family in Hitchhiking Through Asperger Syndrome *by Lise Pyles (also published by Jessica Kingsley Publishers).*

10

Being himself
Tristan's story

Anne Bedish

Our son Tristan is now eleven years old. He has Asperger's syndrome. We suspected this was so from about the age of six, when we came in contact with other families with children on the autistic spectrum. However, we found it neither necessary nor desirable to get a professional diagnosis of it until he was nearly ten. We live on the outskirts of London and Tristan has never been to school.

Tristan is a very sensitive, guileless, loving boy, but from very early on in his life it became apparent to us that he finds the world to be a fearful place, and this can cause him much anxiety and distress. It has been our special challenge as his parents to provide an environment in which he feels safe and in which he can develop. We have had to lead a somewhat socially isolated existence to ensure this, particularly during his early years, but we have found that when he feels safe, secure and in control, he is more able to relax and enjoy interacting and learning from his environment.

We began to consider not sending our son to school when he was only a few weeks old. I had gone to a National Childbirth Trust meeting with my five-week-old baby to meet other mums with newborn babies, and the main topic of conversation was which school to send their children to. I was horrified: their babies were already being organised to be packed off to school.

Fortuitously, Tristan was an extremely needy baby, virtually constantly breast feeding and, thinking there was something wrong, I went to see a La Leche League breastfeeding counsellor. I arrived at her house on a regular weekday to be met by her three children. I was immediately struck by their self-confidence and cheerfulness and, on asking them what they were doing at home that day, found out that they were educated at home. This was something I'd never heard of, that I didn't know anyone was even allowed to do. Our initial meeting with this family opened up a whole new horizon for us to explore.

We joined the home educators' support organisation Education Otherwise soon after this meeting to learn more and meet families who were already doing it, to see if it was feasible for us. Unfortunately, when Tristan was eleven weeks old, the first of his major problems began. He became acutely afraid of everyone but us. Initially we thought he'd got the normal fear of strangers that most nine-month-old babies get, though admittedly six months early (but don't all parents think their baby is in advance?). We found it very difficult to see other people, even close relatives, as he would become extremely distressed whenever anyone came near him. I would occasionally try to go to Education Otherwise meetings, and would sometimes be able to chat for a few minutes, but invariably I had to settle with talking on the 'phone.

However, in the weeks and months that followed, we managed to read various books on home education and parenting. The writings of the educationist John Holt and the psychologist Alice Miller especially influenced us. We were intrigued by the idea that children learn best when allowed to follow their own interests in an environment where the parents are supportive of and encourage those interests, and not when they are made to learn what they do not enjoy. We learned that children learn in different ways and at different times from each other, and that every child is unique and has his own needs that should be listened to and respected, not only for the sake of his happiness and well-being, but also for his education. Reflecting on schools made us realise that not only did they not do this, but they also set up poor models of social interaction and 'real life' in contrast to the home environment. By the time Tristan was eight months old, we had decided that home education, where we could fully see to his individual needs, was the path that we would follow.

As to how and when we would do it, we were already doing it. At no point was there a moment when we decided that today our son's 'education' would begin. From the very day that he was born he had been learning.

Still, no one can learn in a vacuum, and we didn't expect Tristan to reinvent the wheel. One of the tenets of educators such as John Holt is that children learn through following their own natural curiosity, but Tristan has never been very curious. He has rarely asked 'why' questions and doesn't seem to have an innate interest in what's going on around him (though I can sense some change recently). This lack of curiosity has a major impact on his learning ability, so we have always tried to provide lots of opportunities through our interactions with him to help stimulate his interest and curiosity, bearing in mind his needs.

Most of his learning comes about through his using the computer and his reading, our talking together, showing him things and doing things together, and our encouraging any interests he does get, but all of this in a gentle, unzealous and non-intrusive manner. However, I cannot emphasise enough that he is and always has been free to ignore or reject any of what we do. He frequently does! We are trying to help him learn to trust his own judgment and initiative, to encourage self-motivation. One of the best things about learning at home is that he can pursue whatever does interest him as much as he likes. How can a person become truly self-motivated if he is always directed and interrupted?

Tristan's learning is not broken up into subjects: he would never experience a computer game about Vikings as 'history', or looking through a microscope as 'science', though we may describe them this way. Learning does not just happen between the hours of nine and three, nor is it separated from everyday living. We are trying to help him learn about life and himself in his own unique way. It is vital that what he experiences has real meaning to him for it to have any chance of an impact.

As a toddler of about a year, he began to want me to read to him and this is what I did, for hours every day. He liked to hear the same stories over and over again. He didn't seem interested in playing with his toys (apart from the switches of our lights, hoover and mixer), so I thought he just didn't like them and bought loads more; but after he had examined each new one and discarded it, I eventually came to the conclusion that he simply preferred my human company to that of a piece of plastic or wood. We didn't realise then that he had a problem with his imagination and play.

Then one day, when Tristan was four, we found out quite by accident that he could read, and read completely fluently. I would like to be able to say how he had taught himself, but I've no idea. There were no indications that he was trying to read, nor do we know precisely when he had mastered it. On a few occasions I had put my finger under words while reading to him, misguidedly hoping to 'teach' him (I was still learning about learning), but he had always taken my hand away. All we did was read to him as much as he had wanted us to. His learning to read by himself seemed a confirmation that child-led learning worked.

We continued to follow his lead in all aspects of his life, whilst providing as interesting and stimulating an environment as he felt safe with, but we were very worried about his fear of other people, as it caused him such distress. In retrospect we can see that there were many signs of Asperger's. For example, he never babbled, but began talking at the normal age, albeit unclearly for a number of years; he didn't do pretend or symbolic play; he never pointed things out and his eye contact was very poor. Nevertheless, we are glad that we didn't interpret these as something 'wrong'. At the time, they bothered neither him nor us, and we feel more than happy with the approach we adopted for him.

Socially we sometimes got together with friends or relatives, and by the time he was three, he had grown to feel less uncomfortable with adults. However, his fear of other children continued, to the extent that whenever we were out somewhere and another child came close by, he would get in a terrified state. By the time he reached the age of four, when so many children are beginning school, we decided to take more active steps to help him with his fear, while realising how lucky we were that we had chosen to keep him at home. We cannot imagine how he would have managed school—or rather, we can only imagine the worst.

A local home-educating family advertised in the Education Otherwise magazine that others would be welcome to visit them, so one day Tristan and I went to their house. We stayed about ten minutes until it was too much for Tristan and then left. We returned a fortnight later, stayed a bit longer and left. This carried on for several months until one day Tristan, huddled in my arms, looked around and saw a toy that one of the other children was playing with. He left my arms, pulled me along and went over to this other child and looked at the toy.

This was the tentative beginning of a relationship with these children. At first Tristan was very wary, pulling me along wherever he went when we saw them, but over the years he became more comfortable and now, although it can still be stressful for him, he looks forward to seeing them. He has now built up a little circle of friends from three different families, a mixture of girls and boys from four to thirteen years old. We visit each other regularly, each family separately, so we have all got to know each other very well.

The wonderful thing about these other children, who have also never been to school, is that they have never experienced the peer pressure or peer dependency that so many school children do, and feel no need to conform to whatever the current peer norm is supposed to be. They are very accepting and tolerant of others. Once, another friend of one of these children was present and mercilessly teased Tristan, even screaming near him once she'd discovered that loud noises hurt his ears. The whole incident was horrible and made worse by the fact that we didn't know it was going on until Tristan appeared at our side very upset (he had been within sight, but not sound of us). Luckily this was an isolated incident for him, although he refers to it still, twelve months later.

It could be argued that in having a rather restricted group of friends, whom we have in essence vetted, we over-protect our child, but judging by the accounts of individuals with autistic spectrum disorders who suffered a lot of teasing and bullying in their childhood, with the resultant low self-esteem and negative impressions, then that is only a good thing, and we will continue to protect him for as long as he needs and wants. Having positive social experiences can only be of benefit to such a person as Tristan. I can see that negative experiences would only exacerbate many of his difficulties associated with his Asperger's.

His friends are also not restricted to children; he has adult ones, too, and he says he has enough friends. We have occasionally tried going to group activities with other home educators, but he hasn't enjoyed these at all; they don't suit him. There are too many people in one go for him. He prefers the company of just one or two at a time, so unless he asks, we won't encourage group events.

Just before Tristan's fourth birthday, we bought a computer. From the first day we got it and installed our first program, *Grandma and Me* from Brøderbund, this computer has had a major impact on him. That first day he spent from 10:00 a.m. until 9:00 p.m. playing with the program. His self-confidence visibly soared. Here was something that he could control and make do spectacular things in a way quite unlike anything else. The computer immediately became the main interest, focus and love of his life, and has remained so.

Over the years, we have purchased many useful and some useless programs. Our first priority has always been that the program should be highly attractive, with lots of variety and novelty. Some so-called 'educational' programs are little more than glorified workbooks and Tristan gives them very little attention, so we made a number of expensive mistakes. Happily, we have managed to find a lot that are very well done.

Tristan usually has a current favourite that he will play for hours and hours every day, for weeks or months at a time, exploring it fully. He has enjoyed all sorts, from 'point and click' programs when he was younger to running simulated worlds and simple programming and experimenting, as well as conventional strategy and fighting games, which are his current favourites. Although he spends a lot of time using the computer by himself, we also do things together on it, not just because he likes me to see what he's doing and sometimes help him, but also because there can be so much to talk about and enjoy together.

We had originally thought to get the computer to help our son learn conventionally 'educational' things and were astonished that it could have so many other benefits. The programs can be expensive, but when we consider the hours he uses them, they translate into remarkably good value. Undoubtedly the computer has become a valuable and important source of pleasure and knowledge that he is unable to get so easily from more conventional sources.

We have filled our house with a wide variety of ordinary toys and games and so-called 'educational' toys and kits, although we don't really distinguish between the types. We have arranged them on shelving where Tristan can easily see and access them, but he hardly ever does. They don't stimulate his curiosity or imagination. I occasionally get something out and start using it myself. I do this in a very casual, non-intrusive way: at the most I will make an encouraging remark, and sometimes his interest will be attracted. He does not have to join in, but a vinegar and sodium bicarbonate 'volcano' or other comparatively attractive activity will sometimes engage him. I always make sure that it is something that I genuinely enjoy doing myself too.

An exercise that we have always enjoyed doing every eighteen months or so since he was four is making a life-sized drawing of himself: Tristan lies on a large sheet of lining paper while I draw around him. Then we draw in his main internal organs, heart, lungs, *etc.*, which he helps colour in and label. We print a photo of his face to put at the top and hang this on a wall. We keep all the old ones together so he can see how he has changed over the years.

We have also found some amusingly written books with suggestions for intriguing science experiments that he has enjoyed. In this way we are not only playing with or making something together, but also exploring various aspects of science and technology and sometimes history and geography.

Playing with toys and doing pretend games also doesn't come easily to Tristan. Although he likes getting them, he can find it hard to 'play' with toys, but he enjoys my initiating play with them for him, which I do from time to time, more so when he was younger. Seeing one of his friends playing with his things is also an excellent way to get him playing more imaginatively (though this has happened only since he was eight years old or so).

This problem with imagination has quite a global effect on the way he thinks and learns. It is not just conventionally creative areas that are affected. The kind of abstract academic work that school children do would be difficult, too. If you find it hard to think creatively, then it's difficult to imagine different possible solutions to problems in life in general, so we try to encourage any interest in fiction, pretence and play to enhance Tristan's imagination.

Topics involving history and geography we can do through conversation, looking at books, using computer programs or watching television, but this does not give him the experience that he really needs to make the subjects interesting or meaningful to him. Occasional visits to historic places such as castles are better, as are 'living history' museums: we once sat for two hours in an Iron Age round house surrounded by a selection of cooking and farming implements that we were able to handle. A beach where one can find fossils has become a favourite place to visit. Another useful thing we have done is to draw a timeline on the wall along our stairs on which we mark things that Tristan has come across in history. We have added little pictures and photos, including a photo of him when he was born, so that he can see himself in relation to historical events and people.

Since he was seven and we felt he was able to cope with holidays away from home for more than a few days, we have been to France a number of times, something he has thoroughly enjoyed. He has fully experienced a country with not only a different language, money and food, but also a different climate and varied terrain, from the hot, dry Mediterranean to the high Alps. We have a number of French language videos that he always enjoys watching before a trip, and he has attempted to speak a bit of French himself. On our last trip, at a favourite *brasserie* in St-Omer, Tristan asked for *'Un Cacolac, s'il vous plaît?'* and was very pleased when he not only got his *Cacolac*, but was rewarded with some sweets from the friendly *patron*.

Visiting places can be hard for Tristan and he is extremely reluctant to go out; he can't predict what is going to happen, and this can make him feel unsafe and anxious. He doesn't like strangers talking to us either. We plan and talk about our trips well in advance, and make it clear that we will respect his decision if he doesn't wish to go. Once there, he usually enjoys himself. (I only wish he'd remember that!)

We have found it best to revisit places several times over the years to help him feel more familiar and comfortable there; for example, visiting London Zoo frequently over a period of years has meant he now not only feels fairly safe in the environment, but has seen the animals grow and change with time. Being able to visit during school term time means that places are relatively uncrowded and quiet, which suits him. Belonging to Education Otherwise or having season tickets also means that we don't have to stay long if the visit is not going well. We don't feel we have to see everything in one go or stay for ages, and short visits are better for him anyway. If his attention is drawn to one particular thing, we will spend a long time just on that and then go home, the whole experience leaving a greater impression on his mind.

I will sometimes take photographs of places we visit and things that have attracted his attention there, and of things we've done or made at home. I try to make sure that Tristan is in the photographs; that gives them a special meaning for him. We arrange them in folders that we look at and talk about from time to time. We find this a very helpful way to keep alive what we have done and to give relevance to new but related things.

Tristan has always enjoyed talking a lot, but he finds it difficult listening, keeping track of and making sense of conversation in general. Being at home and having two-way conversations with me is good practice for him. Of course we don't experience it as 'practice', but in effect it is, and far easier for him in the peace of our home than elsewhere.

In fact, it is through our conversations and discussions that a lot of informal natural learning takes place—in both directions, I might add. I remember an occasion when Tristan and I were travelling on an Underground train some years ago. He was telling me enthusiastically and in great detail in a loud voice all about the different types of cloud there are, which was his current interest. The other passengers were staring in amazement. I felt so proud that he knew so much about clouds, far more than I did—most likely far more than the other passengers, too!

Reading continues to be an important activity for Tristan. Despite the fact that he could read fluently from an early age, he continued to want me to read to him for long periods each day. It is actually only since he was ten that he has begun to read fiction books previously unread by me to himself. Reading non-fiction books was no problem, and through them he has been able to enjoy learning a lot of fascinating and useful facts about subjects that have interested him deeply from time to time. Unfortunately, a phobia of snails and slugs means that he has got rather wary of looking in a lot of non-fiction books, especially nature books that might contain pictures of molluscs. We've put away all the nature books and are trying to restore his confidence in reading others. Fortunately, a television series about dinosaurs has led him to reading books on the subject, and he is now becoming quite knowledgeable about them.

We will happily encourage and feed any interest with books, computer software or whatever; his interests can be a wonderful way of learning. Through this current one he is not only learning about dinosaurs, but also the written word, science, history, geography and arithmetic. He likes to find out how long and tall those dinosaurs were and compares them with each other.

Needless to say, we spend a fair bit of money on books, though we try to take advantage of bargain bookshops or library sales. Some of his books Tristan has not even bothered to look at, but we continue to provide him with those that we think he might be drawn to, as he finds it too difficult to choose for himself. When we purchase a new book, Tristan might look at it straight away, but if he doesn't, I place it in a prominent place and draw his attention to its location. If after a week or so the book is still unread, I put it in one of his bookshelves, making sure that he knows where I've put it. He does tend to re-read the same books over and over again, but he gains a lot of pleasure and knowledge doing so.

Although there have been times when he's enjoyed watching a particular video over and over again, he doesn't watch much television, only the occasional film or comedy, or sometimes a documentary. However, one serial he nearly always watches is *Star Trek: The Next Generation*. This has proved not only highly enjoyable, but also very helpful in an unexpected way. It's not so much an interstellar 'shoot up' as a psychological or philosophical drama, and this lends itself well to discussions about the characters and why they are behaving as they are. Other people's feelings and the reasons for those feelings can elude him, so it's nice having such an exciting way to talk about them. Of course, in this situation he is an onlooker, which makes it easier for him to work things out; real life is more problematic, but we think this is still helpful, and it is enjoyable and non-threatening for him. Talking about his and our feelings is, of course, helpful too towards understanding them.

Arithmetic is not something that Tristan has ever been keen on, though we have tried various ways to make it attractive for him, mostly without success. It has proved difficult to bring it into his life in a meaningful way, apart from the measuring of things and spending money. When he was about six, I bought some 'educational' products aimed at helping children with maths, but these all relied on their being played with, something Tristan didn't do. I spent several hours enjoying making patterns with Cuisenaire rods, but Tristan gained nothing from them.

We bought maths software which, of course, enjoying anything to do with computers, he used for a while, so he absorbed some of it, but those programs were never a big hit. At six, he learnt all the times tables from a song tape that he liked, but he didn't know what multiplication meant and got furious whenever I tried to explain it, even with objects so he could see it. At one point we panicked and bought attractive workbooks, but he hated them; to get him to use one was a losing battle and didn't teach him anything, so we quickly realised this method would not work.

Eventually, with occasional talking about it, the odd bit of software and the passage of time, he has come to understand basic arithmetic. I bring into our everyday conversation ideas about percentage and fractions, but only in the sense that he'll meet them in life (when was the last time anyone bought 3/20ths plus 5/17ths of something?). Mathematics, as opposed to everyday arithmetic, is too abstract for him, so unless he asks or it crops up naturally, we're not planning to do any of it.

Actually, he enjoyed doing a bit of geometry when he was seven. He has always been fascinated with the lengths of things, and wanted to know how tall the trees in our garden and elsewhere were. I discovered a nifty gadget in an educational catalogue: a clinometer, with which an observer can measure the angle of their eyes between the horizontal and the top of a tree or building and then, using the principles of a right-angled triangle and a scale drawing, calculate the height. The clinometer came with detailed instructions that made it very easy to do the calculations. Together we found out the heights of everything he wanted. This was an application of mathematics in an entirely practical, meaningful and interesting way to him.

When Tristan was little, I purchased loads of art materials, paints, felts and colouring pencils, misguidedly thinking all children like those sorts of things, but painting and drawing are things he has not been able to enjoy. His imagination, again, doesn't help him, but that doesn't mean he doesn't like looking at art, and he has enjoyed the occasional visit to art galleries.

Writing stories is also problematic, not only for the same reasons of imagination, but also because of his awkward handwriting, due to problems with hand co-ordination. When he was younger he used to get extremely angry with himself, because he could see that his handwriting was very ill-formed (we weren't judging it—he was), so we encouraged him to dictate to us or type on the computer instead. This is more satisfactory to him, especially as his spelling and grammar are good because of all his reading.

He is finding it useful to do a few physical exercises every day. This is helping to improve his hand co-ordination, but activities such as swimming, ball games, riding a bike or using playground equipment are difficult for him and he doesn't enjoy them at all. Luckily, he's not under any pressure to do them.

Trying new things and making choices and decisions are very hard for Tristan, undoubtedly partly due to a preference for sameness and a dislike of change. These are challenges he will have to face if he is to become self-motivated and independent in all aspects of life. Being able to practise these skills in simple everyday situations in a safe environment, *i.e.*, at home with no pressure, we hope will help him.

For example, when he was younger he ate mostly the same foods all the time, so we gave him what he wanted while we had the same with something else. For example, plain pasta was his favourite for years; we'd have sauce and cheese with ours. Eventually he tried it with a bit of cheese and later with sauce as well. We never put pressure on him to try new foods, just made them available (fruit, milk and a vitamin and mineral supplement meant he was getting a nutritious diet) and now he eats a more varied diet. He enjoys reading cookery books and, although he won't cook himself, he asks me to make new dishes from them from time to time. Even if he rejects these, it is enough progress for him that he has wanted to try them.

As another example, Tristan always likes to wear the same clothes. To avoid distress when he was younger, I just bought the same of everything. Once I bought a different colour but same style top and asked him to choose which to wear. Even rejecting the new top was now, in a sense, a choice, and so he is progressing from there. He still wears more or less the same clothes every day, but he now chooses them himself. He finds it difficult to choose clothes in shops, so I always buy from those that it's easy to return the things to, in case he can't decide or dislikes them or they're uncomfortable for him, as his skin is very sensitive. I make sure his tops and trousers all match, so that even if he takes the first thing he sees from his clothes rail, he will still look well dressed.

Of course, the biggest single factor in helping our son towards a self-motivated life is enabling him to follow his own interests, to choose whatever he does or doesn't do, whilst maintaining a stimulating and interesting environment and respecting his choices.

Learning life skills is very much a part of Tristan's everyday living. He doesn't need to learn them as a separate exercise. Simply being at home with me means that he is exposed to some of the daily work involved in running a house. As I don't drive, we use public transport to get around when my husband (our driver!) is at work, so Tristan is familiar with the whole concept of buying and using tickets on trains, the Underground and buses, and in working out a route from A to B. He sometimes accompanies me with shopping, and enjoys buying himself things with his own money and planning to save for things he wishes to purchase—all of which helps with his arithmetic skills, too.

Despite his tendency to be fearful, Tristan has always been an exuberant person and able to get a lot of joy out of life, but with increasing awareness he has become very anxious, developing obsessive compulsive behaviours and repetitive questioning. It was in fact this greatly increased anxiety that prompted us to get a professional diagnosis of Asperger's syndrome in order to gain access to help and advice. Although it is very disturbing for us to see him like this, we feel it is fortunate that he has the freedom to express his anxieties in the way he needs to in the safety of our home, without the pressure to change his behaviour or conform to suit others. By the same token, he is also able to express himself in ways he just simply enjoys without risking censure or ridicule from others.

An obvious way we've found to help him with his anxiety is to maintain a calm atmosphere at home, mainly by being calm ourselves, and to give him the verbal reassurance and extra cuddles that he needs. Keeping the house organised seems to help. Having soothing music on has a good effect too: Tristan gets distressed and anxious by what he perceives as loud noises, so calming ones are beneficial to him. We find pieces of Baroque music are particularly helpful in this respect. We have also found some pieces of music, combining music and nature sounds, which are specifically designed to entrain the brain and induce a more relaxed state. Whether or not they do that, Tristan really enjoys them.

On a suggestion, Tristan drew up a schedule of his day: not a very detailed one—mealtimes, washing and brushing teeth, that type of thing. He does not feel he has to stick rigidly to it, but it is enough to have drawn up a framework on which to 'hang' his day and give him a sense of direction. His own personal calendar that we make, showing twelve weeks at a time instead of the usual month, is very helpful, too.

He writes on it when we are seeing friends or going out to places, or special dates like birthdays and Christmas. He crosses off each day that has passed so he can see at a glance the current date and what is happening when, which helps him feel more secure. He finds it easier to keep in mind any future plans with this.

As a result of his Asperger's syndrome, many things in Tristan's ordinary everyday life can be hard for him to manage, but being very aware of these things, we are able to engineer his environment to make sure that he has as many successful experiences as possible without too many frustrating ones. Frustration has an extremely deleterious effect on him, damaging his self-esteem and making him more anxious: it in no way enables or stimulates a desire in him to succeed. Success is vital for him first time; life itself presents him with enough frustrations. He doesn't always understand things that can seem obvious to others, and he needs frequent reassurances every day about many things, but I am able to be there for him all the time that he needs me. However, his ability to become so focused on whatever interests him is a wonderful asset for him, as is his ability to keep himself occupied, in whatever way. He has never in his whole life complained of boredom or of not knowing what to do.

All of us have only one childhood. When we are adults, this just consists of lifelong memories and impressions of our childhood that have a profound effect on us. There is no second chance. In choosing to enable our son to learn, or rather experience life, at home rather than at school, this is something we can bear in mind all the time. How will he remember his childhood? How will it affect him as he grows towards, we hope, a self-fulfilling adulthood?

We listen to Tristan and try to imagine what we would need from parents if we were in his position, with his particular needs and outlook on life, and act accordingly. That is the best that we can do. Being his parents and loving him and knowing him as well as it is possible to know another person, we are in the unique position of being able to be totally adaptable, flexible, empathetic and responsive to all his needs, and we feel enormously happy and privileged that we can do this.

One afternoon recently, quite out of the blue, Tristan said he'd like to go mushroom hunting. This is a boy who has never asked to go out! So we did, there and then. As luck would have it, we found many different kinds, and as I watched his delight in finding them and identifying them from a little book we happened to have, I reflected that being able to give him such freedom to explore his world as and when he feels safe to is a joy to see.

We are not perfect. There are times, I'm sure, when we have made mistakes. We are sometimes filled with doubts about what we are doing, but this is actually always helpful, as it makes us review critically what we do and reaffirms our commitment to our chosen path. It does require a lot of emotional energy and we often get very tired, but despite all the difficulties, we can have a lot of fun together, and… after all, he is our son.

11

The difficult child
Alexandra's story

Rachel Cohen

First steps

Alexandra was a very much wanted child. Although I didn't become pregnant until I was thirty-nine, once it happened I was very excited. I felt very alive and well throughout my pregnancy. I enjoyed shopping for the nursery furniture and picking out baby clothes. I bought a little stuffed monkey, which we still have today, as Alexandra's first toy.

Alexandra was a beautiful baby, as all babies are. I loved to dress her up in pretty clothes. When I walked her down Queens Boulevard in Forest Hills, a quiet residential neighborhood in New York City, people would stop me on the street to tell me what a beautiful baby she was.

Language development was quite normal. Prior to her first birthday, she spoke the words 'Mama', 'Dada', and 'Nana'. She said the word 'boont', meaning balloon. 'Shoe' was another early word spoken, although with a lisp on the 's' sound. Other simple words, such as 'cow', 'man', 'cat', *etc.*, soon followed.

I remember her first sentence clearly. We were on a vacation trip to Barbados when Alexandra was eighteen months old. When she saw one of the hotel staff walking towards us, she said, 'Man coming.' Other sentences soon followed. Her mischievous nature began to show during this trip. She managed to get herself locked in the bathroom, necessitating being rescued by one of the hotel staff.

I was fascinated watching Alexandra's developing language. By the age of two, she had some real speech ability. I talked to her as much as I could, and spoke the words back to her to enable her to develop clear speech. Her language skills continued to develop, and she could definitely make her needs known by age three.

Her early physical development proceeded normally. She rolled over before the age of three months, sat up at six months, and was walking at eleven and a half months. Very shortly after she took her first steps, she began climbing all over the place. Alexandra soon found her way out of the crib. I did not notice any of the difficulties with small motor co-ordination which were to become a problem later on. She seemed able to manipulate her toys quite well and to pick up small objects with ease.

Early differences

I was unaware of Alexandra's being different from other children until she started Kindergarten. As I look back, however, there were some differences. Alexandra would not cuddle when she was picked up. It was almost as though she were trying to move away from me. She was often very restless in her crib, and would not sit still in her stroller, even to the point of getting her leg twisted in the safety strap one afternoon. I needed to comfort her with a bottle quite frequently.

If you looked straight at Alexandra, her eyes would be diverted either to the side or straight up at the ceiling. She still has this tendency today, and does not like to be stared at. She also developed quite a collection of stuffed animals, which she would line up carefully in neat rows. I thought that this was quite clever at the time, but I now realize that it was an early sign of Asperger's syndrome (AS).

The terrible twos

Most toddlers go through the 'terrible twos'. With Alexandra this stage began before the age of two and lasted well beyond toddlerhood. Her hands were on everything. She had the need to be constantly touching things. I removed all breakable items from any place reachable. My end tables and coffee table stayed bare for years. In fact, my first attempts at restoring knick-knacks to the end tables resulted in a broken Lenox bud vase and candy dish. I continued to leave the tables bare for another few years.

Temper tantrums were frequent and remained a problem for years. Only a bottle seemed to comfort her. Sometimes she would be inconsolable. I would try holding her firmly during tantrums, but she would break away. Temper tantrums remain a problem even today, but fortunately are much less frequent. She can really get worked up if she is angry.

Going to a restaurant was always a problem with Alexandra. She was a picky eater for anything except sweets, and going to a restaurant was not a pleasant experience. She would leave her seat and start rolling on the floor as we finished our meal. Sometimes she would become hysterical, and we would have to leave the restaurant. Many a restaurant meal had to be wrapped and taken home.

On a trip back from Disneyland in California when Alexandra was two, our airplane had to return to Los Angeles airport due to a mechanical problem. This caused a delay of several hours. It was very difficult keeping Alexandra amused all of those hours. In the middle of the busy airport lounge, she started rolling around on the carpet. When I tried to pick her up, she pulled back like a reluctant dog on a leash.

Pre-school years

I have always been an advocate of early education, believing that it would stimulate a child's learning ability and natural curiosity. I lined Alexandra's crib and playpen with board books opened to brightly colored pictures. When she was a little bit older, I enrolled in a children's book club, and spent many hours reading picture books aloud to her. I bought *Kid Songs* and *Sesame Street* videotapes, which were played over and over. We watched the *Sesame Street* television program. As a result, Alexandra easily learned her ABCs and numbers prior to entering Kindergarten.

As eager as she was to learn to recognize her ABCs, she would refuse to let me show her how to write her letters. Using a National Geographic book, I taught her the names of all but the least commonly known North American mammals. Friends of ours were quite impressed when our daughter was able to name the animals on practically every page of that book.

I also picked up a puzzle of the USA for Alexandra. She not only learned to recognize all of the states from their shapes, but she personalized the puzzle pieces as well. She would line them up in rows and tell stories about Arizona, Maryland, California, *etc.* Again, I thought that this was very clever behavior, but did not recognize the autistic nature of it.

I had bought a magnetic letter board for Alexandra. My mother, who lived in the downstairs apartment of our house, used it to teach her to read rhyming words such as 'bit, hit, sit' and 'bat, cat, mat'. She had an excellent memory for words, and was soon able to read simple story books.

We also used reading flashcards. These flashcards had both the word and picture on one side and just the printed word on the other side. With her excellent memory, Alexandra soon learned to read the word side of the flashcard. After a while, she began to create a variation of this game. Instead of saying the word 'baby', she would say 'the one who sleeps in a crib', or instead of 'cat', 'the one that says meow'. She would refuse to tell me the real word for the card, but would instead make up a riddle to identify the word. She would really get quite worked up if I insisted that she tell me the actual name. Again I thought that this was a sign of real cleverness, and didn't recognize the true autistic nature of this behavior.

As her reading proficiency increased, I bought some of the early readers such as *Hello Reader* (Scholastic Books) and the *Step into Reading* (Random House) series. Alexandra's mind was always extremely creative and active. She would be constantly thinking of ideas while she was trying to read. It was difficult for her to read more than a few words at a time without stopping to ask a question or tell me something. I knew that she was thinking of things at the same time that she was reading the words.

Kindergarten and first grade

We moved to the suburbs shortly before Alexandra's fifth birthday. I had fond memories of growing up on Long Island, New York, and having beautiful parks and a nice yard to play in. I certainly wanted the same for my daughter.

Having always been very education oriented, I was really looking forward to September and the start of the school year. I got very involved in all the pre-Kindergarten meetings at the local elementary school, including having my daughter visit the Kindergarten class. At one of the meetings, we received a little book stating what your child should know before entering Kindergarten. I felt very proud that Alexandra knew all of her letters and numbers, was familiar with many children's songs, and could read simple rhyming words. I was a bit concerned that she had no interest in learning to print her name, but was sure that the Kindergarten program would be able to teach her. Overall I felt very confident about our new venture.

On her first day of Kindergarten, Alexandra had no problem with my leaving her behind. Every morning I would park the car, walk her to the meeting place where all the children would line up with their respective teachers, and then go home to start my day. Three weeks into the Kindergarten program, her teacher walked up to me at the morning meeting place and said very emphatically, 'She's not adjusting!' I was shocked. Thus began our two-year nightmare in the public school system.

Our elementary school was privileged to have an all-day Kindergarten program. However, because of physical space limitations, fifty-four children shared one large room with two teachers and two teaching assistants. Obviously this is not the kind of environment that you would want to place any child in, let alone an AS child. When I visited during observation week, there was a constant din in the room and much distraction and overstimulation. No more than twenty minutes were spent on any one activity, as the children were moved from one learning center to another. Nine notes on a glockenspiel signaled the start of the next activity.

There followed numerous meetings with both Kindergarten teachers, Mr. LoCascio, a dour-faced middle-aged man, and Mrs. Silverman, a perky young first-year teacher. Each time that I came home from one of these meetings I was emotionally drained, exhausted, and even reduced to tears.

Apparently Alexandra had tested at the low end of the screening test. Unfortunately, teachers are often very influenced by these test results. What I did not know at the time was that I had a right to refuse these pre-Kindergarten screening tests, which had been administered early in the morning, not Alexandra's most alert time of day.

I was told by the Kindergarten teachers that she was behind in many areas, especially small motor co-ordination. They were concerned because she spent so much time by herself at the doll house during free play and seemed withdrawn. I was told that she could not follow simple directions and was disorganized. I was really disturbed when Alexandra was not allowed to visit the fire truck that visited the school one after-noon because she failed to come when her group was called.

At first the Kindergarten teachers tried being helpful and suggested activities for developing small motor co-ordination. At later meetings they suggested testing. My response was that since I did not see any of the problems that they were speaking about when I worked with Alexandra at home, I saw no point to testing.

At a subsequent meeting, Mr. LoCascio and Mrs. Silverman said that they were recommending to the principal that Alexandra repeat Kin-dergarten. They did not even feel that she would benefit from the tran-sition (slow) first-grade class. In anger, I responded that I did not feel that another year in this fifty-four–child 'zoo' would be beneficial, and that repeating Kindergarten was an outlandish idea for a child who was beginning to read. I also stated that since Kindergarten was not a man-datory grade, my decision was for Alexandra to begin first grade next year. I immediately made an appointment with the principal, who agreed to place my child in a regular first-grade class.

When I visited the Kindergarten during observation week, I did get a glimpse of what the Kindergarten teachers were talking about. I was absolutely shocked. The children were reading aloud from an oversized book on an easel. My child was totally withdrawn and in her own world. She did not respond to any of the questions, even when asked directly. It was almost as though she were in a stupor. We had discussed more difficult stories during read aloud time at home, and Alexandra could readily answer most questions. At the same time, she was always very talkative and energetic at home. Here was a totally different child from the one that I knew at home. Apparently she could not function with other children around her, and withdrew from the noise and distraction in the classroom.

The only compliment I received that year was that Alexandra was a beautiful child, and that she had been the only child out of the fifty-four children to learn all of the dinosaur names. A year later, while visiting a children's park in Sarasota, Florida, which had dinosaur sculptures, I was amazed that she could still name most of the dinosaurs. Another positive was that Alexandra's *papier-mâché* sculpture made it to the display case at the school entrance hall.

On one of Alexandra's Kindergarten report cards, the speech teacher wrote:

> Although Alexandra has made some progress, she still has a great deal of difficulty responding to questions that require a response other than 'yes' or 'no'. She often has a blank look on her face and seems to have learned to smile as a way of masking her inability to process language.

I think that this teacher was giving a fairly accurate description of Alexandra's autistic tendency to withdraw in a situation in which she felt uncomfortable. She would withdraw into her own world of thoughts and ideas, a world in which she felt comfortable, happy, and able to smile. I do not believe that Alexandra was 'masking her inability to process language.'

Although the first-grade class had only twenty-five children, it was not much better for Alexandra. Mrs. Farrell was a stern teacher about two years away from retirement. Alexandra was able to keep up with the class in reading, partially because the parents received the word lists for reading and spelling each week. Alexandra memorized the words quite easily when I worked with her. I would make cards for each word for flashcard drill, and we would use the cards to make sentences. Because the actual readers rarely made their way home, I purchased my own copies so that we could practice reading at home.

Unfortunately, we were unable to use the same strategy for math. The school was experimenting with a new math program (the *University of Chicago Mathematics Program*), which used co-operative learning, math stories, and pre-algebraic concepts to teach primary school math. Basic addition and subtraction facts were not stressed, and the children were not given any homework. A child on the autistic spectrum has difficulty learning in a co-operative group setting, and without homework I was unable to help Alexandra at home. Without a good beginning foundation, mathematics remained a problem for years.

Among Mrs. Farrell's complaints that year were that Alexandra was disorganized, had poor work habits, and was not able to work independently. I always heard negatives whenever I came to pick up my daughter after school. I even asked, 'Don't you have anything positive to say?'

When I visited during parents' observation week, I noticed that Alexandra would sit outside the group during circle time. She was withdrawn and did not respond when asked a question directly, although when one child did not know a reading word, Alexandra raised her hand and responded correctly. As Mrs. Farrell stated in Alexandra's first report card that year, 'I am concerned because sometimes Alexandra seems self-absorbed to the point that she is completely unaware of what's happening in class.' This school persona was very shocking to me. Alexandra was very different at home.

Mrs. Farrell was at a loss how to deal with this. She suggested meetings with the school psychologist. She also suggested that Alexandra be placed in a remedial reading class, not because she could not read, but in order to work in a smaller group of children. I personally didn't feel that she belonged with children who were having difficulty reading, but I hoped that the remedial class would help her with other skills as well, such as penmanship.

Penmanship was to become a big problem for Alexandra. She learned to print her letters, but did not really learn to form the letters correctly. She had great difficulty staying within the lines, and her letters were often distorted or incorrectly sized. The same problems were to turn up later in cursive writing.

Throughout her school years, Alexandra was apparently just allowed to sit withdrawn in class and not do any work. It was all right if she stayed outside the circle and failed to participate. I used to check her backpack each day, only to be disappointed to find that little if any completed work ever made its way home. Even at the end of the year, her workbooks would have only a few pages completed in them. The only real learning seemed to be the work that we did at home together.

There were some positive notes in that first-grade year. Alexandra was given a small part in the class play, called *Wack-a-doo Zoo*. She memorized the entire play from beginning to end, once again demonstrating her fine memory. My mother and I were treated to a complete performance (all parts) every night for weeks. An impressionistic watercolor done in the style of Monet, whom they were studying in art class, also made it to the display area at the public school.

I began to feel anxious and stressed from the constant complaints and meetings with the teacher, the school psychologist, and the principal. I told my husband that I just could not take this harassment any longer. We agreed to take Alexandra out of public school and send her to private school.

Private school years

The Meadowbrook School was a small private school with a nine to one student/teacher ratio. The tuition was moderate compared to some of the other private schools in the area. Alexandra's admission was contingent upon spending a full day at the school with her new classmates and being evaluated by the classroom teachers.

The teachers, director, and staff seemed very pleasant and the atmosphere was relaxed. I was, of course, nervous after all the negative opinions from the public school teachers, but everything went very well. Claire, the first-grade teacher, told me that Alexandra had done a good job reading for her, only getting stuck on a few difficult words. She remarked that she seemed especially to enjoy playing in the clay area. Fortunately the school had two openings. Alexandra was invited to join the second-grade class.

We were quite pleased when we received invitations to a beach barbecue from one of the parents and also to the birthday party of another child a month before classes were to begin. The other parents and children seemed lovely, and we eagerly anticipated the start of the new school year.

Children did real work in the Meadowbrook School Kindergarten. They had already learned to read and do some simple math in the Kindergarten year. Many of the children in Alexandra's second-grade class were already multiplying and dividing and adding long columns of numbers. With a few exceptions, this seemed to be a class of extraordinarily precocious children. Lorraine had been at the school for a number of years and was the head teacher; Barbara was the assistant teacher in this class of eighteen children.

One of the premises of the school was that each child would be given his or her own individualized program to follow. This concept is great in theory, but unfortunately not always practical to implement in a class of eighteen children. My biggest complaint was that the math exercises given to Alexandra were either too easy or too difficult, never quite matching the level that she was up to.

Since Alexandra traveled to school by bus, I only had occasional interaction with the teachers. Generally the private school was much more relaxed. When you pay the bill, the teachers treat you more kindly. The director of the school, Mr. Jameson, although he expressed concern with Alexandra's learning, tried to be helpful. When the school bought new computers, Mr. Jameson sold us one of the school's older models, already loaded with about forty educational games. Alexandra and I spent hours playing these games.

At a parents' night and at conferences, Lorraine stated that Alexandra was slow and behind the other children in the class. She had poor work habits, was disorganized, and was unable to work without one-on-one assistance. Sometimes she would have some of the other children help Alexandra. I asked her not to compare Alexandra with other second-grade students who were already doing multiplication and division and working at a third- or fourth-grade level. I also asked her whether she had anything positive to tell me. What about the excellent stories that Alexandra had written? Alexandra had dictated several stories to me, which I diligently wrote down over the course of the year. I thought that they were rather good for a second grader. I submitted them to Lorraine only to receive no feedback on them. I have found that school teachers seem to dwell on your child's negatives. What about my child's creativity, excellent imagination, and good writing skills?

Third grade was a more positive experience for us. In fact, when Alexandra looks back on her entire school experience, she always remembers that she liked third grade the most. Nancy and Liza were very encouraging and supportive. For the first time, I actually got some positive feedback during conferences and on report cards.

All of this was to change when Alexandra entered the fourth grade. The director of the school, Mr. Jameson, was head teacher of the class. He was determined to get his fourth-grade students prepared for junior high school.

The backbone of his program was the *Scholastic News*, which the children had to learn verbatim. The fourth graders were given a test each week to see whether they understood this material. The test was rather difficult, including essay questions, vocabulary, short answers and definitions. It appeared to be closer to a secondary school level examination than one meant for primary school students. In order to pass, the child would need to have practically memorized the entire *Scholastic News*. Needless to say, with Alexandra's inability to work independently, poor focusing and concentration skills, and her difficulty in printing, she did very poorly on these tests.

She was also placed in the slower math group along with three other children. Only three days a week were devoted to math study. Instead of building these poorer math students' self-esteem and confidence and giving them additional hours of remediation, they were told by Mr. Jameson that math was not 'their thing'. Alexandra was told to pay attention several times in front of the group. For Alexandra, who has never taken well to criticism, an experience like this could be absolutely mortifying.

Here are some comments from Alexandra's fourth-grade report card:

> Alexandra requires much supervision in completing her work. She has difficulty moving from one task to another and requires continued attention. Her work pace is also slow.

> Alexandra is very confused in gym. She has not learned any positions. She does not remember what team she is on right after they have been selected.

> Alexandra is very likable and her peers accept her readily, albeit often as caretakers. She is welcomed into social situations, but she acts uninterested and chooses to stay by herself most of the time.

Mr. Jameson began to express concern about Alexandra's work and her isolation from the other students in the class. In his final report card comment, he wrote:

> It is our firm opinion that Alexandra's needs exceed the capacity of a teacher in a normal classroom setting to address. With proper one-on-one instruction, Alexandra's progress would increase and her time in school would be better utilized. Alexandra is very capable of learning, and although she is progressing, her peers are progressing faster, and the gap between them widens. She then becomes increasingly lost as class discussions and projects exceed her independent capacity.

Mr. Jameson made it clear to me that Alexandra could no longer continue at his school unless I had a special education teacher from my school district come to work with her at his school. I told him that I had sent Alexandra to private school to avoid having to deal with the local public school district, and that this option was certainly out of the question. I then began my search for a new private school.

I spent some time researching new private schools within a reasonable distance from home, and eventually enrolled Alexandra at the Forest Valley School. The director, Mrs. Evans, was a very warm and caring person. It was also a very beautiful and pleasant campus. The Forest Valley School was more structured than the Meadowbrook School and had a similar student/teacher ratio.

Mrs. Ross was an energetic and enthusiastic teacher with creative teaching ideas who was able to recognize my daughter's creative potential. There were still problems in Alexandra's ability to be organized, work independently, and be responsive in class. I did receive some assistance from her teachers in making sure that the homework assignment and proper books made their way home. Imagine my surprise when Mrs. Ross told me that Alexandra had done well on a practice standardized reading test! I was so used to hearing that she can read the words but she cannot comprehend what she reads.

We continued on to sixth grade at the Forest Valley School. Alexandra was placed in the smaller of two combined fifth- and sixth-grade classes with Mrs. Weiss. Mrs. Weiss was friendly and supportive, but proved to be an inexperienced first-year teacher.

In the sixth grade, there was increasing pressure to prepare the children for junior high. The children were given considerably more homework than they had received the previous year. Again Alexandra had a problem writing down the necessary homework assignments or remembering to take the proper books home each afternoon. Although she had been eager to attend fifth-grade classes the previous year, she began asking for days off, even pretending illness.

Since very little learning took place in the classroom environment, I was again spending hours each night trying to complete the excessive amount of homework and also seeing to it that Alexandra managed to learn something. This would often involve late hours and considerable stress.

As a piano teacher, my work day first starts when children come home from school, usually around 3:30 in the afternoon. I often do not finish my teaching until 8:00 or 8:30 in the evening. After a late dinner, Alexandra and I would first sit down to homework. Both of us felt very pressured by constant homework deadlines.

Deciding to homeschool

By October of the sixth-grade year, I realized that I was doing most of the work involved in teaching Alexandra. I also realized that I was expending much effort working on someone else's educational plan rather than one more suited to my daughter's needs and our interests. I began to feel that if I had to do so much of the school work at home, I might as well do it all, and at hours more suited to our schedule and sleep habits.

I was also concerned with how Alexandra would adjust to the junior high environment the following year. I knew that she would have trouble remembering to bring home her books each day, would daydream through classes, might get confused finding her classes, and could be taunted by the other children. Having her classified and placed into special education was not an option for us. I felt that she was too bright to receive a 'watered down' education.

I had begun to hear of homeschooling as a viable educational option and had recently read a *Newsweek* article on homeschooling. I began to do some research on homeschooling in the library and on the Internet.

One of the homeschooling books that I read listed local homeschooling support groups for each state. I contacted and later joined one of these groups and received helpful information on obtaining the New York State homeschooling regulations. Homeschooling is legal in all fifty states in the USA, but requirements vary from state to state. I subscribed to our group's newsletter and had Alexandra skip a day of class to join the homeschoolers on a tour of a local newspaper plant.

I now had to tell my husband that I was seriously considering homeschooling our daughter, because I seemed to be the only one who could teach her. I thought that he would think I was crazy, but he had seen us working late into each night, trying to complete the homework. He realized how much pressure and stress the homework assignments were causing us. He suggested that we let our daughter finish sixth grade and have the experience of graduating with her class while I researched homeschooling.

At about the same time that I had decided to consider homeschooling, Mrs. Weiss suggested a meeting with herself and Mrs. Evans, the director. She was concerned about Alexandra's inability to work independently, her withdrawal in the classroom, and her tendency to go off by herself during recess. During our meeting I brought up the idea that I was very seriously considering homeschooling for the next year. To my surprise, Mrs. Evans stated that she had heard of children being homeschooled successfully, and offered to help me in any way that she could.

Our first homeschooling year

I began by ordering middle school textbook catalogues. With Mrs. Evans's help, I was able to obtain review copies of most of the textbooks that interested me. This was especially helpful for my first year of homeschooling.

I ordered science lab kits from science equipment catalogues, and was also able to find science equipment through some small companies that specialize in the homeschooling market. It was very important to me to try to make science as interesting and 'hands on' as possible. I wanted my daughter to have a real lab experience.

After assembling all our books, CD-ROMs, and science equipment, we were ready to begin homeschooling.

Although the idea of 'unschooling' was attractive to me, I decided that a more structured approach would better suit us. Alexandra was prone to being easily distracted and unable to focus for very long. She also had difficulty in being able to work independently, and needed me to sit with her constantly. At the same time, she was totally 'turned off' to anything educational. In addition to providing structure for her day's work, I needed to keep things interesting and motivating.

I have found it helpful to spend a few minutes at the end of each day writing brief lesson plans for the next day. The plans are always flexible, and anything that we don't finish or that we are not in the mood for can always be done another day. I also take a few minutes to record what we actually worked on each day and approximately how long each activity took. This small amount of record keeping is most helpful when it comes time to file any necessary reports required for your area.

Basically, we approach our homeschooling from a wellness point of view. We do not dwell on the disabilities. Unlike traditional schooling, there is no need for labels or special classes. This labeling can be very damaging to a child's self-esteem. Instead, the homeschooling parent can choose work suitable for the child's level, spend as long as is needed to cover the material, and with one-on-one instruction, make sure the child is understanding the material.

Math was an area in which we seriously needed to do remedial work. Alexandra needed a thorough foundation in mathematics to fill in the gaps from her years of traditional schooling. Although she had tested at a composite level of grade 3.8 for math, I knew from working with her that she was capable of working on a higher level. I chose the Glencoe McGraw-Hill *Mathematics Applications and Connections Course One* textbook and the combined *Study Guide and Practice Workbook*. This is the first volume in this middle school math series and is designed for sixth grade. I also purchased the interactive CD-ROM to accompany the textbook.

What I particularly like about this textbook is that it is well suited to the average learner. It does not have so-called 'challenge' or thinking problems. If the child understands the concept, he or she will be able to complete all problems and examples successfully. I truly believe that a child needs to experience success in order to develop both self-esteem and motivation to do well. The textbook explanations are clear, and the pages are liberally sprinkled with sample problems. This helps to make it easier for parents to teach. The book is attractively illustrated with color photographs and contains some 'real world' math problems, including a chapter project. For the less able student, a *Transition Booklet* and *Investigations for the Special Education Student* are available to accompany this math program.

We spent the summer prior to beginning our homeschooling year doing fraction problems, since this had been neglected by her sixth-grade teacher. I did not want these problems to be totally new when we went through the *Course One* book during the year. This plan worked: Alexandra was able to understand difficult fractions concepts when we studied these topics again later in the year.

Alexandra did very well with the pre-algebra problems. Other mathematical concepts were routine and easy to learn. However, she had serious problems with multi-step calculations such as those involved with long division. It is difficult for a child whose mind is filled with constant extraneous thoughts to keep focused long enough to solve a multi-step calculation. She would chat constantly throughout a long division problem.

What I did as an aid to learning was to make a chart of all of the steps to be referred to while working on problems, and we just did a lot of practice. I would first select easy long division problems and have Alexandra practice these until she could perform the calculations with ease. I would then advance to more difficult problems. For more practice, I even made up some of my own examples and problems to help in mastery.

To keep things interesting and for practice in knowing which operation (addition, subtraction, multiplication, or division) to choose for a given word problem, I either chose suitable problems from the textbook or made up my own, using television show characters that she liked. 'Real world' math problems are always interesting for the student. Alexandra especially liked a statistics problem in the textbook in which we had to construct a frequency table comparing grams of fat in different foods. We had fun pulling foods out of the freezer, refrigerator, and pantry and creating our frequency table.

To keep math from becoming tedious, I do allow use of a calculator for some of our work. This can be extremely helpful for the student who understands mathematical concepts but has difficulty with calculations.

One math computer game that Alexandra has found both entertaining and educational is *Math for the Real World* by Davidson. The game follows a rock band as it travels across the USA. The group must solve everyday math problems, stop for gas, and pay for food at a diner along the way.

Foreign language study is always a challenge for the homeschooling parent, especially when your child chooses a language that you have never studied. Alexandra refused to work with a tutor, so I decided that we would learn Spanish together, using the McGraw-Hill textbook *Bienvenidos Spanish 1A* for seventh grade and the accompanying CD-ROM. This has worked out very well. We both are learning Spanish and enjoying it.

Social studies was probably the subject that Alexandra liked the least. We decided to begin with geography. To make it more interesting, in addition to a well-illustrated middle school textbook, I purchased the *National Geographic Picture Atlas of the World* on CD-ROM, which has excellent maps, beautiful photographs, music clips, important facts, and a brief essay for each country. We rented travel videos from the local library and reviewed travel brochures.

We also colored beautiful maps using the *Geography Coloring Book* by Wynn Kapit. This book has detailed physical and political maps of each country, maps on world-wide climate, religions, and water currents, and accompanying text. It is suitable for both middle school and high school. My daughter truly enjoyed coloring these maps.

Alexandra continued to have difficulty both in working independently and in being able to look up answers to questions in textbooks. One day, as I watched her 'drift off' while we were attempting to read a geography section aloud, I decided to try another tactic. I read the chapter myself and prepared a thorough set of questions based on the reading. I then requested that Alexandra read the section and answer the questions as she went along. Not only was she able to do this successfully, but she did a better job in preparing the questions each time that she did this exercise.

Science has always been a special interest of mine, and I hoped to convey some of this excitement of learning to my daughter. I chose the

Prentice-Hall *Science Explorer* series for middle school students. It consists of fifteen books on various topics in the life sciences, earth sciences, and physical sciences. This series lends itself well to unit studies, and is well suited to those homeschoolers who enjoy working on topics of special interest. For our first year of homeschooling, we completed the *Electricity and Magnetism, Weather and Climate*, and *Sound and Light* textbooks.

I was determined that my daughter would have a real, 'hands on' laboratory experience. I purchased an optics kit, a low-cost weather station, a circuit board, and a magnetism kit. We built an electric bell, an electric motor, a chemical battery, and an electromagnet. One-day field trips and family vacations can also be used to supplement both science and social studies. These field trips will be remembered long after book lessons are forgotten.

This year we will be focusing on life science, using the Prentice-Hall books *From Bacteria to Plants and Animals*. I have ordered a new micro-scope, slides, a bacteria culturing kit, a protozoa discovery kit, some nature kits, a flower model, and a classification CD-ROM.

I have found language arts the most challenging subject to teach, because it really consists of several different topics, each a study in itself. Most traditional middle school language arts programs focus on spelling, vocabulary, reading comprehension, literature, and writing. How do you find time to teach all of these different subject areas and still keep things interesting and unified?

Fortunately, English is my daughter's strongest subject, and this has become an area where she has learned to work independently. She easily handles workbook exercises on spelling, vocabulary, and grammar after I briefly go over the instructions with her. Focusing on what a child does well is excellent for building the self-esteem of your special needs child.

For literature we selected Newberry Award and Honors books. These are excellent novels, which I have enjoyed reading along with Alexandra. This year I have added an anthology, so that I can introduce short stories, poetry, and drama in addition to the novels that we will continue to read. Keep in mind that you are also doing language arts every time that you pick up a textbook on geography, history, science—or any other subject, for that matter.

Because Alexandra had a great deal of difficulty printing in the early grades of school, her earliest written work was very poor. Her printing was sloppy at best, and many words were incorrectly spelled. She always had an ability with words, so I encouraged her to dictate some of her stories to me. Later she was able to write the stories on her own, or type her work on the computer. I found that when she typed, her spelling greatly improved.

One way to improve your child's spelling and command of the English language is to encourage reading. This is, of course, difficult in the modern world of cable television with its eighty or more channels, computers, the Internet, and video games. In our case, television proved helpful in stimulating reading interest. Many of the popular television series, such as *Charmed, Seventh Heaven, Sabrina the Teenage Witch,* etc., have book series that are available in local book stores. Reading should be fun, and giving children books that they will want to read will encourage a reading habit.

Spending time on the Internet can also be helpful for developing good language skills. The child does have to read and write to participate on the Internet. Over time, I found that Alexandra's reading fluency and spelling ability improved greatly. She actually became a good speller! For those families that want a more structured approach, there are some good spelling books and CD-ROM spelling games on the market. One game that we especially enjoyed was *Spell It Deluxe* by Davidson.

Miscellaneous subjects such as music, art, drama, and sports can be excellent for developing co-ordination and concentration skills. Success in these areas can help to build your child's self-esteem and ability to express herself creatively. Encourage attendance at shows, concerts, and art workshops. Many autistic spectrum children have definite talents in these areas, and these events can help with socialization skills as well.

Some problems and successes

Alexandra is fourteen years old now, and we are well into our second year of homeschooling. As we homeschoolers like to say, there are good days and bad days. Alexandra is a bit of a hypochondriac. On days when she had even something as minor as a blemish, she would be very distracted and unable to work well.

One of our biggest problems involved the bodily changes of adolescence. It took her months to adjust to the onset of puberty. At certain times of the month, she would be very distracted in her work and refuse to go out of the house. Things are getting better as she gradually adjusts to the changes in her body.

Another problem that we continue to have is that Alexandra can be a regular chatterbox during lessons. She has no shortage of ideas she is thinking about. Her mind is constantly working. It is still difficult to get her to concentrate on a lesson long enough to complete it. I am often amazed that she can complete a long division problem while talking non-stop.

On a good day, Alexandra understands math concepts readily, finishes her language arts workbooks quickly, and enjoys her Spanish computer program. On our best days, we find the perfect geography video at the library and our science experiments work just as they are supposed to. Occasionally, lessons will lead to a discussion on a topic of special interest to Alexandra.

Overall, our homeschooling venture has been quite positive. Alexandra went from a 4.8 composite score on a sixth-grade standardized test to a 7.9 composite score on another standardized test taken after just one year of homeschooling seventh grade. At the same time, her math scores rose from a 3.8 to a 7.5. In spelling, she scored one full year above her current grade level, at 8.7.

More important than test scores, I feel that real learning took place. Alexandra's confidence in math grew when she found that she could solve a page of math problems quickly and correctly. When we first started to homeschool, Alexandra read aloud with some hesitation. She is now able to read fluently, and her spelling and writing have improved. At the end of the year, our portfolio was filled with completed worksheets and workbooks—all this in fewer hours than she would have spent in school.

Before we started to homeschool, I felt as though Alexandra had lost all interest in school work. She now tells me that she enjoys our work in English and Spanish. I still hope to get her more motivated with social studies and science, although more recently some of our science lessons have led to some interesting discussions.

Alexandra's confidence has grown as well. She enjoys having some real time to herself, which previously would have been spent on homework. This is important to the AS child. In Alexandra's own words, 'I am happy with my life. I have found myself with all the extra time that I have.'

I still worry about her future. How will she do when she is ready for college? Alexandra was heading for real academic failure when we first started to homeschool. Things are beginning to look brighter.

12

Three springs for a summer
David's story

Margaret R. Paton

It was nearly Christmas and the short, dark days of northern Scotland seemed to engulf us with despair. We had been so full of hope. Our elder son, David, the victim of a birth trauma which had never been openly explained, had been progressing beyond our wildest dreams and the expectations of all who knew him. His early educational experiences, though fraught with difficulties of perceptual and physical abnormalities, had become a fascinating journey of discovery. We were so fortunate to be working with gifted teachers who, even if not always able to enter directly into our struggles, were ready to listen and to learn.

Our journey now was much more painful. Just before his eighth birthday David was transferred, with many tears at parting and yet much excitement and anticipation, from the Scottish National Society for Autistic Children's school, Struan House, to a local primary school which contained a special unit designed for children with communication problems. The aim was to integrate him gradually into normal schooling, though we discovered later that the vision held by the educational authorities was very different from our own. Ours had no boundaries. Theirs was qualified by preconceptions and irrational fears for their professional reputations and prestige.

At first all seemed well. The class was small and the head of the unit was a lady of wide experience. As the class grew, however, the difficulties became more obvious. The unit catered not only for children such as David with autism, but also for others who had never been diagnosed or who were perfectly normal in every respect except that they had physical speech impediments. Before the end of his fourth term, at the age of nine, David was losing ground rapidly, with severe tantrums, constant over-excitement, nonsensical talk and a severe deterioration in his concentration. On that dark, cold day in December, after a series of violent tantrums and with total frustration that our queries and concerns were never directly addressed, we decided not to return him to school.

We were no strangers to educating a child in the home. Jeremy, David's younger brother by eighteen months, had already taken shelter from the problems raised by an environment which could not cater for his needs. In his case we were dealing with exceptional musical and academic ability, and he had now departed to a music school after nine happy months at home. It was later suggested that David had deliberately manoeuvred us into removing him from school because he was so taken with the idea of 'lessons at home', as he expressed it, and wished to be placed in the same privileged position as his brother. Whatever the cause, David's need for physical and emotional respite was as easily recognisable as Jeremy's and we knew that, for the time being, home was the right place for his education.

For David it was a question of bonding. The bonding he was achieving at home was safely in place. There had been no bonding in school, because his abnormal perceptions and his difficulties with making connections were not recognised. His true misery had revealed itself when he arrived home from school each evening. Having been passive and fairly inactive during the day, he had not used the skills he had learned and had been introduced to few others. Consequently he had descended into limbo. On arriving home he would immediately let go of his unconscious restraints, physical and emotional, as he stepped over a threshold which, for him, represented a boundary between oblivion and recognition. Once the symptoms of this release had been treated, there was little time left for productive activity.

This was in extreme contrast with his previous experience at Struan House, which he had attended from the age of six until his progress demanded he should leave them for a wider world a year and a half later. At Struan he had gained a sense of importance which had done him no harm, and his self-discipline had increased as he learned the joys of rewards as well as sanctions. He had trusted his teachers and carers as he trusted us, that they would give him a secure and happy life. They had taught him that the reality which we accept without question is worth living. Two such dissimilar educational encounters were bound to cause confusion and tension, which resulted in the traumas we now underwent.

Jeremy was probably the first child ever to be home educated in our region, and we had discovered then that we were completely isolated. The home educators' support organisation Education Otherwise existed, but we had no means of making contact. With the help of an understanding lawyer, we had no difficulty in deregistering Jeremy, and I still possess the historic newspaper cutting which states that the parents of an unnamed child were given permission to educate him at home.

David's regime, however, was very different from Jeremy's, as were the attitudes of the authorities. Because he had special needs, it was automatically assumed to be impossible that he should remain at home, even though both his parents were highly qualified teachers. We were not 'experts', and this was probably the difficulty which lay at the heart of all our negative experiences from this time onwards.

By the time we removed David from school, we were not dealing so much with systems as with individuals. If ever I learned the lesson that teachers, whether inside of school or out, stand or fall by their own strengths and weaknesses, not by any methodology or educational philosophy or even financial and material resources, it was now. This has remained a theme throughout David's life and still applies today. It is the people around him who count. Physical environment is important in so far as it takes account of any organic difficulties he might have and provides him with a reliable structure. But if his instructors and colleagues have an inner completeness, then he participates in it to the extent that his own persona blooms with the fullness of summer.

So our true battle began. In David's babyhood we had struggled with the medical profession for a diagnosis and for a recognition that this diagnosis was meant to open doors, not close them. Now, after five years of undeviating support and co-operation, we were to face an even worse enemy: the belief that because David was autistic, his future was already laid down in minute detail. In his earliest years, we had been recommended to place him in residential care. Now we were advised that he would never go beyond the earliest stages of primary education. Later on, it was decreed he would not pass examinations. Constant themes also were that he would never make friends and never possess a sense of humour.

Our own experience contradicted these gloomy predictions. We had seen evidence of friendship when, at the unit, a perfectly normal little boy with a speech impediment had been one of his most constant companions. His sense of humour still never fails to give us delight. One day, not long after our early efforts in home education, I was getting things ready for our evening meal. 'Go to the bathroom if you have to,' I said to David, 'and don't be too long.' He still had difficulties with water, washing his face and hands too often and splashing the water all over the floor. I went upstairs after him. 'Who's been throwing talc all over the place?' I complained. 'I only bought that box last week and it's nearly finished.'

'Well, it wasn't me,' said David, 'and it wasn't you, was it? And it wasn't the spider.' My husband heard and laughed with us. That only left him, as Jeremy was away. 'They said he couldn't make a joke,' I remembered. We sat down to our meal with laughter in our eyes.

Our first task was to obtain an independent and detailed assessment of David's educational level. We enlisted the help of a wonderful educational psychologist who worked at the university. The truth was clear to see. There was an enormous discrepancy in David's scores. He was in the top two per cent of the population in his ability to analyse and reproduce abstract design, yet in the bottom one per cent for general knowledge. The latter naturally reflected his early difficulties and restricted environment and the fact that he was unable to learn incidentally.

Our own analysis, however, brought us to the conclusion that he had regressed from where he had previously been, and the areas upon which his last placement had appeared to concentrate, such as sequencing, were exceptionally poor. We therefore set about trying to carry out the implications of the tests, working hard at the areas of misapplication and deficiency which they had highlighted, such as information, his lowest score on the Wechsler intelligence scale, comprehension of reading, where his score was two years behind his accuracy and fluency, digit span and picture arrangement.

With regard to reading, for example, we moved from a 'look and say' approach to a phonetic method. Comprehension could be enhanced by presenting the questions to be answered first, thus providing the direction in which his learning should go. His poor short-term memory was aided by visual formats: for example, using colour coding, underlining and outlining as aids to recall. His poor sequencing skills had resulted in gaps of knowledge in areas such as seasons, months, days of the week and clock time. Many of these things were not caused by environmental factors, but by his poor auditory and sequential memory. Verbal rehearsal, too, was very important to help him to understand what he was going to do and to develop his awareness of the 'why' of social rules.

A wonderful example of his bizarre logic emerged from the teaching of units, tens and hundreds. He came into the kitchen one day when I was doing the washing-up. As I laid the cutlery on a shelf, ready to put away, he started to arrange some of the forks and spoons. Suddenly he announced proudly, 'Spoon hundred and forkty-fork!'

Each progressive stage in our programme resulted not only in greater understanding in, for example, the way language works, but also in some obvious release of his frustrations. As we opened more new doors, he grew in his ability to see not the narrowly confined areas he had created for himself in his earliest years, but the whole room. So he gained a sense of freedom and happiness and a greater ability to play. He also acquired a social personality, delighted in our regular trips on the train to collect Jeremy and became well loved by Jeremy's house-mother, who has remained a close friend.

The influence of our railway journeys still survives on the home education timetable I have in front of me. David has drawn cups of tea in the spaces marked for break entitled 'buffet', as distinguished from knives and forks for 'lunch'. It was natural for me to adopt a firmly struc-tured timetable, since I had been used to working this way in my teaching career. When flexibility was needed, however, it was there. Much of his 'free' time was spent in doing the things he did well, such as Lego construction, and although there was a conscious break between lessons and a time when he could have a wider choice, this in itself was a lesson.

One of the most difficult areas in the special unit at school had been a session called 'choice'. David did not really know how to choose and would often, I'm sure, dream the time away. Even now, choice is a serious matter and tiredness can lead to a mental struggle over whether to have a cup of tea or no, a struggle which we can only watch and guide. Even as parents, our imaginations cannot extend into the indecisions and concerns which our children face daily.

The important thing for all of us was that there was pattern. As parents, we needed an accepted structure to hold onto through the stresses of the day. As a child gradually learning responses and areas of knowledge foreign to all his inner inclinations, David needed that same structure to give him security in a challenging world. This pattern might have very clear outlines or it could, like chaos, be idiosyncratic.

The outlines had to be especially clear when it came to social behav-iour if he were to be accepted in the outside world. Forbidden areas, such as continual interruptions into other people's conversations or inappropriate touching, received an immediate response, which usually involved raised voices. One of the most severe punishments David can still receive is to be shouted at. The element of pain was felt to be neces-sary to impress upon him our absolute rejection of such behaviour, although it could result in outbursts, which were usually contained by 'holding'.

Such a technique is sometimes criticised. I found, however, that the strength required to hold close to me an unwilling and physically violent nine-year-old child was well worth the result, and was never wrongly interpreted by David. He knew that he needed the physical contact he sometimes found so hard to accept, and he told me so one day in a very moving way. I asked him some years later, when he was in his teens, if he remembered not only the pleasures of 'lessons at home', but also the times when his words would only come if I withheld what he wanted, or when the contact I imposed upon him to subdue his resistant behaviour could be physically painful. 'Oh yes,' he said, smiling, 'but I always knew that you loved me.' Whatever mistakes we make are healed by the power of love, sometimes unbeknown to us. How fortunate I am that he can tell me!

So we proceeded with all the excitement that knowledge and understanding can endow. He was musical, and I had already taught him the rudiments of reading music at the age of three, in the same way as I taught him to read words. We simply held up pictures of notes on a stave and demonstrated them on the piano, later making chords and tunes until he was ready for a teaching book. During our time at home, he developed his piano playing, and at the age of fourteen was able to take up the trombone with exceptional success. He had a lovely singing voice and we sang every day, starting the morning with prayers and songs and placing plenty of musical activities in the timetable.

Drawing, particularly of human figures, was stereotyped and without perspective. Here we had help from a gifted teacher at a community centre. We had consciously encouraged David to be involved in activities with normal children at the weekends during the time he had attended the autistic school. The art class and a similar class in dancing were extremely successful, and gave David an enhanced understanding and better use of space. These activities were continued without interruption during his period at home.

Of course he was noticeable. When other mothers left their children and went shopping or to have a coffee, I had to stay. David had to be taught to stand in the queue at break, choose his snack and pay for his food. This fifteen minutes was a dozen lessons in one! Eventually I only had to return for break, so would go down the hill, back home again, back again for break, back home again and then finally collect him. But it was important for him to know that he was becoming independent of me, important for the teacher to know that I trusted her and important for me to see a glimpse of what might one day become an independent life—not only for David, but for myself.

The same thing happened with 'Young Church', or Sunday School, where he again had loving and competent teachers. I remember him carrying—oh, so carefully!—the sacred elements up to the altar in a Sunday morning procession when he was only seven, an important lesson that rituals are not always destructive. As parents of autistic children, we grow so used to trying to break down ritualistic behaviour. In such an instance, it was wonderful to see rituals being used in the service of beauty and meaningful ceremony.

The local Cub Scout pack also taught him numerous skills in a small group and enabled him to display his own special abilities, such as playing chess. One evening, not long after his ninth birthday, the Scottish winter had descended extra early. The night was black and the roads were frozen. We drove very slowly to the Cub Scout hall to collect him, torn with fear that he would have wandered or been frantic with apprehension. He stood there, with his uniform covered in badges, no signs of panic, staunchly and patiently waiting. Oh, he was so pleased to see us! For us it represented another landmark on his way to self-sufficiency.

Yet we had always known he would return to school. It was never a case of one method versus another. It was always a case of what David needed at any particular time, with an eye, too, on that distant future when he might just conceivably be counted as an ordinary member of society—or, perhaps, an extraordinary member, but for different reasons from the ones we would have been given at this time.

To facilitate the process of this return, we paid another visit to the educational psychologist who had seen him six months previously. We were conscious that it was now only a matter of weeks before his tenth birthday and that the arena of his life was still very limited. More extensive social interactions could be an opening to further development, as long as his difficulties were contained within a sympathetic and individually geared tuition structure. We were also conscious that this second test was not so much of David as of our home education, and I'm happy to say that our efforts were well rewarded.

David had made tremendous progress. His reading age was now only eight months behind his chronological age, and his comprehension of reading only nine months behind instead of two years. There were still some problems with decoding longer words and sequencing, but his grasp of sequences, such as months and seasons, was greatly improved. He still struggled with free writing and conversation, where he found it difficult to keep to a point or to examine the meaning of a question rather than persevering with what he wanted to say, but it was clear that his progress had been considerable, and that regular socialisation with a peer group would be an important next stage in his development. We therefore decided to try to find a suitable place for him to be.

We could not face the possible results of a further experiment in a state school at this time. The treatment ultimately meted out to us before and after we removed David from school was cruel in the extreme. The fear of those in authority that their expertise was in danger of being questioned had brought dissimulation, persecution and ridicule of our methods and expectations.

These attitudes had continued during David's time at home. Whereas Jeremy's deregistration had been comparatively simple, David's was never officially achieved, because of his special needs. Correspondence and personal encounters with the authorities were acrimonious. Because David was not deregistered, if he had remained at home, we would probably have been forced to defend ourselves in court. However, once the authorities knew that we were actively seeking a school placement, we were left in peace.

The choice was limited, but there was one school where he was kindly welcomed, a preparatory school about twenty-five miles from our home. By this time we were making extreme sacrifices of money and time to educate our children. Both our children were 'abnormal' in that they had special educational needs. Home education is not cheap, nor are the additional aids such as special classes and activities which are required to give such children as full and happy a life as possible.

It was a hard time in our lives. My husband and I were convinced, however, that these sacrifices were necessary, not only for David's short-term happiness, but also for the fruition of his potential in the future. So just before his tenth birthday, David went to his preparatory school without any hesitation on our part and with the blessing of the educational psychologist at the university who had tested him for the second time.

One of the happiest memories is of the bright summer's day we took him for his interview, in the hope that he would be accepted for the autumn term. Having given David some quite taxing tests, the headmaster came out onto the top of the flight of steps leading up to the front door. My husband and I were standing in the drive, enjoying the sunshine and waiting for a verdict. 'You have taught him well,' he exclaimed. 'I could see his mind working through the processes you had given him as I gave him the problems.' I felt warm inside. It was good to have some approbation, after the months of hard work and the acrimonious struggles with the authorities.

David was never really happy in his new school, but he survived for the period that was necessary to give him a wider experience of a peer group. As time went on, however, the ethos of the school and the attitudes of some of the parents and children became unpalatable. The four terms during which David remained there were fraught with challenges for him. He loathed rugby and suffered some contempt as a result. He and another child who had muscular dystrophy were largely isolated by the rest of the class, and David would often be the one caring for the other child. Parents would appear to be friendly and then ignore us for no apparent reason.

Yet there was one outstanding benefit. His teacher was a young woman with few formal qualifications, but she was an outstanding example of the archetypal teacher who is born and not made. The school made grandiose claims to great achievements, some of which were misleading, but she came the closest to fulfilling what the school claimed to accomplish. With the Common Entrance to Public Schools examination always in mind, great stress was laid on English and mathematics, and David flourished in a small class under her individual care. As a halfway house between special education and the wider world, it helped to prepare him for his next stage of integration.

The greatest gift of all given to us by that generous-hearted girl was that she realised that David could sing. Just before the Christmas of his first term, the children prepared a nativity play and David, now ten years old, sang with a pure, clear voice the song of the angel to the shepherds. 'Fear not,' he carolled, 'glad tidings of great joy I bring to you and all mankind.' We wept with tears of happiness. It was a beautiful outcome of the work we had done at home and the sensitivity of his young teacher.

Our gifted friend left at the end of David's first year, and he limped through the first term of the next. By Christmas we knew he could not go back, and once again we had to make a choice. Our first intention was to give him some rest and at least a term's education at home. Another springtime to bring forth more flowers seemed to be what was needed. Without a kind hand behind him he was lost, yet at the same time we realised the pattern which was beginning to emerge. David's education had to be empirical as far as systems and individuals were concerned. We took what we could and then moved on. This might appear to have been a selfish, manipulative attitude, but it was necessary for David's survival.

David therefore spent one term at home with a timetable that continued the good work which the school had done in mathematics and English. We also needed to relieve his emotional anxieties, which had increased towards the end of the previous year, and give him plenty of exercise and creative experiences. This was not difficult, since Jeremy was still at the music school as a pianist and full chorister, and we were continually travelling backwards and forwards, enjoying the benefits of a rich artistic environment. It meant that we were able to revert to our pattern of frequent railway journeys which we had enjoyed in David's first springtime at home.

His music sessions were emphasised again, but at a more advanced level, for he was now eleven years old. He was also able to develop his creative writing. Much of his work at school had been formal sentence structure, and he now needed to nurture the one thing many people believe an autistic person can never have: an imagination. Games were a very important part of our programme, and had been from early childhood. Jeremy had been a willing aide in developing David's ability to place himself in imaginary situations. From 'playing' concerts for the toys, they had progressed to *Star Wars*, *Masters of the Universe* and *Dungeons and Dragons*. Now, with Jeremy away, David and I continued to play, although never once was David allowed to win anything under false pretences. This pattern has endured throughout our lives, and board games in particular are still a part of our relaxation when we are all together.

At the time of this second withdrawal from conventional education, David was eleven, and could not have remained at a preparatory school for much longer. It seemed right that we should look for a more long-term solution fairly quickly. We still felt that our ultimate aim should be to enable him to comply with the standard expectations of the outside world. That meant not running the risk of bypassing valuable opportunities which could be more easily accessed through conventional channels if those channels were supportive. We had yet to discover anything that David could not be taught if the processes were analysed into minute degrees of progress.

The local education authority had now washed their hands of us and we of them. We knew, however, that at some point, if we wanted David to gain any kind of qualification, we would have to raise our heads above anonymity. It was better to try to find a placement in our own time than to be forced into something inadequate. On this occasion we had no choice. Competitive independent schools were out of the question, since they would have duplicated the problems David had recently faced, and they could not offer sufficiently specialised understanding of his condition. There was only one organisation within the approved systems which we could consider. We turned, as many other perplexed parents have turned, to a Rudolf Steiner school, which catered not for disabled but for normal children, a move which again involved enormous changes in our lives.

David was accepted by the Rudolf Steiner school in an atmosphere of full understanding and sympathy, but there were enormous physical difficulties. We could not entertain the thought of his being a boarder. As a little boy he had not been sufficiently aware of relationships for it to be a major problem. As he used to say himself, with reference to the autistic school, 'I've got two lovely homes.'

Now, at eleven and a half, with his enhanced self-consciousness, such a complete change of environment would have been too distressing. The family and personal bonds he had made were more important to him even than to others. It was as though, having not possessed them in the first instance, they were, when found, too precious to be out of sight. This still applies to a considerable extent, and his attachments to people and places are strong and enduring. Because the school was seventy miles away, the only solution was for us to rent a flat and for me to go and live with David as near to the school as possible, so that he could travel a reasonable distance daily.

This we did, with my husband continuing his stressful job, long periods of separation and an even greater financial commitment. Within a week or two, David was travelling independently by rail each day from a nearby town and then walking to the school, which was a fair distance from the station at the other end. It was a period of enormously increased self-reliance.

Just a few days after the beginning of his first term, when I was still collecting him from school at the end of each day, he did not appear. A search of the school and an enquiry at the office were of no avail. I went across the road, terror in my heart, to the house where children were looked after who would be collected later. He was not there. I turned round, totally panic-stricken. It appeared that one of his classmates who also travelled by rail had insisted that David had to accompany him to the station. David had been unable to explain clearly that he had to wait for me. He described it later as being 'unable to get away', and his teacher agreed that this particular child would probably have been an insurmountable barrier. So he walked with his companion to the station, saw him onto his train, which fortunately was on a different route from his own, and then walked back again. His face appeared at the corner of the road just as I turned in despair. Sometimes the freak memories which our children have can be extremely useful! Although he had only walked that long and tortuous road on two occasions, he had complete recognition of it, and arrived a little tired but quite full of his achievement.

I asked him what he would have done if, when he returned, I had not been there. 'I would have gone to the music school,' he said. Jeremy's school was near to the station. 'Miss White would have looked after me.' Miss White was Jeremy's wonderfully cuddlesome and practical housemother. I knew then that I had no need to fear.

David stayed at the Rudolf Steiner school for three years, until he was fourteen. Although there are happy memories associated with it—school trips, eurhythmy, theatrical and musical presentations and, above all, his introduction to the trombone—once again the difficulties increased, partly as the result of a change of teacher. There were other factors, however. The syllabus was not conducive to his progress, with a heavy emphasis on languages, which he found difficult. 'Main lessons' were long, and based on esoteric and philosophical material of which he had little understanding and which seemed irrelevant to him.

The air was heavy with authoritarianism and, although David needed and still likes to be with people of confidence and authority, he is easily intimidated by excessive use of power. Many of the children had had behavioural and educational problems in other schools, and their parents had turned to the Rudolf Steiner school, as we had, as the only possible alternative. Bullying was rife, and it eventually became obvious that the stresses upon David were too great. By the time we removed him to give him his last springtime at home before his final emergence into ordinary life, he was on the edge of a nervous breakdown.

Yet we knew that because of—not in spite of—the hardships he had encountered, he was now strong enough to come home, in the fullest sense of those words. He was also travelling one hundred and thirty miles a day. One year after he had started at his new school, I was taken seriously ill and we had to return to our own house. David, still only twelve, had immediately volunteered to do the long journey by himself, and he was now a seasoned traveller with a special mention in the *Railriders* magazine! He rose each morning at five thirty, and I never once had to get him out of bed.

His last period of full-time home education was again a time of rest and recuperation, and also a return to the local authority which we had been forced to abandon so long before. In this we were helped by a psychologist who had known David from his earliest years. At a crucial time in our lives, he returned to our home town from a post in another area and assisted us towards the completion of David's academic progress and to what was probably the most significant move of David's life, for it would be this which would open all the doors for his complete acceptance into normal society. It began to be a practical proposition that one day there might be no 'special needs'. On one occasion he told us that our handling of David and our faith in his potential had completely changed his own attitudes towards the management of autistic children.

This time at home was a preparation for David's final release from the stigma attached to his disability. We had no formal timetable. Our loyal psychologist tested him carefully during these weeks, because we felt that, after a period of recovery, David might be able to attend a school within the state system. I was still extremely ill and awaiting an operation, but we managed, in the security of our home, to heal his mental and emotional wounds caused by the stress of his latest school experience and take him through the kinds of things he might face socially and academically.

At fourteen, he was about a year behind the average scores for his age, but not being too tall, could well be integrated into a slightly lower age group. This time we had no doubts about the school of our choice. It was a Roman Catholic high school, about five minutes' walk from our home, where he would have kindly support from some of the children around us and a headmaster of great renown. The only problem was, we were not Catholics.

With the help of our psychologist friend, David was accepted. His record was still one of special needs, but within a year we were all agreed that this could well be discarded. His headmaster, a monk whose silver cross and powerful charisma boded little argument, made sure that this was achieved.

At seventeen, David sat his exams for six Scottish Standard Grades. At the prize-giving ceremony afterwards, he climbed the steps to the platform twice, firstly to collect the school prize as 'dux' for craft and design (a Scottish award for the most outstanding pupil in the school in any particular subject). He then returned to be awarded his certificate as winner of an advanced trombone class, in a competition which covered most of the east of Scotland.

At the age of eighteen, he went on to become a member of the National Youth Brass Band of Scotland. Later, at twenty-two, he completed a Higher National Diploma in furniture craftsmanship, and a year later, a Business and Technician Education Council (BTEC) award in antique furniture restoration. As far as his higher education was concerned, he had wiped the slate clean: there was no record of special needs. During his BTEC course he even survived the life of a student residence!

It would be wrong, however, to suggest that the organisation of his educational and social progress passed out of our hands in the later stages of his development. Home education never really stopped. All the preparation for examinations took place at a little, rather rickety white table in a bedroom, where he and I would sit with his day's work, his homework and often other exercises devised at home to help him with his studies.

It was still the teacher who was the most important factor. In physics, for example, there were few difficulties. My husband could help with information, but David's physics teacher was so gifted it was mainly a matter of practising logical sequences. With other subjects we might well be starting from scratch. The school provided a social framework which worked and within which there were areas of great academic progress. The gaps had to be filled at home. These sessions would include such things as writing letters of application, learning answers to questions which might arise at an interview and strict monitoring of identifiable mannerisms associated with autism.

This pattern continued throughout David's further education. While the practical elements of furniture making were well within his control under the guidance of a very gifted teacher, other sections of the course, such as setting up a business, were much more difficult. Many hours would be spent working out mythical financial projections or analysing the content of a question so that he could apply his knowledge in an organised way. He loved and still loves history, and we made many fascinating visits to stately homes or exhibitions. Charles Rennie Mackintosh, the great Scottish artist and designer, was a particular favourite, and I, too, was inspired by the knowledge which came my way, often unexpectedly.

David's final placement for his course in antique furniture restoration was many miles away. For the last time, my husband and I took an extra house and suffered separation and a heavy financial commitment. Jeremy was studying nearby and was able to live there too, but my presence was necessary to provide a structure, especially at weekends, when David would leave his student residence and come home. Without that refuge I think it unlikely he would have survived.

My husband remained alone, his other commitments making it impossible for him to leave permanently at that time. He made the final sacrifice, for he died alone, far from us, after a sudden heart attack. Yet he had seen what he had worked for. His autistic son had graduated with confidence and style. He had been present at Jeremy's first full solo recital to hear the deafening applause. There can be no regrets.

At the time of writing, David is twenty-six years old. He has not continued with a career in furniture making, because he finds the ethics of the trade and the work environment uncongenial. Instead, he works full time caring for the elderly, though he still retains his interest in his craft.

The apparent instability in the earlier years of his education, when we had moved him backwards and forwards from school to home, has not been a permanent pattern in his life, even though at one time it was suggested that it might be. During the latter part of his education, he showed an ability to sustain a demanding schedule if given the proper support and encouragement. His full-time employment in a permanent job now proves that our constant adjustments to his needs were justified. One of the ladies he looks after said to me not long ago, 'We'd like to thank you for giving such a wonderful son to the world.'

We all of course played a part, my husband and I with our sacrifices, Jeremy with his continued love and support and the friends and sympathisers we met on the way. At that triumphant school prize-giving, our dear monastic headmaster had given the final word. 'Well, son,' he said, 'you've proved your point.'

13

Liberated by the label
Mark's story

Mark's Mum

Mark is reading in his bedroom while I write in my study. He hums loudly as he reads. I am three rooms away, but the sound fills the house. I try to ignore it, but today it's disturbing my concentration. He bursts into singing aloud. I get up, tap softly on his door and ask him to hum more softly, as I'm trying to think. He leaps up, startled, flapping his hands in the air. He opens and closes his mouth several times. Then he sits down again.

'I'm sorry,' he says, in his dignified, oddly formal voice. 'I was not aware that I was humming.' He is confused by the unexpected interruption. It takes him several minutes to calm down and settle back to his book. For a few minutes after I leave, he tries not to hum.

Mark is eleven years old. He has Asperger's syndrome. He used to hum while working at his desk at school. It annoyed his teacher, Mrs. Chipperton. Many of the things he did annoyed her. He liked to roll a pencil off his desk and watch it clatter to the floor, over and over again. Mrs. Chipperton referred to this as 'Mark's attention-seeking behaviour'.

I remember attention-seeking behaviour. We had that at my school, too. I can still picture it: a boy nudges a pencil across his desk, sending it clattering to the floor. The teacher's back is turned; she is writing on the blackboard. The boy glances around out of the corner of his eye, enjoying the reaction of his classmates. The teacher turns around, and the boy instantly focuses his eyes on his book, pretending innocence.

With Mark, there are no sidelong glances, no suppressed giggles, no feigned innocence. All his attention is focused on the pencil: on its fascinating trajectory from desk to floor, on the shifting angle of its length as it drops through the air, on the sound of wood striking linoleum. He is oblivious to the sniggers of the other children and the growing irritation of the teacher. The attention, when it comes, is unsought and unwelcome.

Mrs. Chipperton has been teaching for ten years; she understands children—but she doesn't understand Mark. I understand Mark.

We've been home educating for three years now. It suits us. 'I love this life!' Mark declared today during our morning walk. 'I'm glad I'm alive.' He didn't always feel this way.

When Mark was six, he came home from school one day and announced that he was going to kill himself. 'I mean it, Mummy,' he said, 'I'm really going to do it. I wish I'd never been born.' I was terribly shocked. I was at least ten before I said that.

Of course, I knew he wasn't learning anything in school. Mark was a fluent reader long before he entered school at age four. In fact, he had been reading for pleasure since about age two, but he still had to sit through class lessons on basic literacy every day. He was good at maths, but he couldn't colour in pictures, so he was stuck on the first maths workbook, on the concept of counting to five, for six months. I was told that he could move to the next level when his writing skills improved. They never did.

I had hoped he would make friends at school, but he seemed strangely detached from the other children. At the start of the school day, he would enter the classroom, open a book and sit reading, ignoring everything around him as long as he could, while the other children chatted and played together until lessons began. We used to say, jokingly, that he was born without a herd instinct.

There were other problems. Mark took no pleasure in the ball games and races that other boys enjoyed. Occupational therapy was recommended to improve his co-ordination and balance. He also had difficulty communicating: his speech wasn't very clear, and he had an odd habit of repeating the final sounds of words and syllables. Speech therapy was added to his timetable. He didn't seem to hear instructions given to the class; a visit to the audiologist was arranged.

After school we did handwriting practice every day, trying to bring him up to the level of his classmates. It was a struggle. Mark had never shown the slightest interest in writing or drawing. Stacks of colouring books and boxes of crayons gathered dust on his bedroom shelves. After months of tedious effort, he finally learned to hold a pencil and form recognisable words.

I thought that being able to write would enable him to survive at school. Indeed, when the time came for him to move up from infant school to junior school, at age eight, he easily passed the entrance test for a selective private school, where I felt certain his intellectual ability would be appreciated. It wasn't.

After only one term, just before Christmas, the headmaster informed us that Mark was not to return to school in January. His behaviour was too distracting to the other children and too embarrassing to the other parents. He skipped along the path to class instead of walking. He spoilt football practice by spinning in circles in the middle of the playing field. He laughed too loudly in assembly. He hummed in class. He had no friends.

I was overwhelmed by grief and disbelief. Mark was such a gentle, peaceful boy. How could they throw him out of school for skipping? He hadn't broken any rules or done anything dangerous. There were other children whose behaviour was far worse. Why Mark? He was only eight. I was thirteen before a school asked me to leave.

The headmaster advised us that Mark was obviously severely brain damaged and belonged in a residential home for the disabled. 'But what about his academic ability?' I asked. 'Mark is so bright. He won't be stretched in a special school.' To my amazement, he lost his temper. He shouted at me that Mark's ability was below average, and that he didn't belong in a school with normal children. Mrs. Chipperton nodded in agreement. I was stunned.

For three months after Mark was asked to leave school, we fought the decision. For another three months after that, we searched for alternatives. We visited other schools, but the good ones demanded letters of recommendation from his previous school, and quickly lost interest when they heard that he'd been asked to leave. In desperation, I spent a day looking at one of the special schools that had been suggested. There I saw violent, destructive, illiterate children who had been excluded from every other school in the county. I didn't see anyone like Mark. I cried every day.

We turned to the specialists, hoping they could 'fix' our child so that he could return to school. I drove back and forth to an army of experts: occupational therapist, speech therapist, audiologist, sensory integration practitioner, educational psychologist, neurologist, consultant paediatrician. Whenever the NHS waiting list was too long, we paid for private consultations. Mark was tested and tested. We learned that his intelligence was in the 'very superior' range, and that he showed some features of autism. I cried even more.

I didn't want to believe there was anything wrong with my beautiful son. I decided that Mark was simply too bright for school and was probably acting silly out of sheer boredom. I would have to teach him myself. We decided to try home education for one term.

With that decision, a great weight fell from my back. We didn't have to please the teachers any more. We could choose to do things our own way. With no pressure to return to school, there seemed no reason to keep making the rounds of all those experts with their useless therapies, so we stopped all that, too. We were free at last.

Our first act was to scrap the hated chore of handwriting practice and replace it with touch typing and computer skills. We forgot about football and cricket, and took up swimming and trampolining instead. Mark was about two years ahead in maths, so we threw away the boring year four maths syllabus he'd been working on in school and started on year six maths instead.

I enrolled Mark in every after-school activity I could find, so that he would spend time with other children: art class, dance class, maths club, chorus. After a while, though, it became obvious that he was not getting any benefit from being in a group; more often than not, he simply tuned out and spent the class time day-dreaming or spinning. Gradually I reduced the number of classes he attended.

I wasted a lot of money in that first year buying course materials and assessment tests for every National Curriculum subject on the syllabus. I recorded the overnight broadcasts of educational television programmes, and sent off for the revision guides and computer software to accompany them. I stocked up on workbooks and mock exam papers from bookshops, and ordered even more from educational publishers.

Most of those materials were never needed. Over the next three years, I gave them away to new home educators going through the same initial panic buying phase. We eventually found our own way of working, and settled into a pattern that suited us.

Every Sunday night, I print out our timetable for the coming week and put it on the counter near the dining table. Mark likes to have a timetable that he can look at to see what's planned, although the plans can change. I don't think we've ever kept exactly to our timetable, but he still insists on having one.

Our typical day begins with a morning walk. I had the unpleasant experience of being an overweight, inactive child, so I try to build some physical activity into our daily routine. Mark, like me, is naturally sedentary. Although he enjoys our walks once we've started out, he has never spontaneously set foot outside the house. When we had builders in last summer and I had no time to organise any exercise, he didn't see daylight for three weeks.

After our walk, we both have free time for an hour. Mark plays his favourite computer game, *Creatures 3*, while I catch up with housework and mail. Then we have a maths lesson and music practice before lunch. Mark likes to eat exactly the same lunch every day: a turkey and cheese sandwich followed by a KitKat bar.

Afternoons are more varied: we might watch a recorded television programme together about science or history, or do some writing on the computer, followed by more free time. Every evening before supper, Mark plays another computer game, *Ultima Online*, on the Internet.

Recently we spent some of our afternoons working through the BBC *Bitesize Revision* programme for science at Key Stage 3, which is intended to help school children study for their assessment tests at age fourteen. I bought it because I was curious to see whether there were any topics we had neglected at home. Mark was enthusiastically looking forward to the section entitled *The Earth and beyond*. 'I want to learn more about black holes,' he said. Unfortunately, the unit covered only very basic facts, such as that the Earth orbits the sun, and that there are nine planets in the solar system. It was a huge disappointment. Mark learns much more by reading *New Scientist* and watching *Tomorrow's World* and *Horizon*.

Thursday is outings day. Our home is not far from Stratford-upon-Avon, so one of our favourite outings is to the Swan Theatre to see a Shakespeare play. If we're not seeing a play, we might visit a museum in Birmingham, or explore a Roman fort, or join an activity of our local Education Otherwise group. It's a friendly, tolerant group; they cheerfully put up with our eccentricities.

Saturday is technology day, when Mark and his father build things or carry out practical science experiments. This is my way of getting a day off, but it has the added benefit of giving them a special time together. They began by doing every experiment in the *Chemistry 100* science kit, and then branched out into more spontaneous projects. When business travel leaves me without a technology teacher, I rely on Robert Krampf's *Experiment of the Week* from the Internet to fill the gap.

Sunday is non-stop free time day. Mark is on the Internet from dawn to dusk, playing computer games and reading newsgroups. On the Internet, he has to communicate by typing on the computer; this has led to a noticeable improvement in his spelling, without any effort on my part.

When we began home educating, I bought a large desk diary in which I recorded all the academic work we did. I started it because I was determined to have plenty of evidence to show an inspector if the local education authority ever came round to investigate us, but they never did. I still keep up the diary, though, because it's so satisfying to look back and read about all the things we've done.

I don't know what an inspector would make of our educational programme. It's highly structured, but it's also very different from what school children do. Freedom from school means freedom to ignore the National Curriculum, much of which is unsuitable for children on the autistic spectrum. For example, National Curriculum mathematics is taught as a social activity, through teamwork and group discussion. Maths is Mark's best subject, but he could never learn it like that.

There might be pressure from the local education authority to follow the National Curriculum, but I have personally felt even greater pressure from other home educators to embrace autonomous education, where the child learns by following his own interests. Left to pursue his own interests, Mark reads science fiction and plays computer games and does very little else. I want him to have a broader education than that. He does have a say in what we choose to study, but not studying is not an option.

In teaching Mark, I have always had the advantage that our brains seem to work the same way. His reactions are second nature to me. I can often sense his thoughts and translate his questions into understandable form. It always puzzled me when his teachers complained that they couldn't figure him out, because I always found his reactions logical and predictable.

Perhaps because we are so much alike, I never thought of Mark as handicapped or disabled. However, even I had to recognise that Mark's behaviour was very different from other children's. He couldn't catch a ball or ride a bike. His speech was slow and laboured. He made odd flapping movements with his hands.

At the age of nine, he began doing what I call the 'eye thing': rolling his eyes sideways and upwards while tilting his head. He explained to me that he enjoyed the interesting effect of double vision this produced. Soon he was doing it almost constantly—during meals, on our walks, everywhere. The eye thing distorted his features and gave his face a monstrous appearance.

I felt more and more self-conscious about Mark's quirks. One day, when we were shopping in town, Mark happily launched himself down the street, spinning, flapping and doing the eye thing as he ran along.

Then he added a new twist by jerking his head sideways against his shoulder on every fourth step. At that moment, I suddenly felt utterly humiliated by the obvious strangeness of my child.

I began to accept the fact that my child was different, and that his difference had a name. I joined a local support group for parents of children with Asperger's syndrome, and poured out my feelings in public for the first time. At the time, the pain seemed unendurable—yet here were parents who seemed to be coping, some happily. How could they bear it? One mother told me, 'The problem goes away when you stop expecting them to be normal.'

That has proved true for us. Mark's quirks are not harmful, either to him or to others. They make people stare, because normal people don't walk around flapping their hands and rolling their eyeballs. But they are not problems in themselves. They are not problems at home. They are only problems at school.

I was the only home educator in the Asperger's support group. Some of the children attended special schools; others were in mainstream schools supported by classroom assistants. A common thread ran through their stories: the parents spent most of their time and energy trying to educate the teachers about autism, while the teachers spent most of their time and energy trying to make the children act normal. I began to realise how lucky we were to be free of school and able to devote our time and energy to education.

Acting normal, at school, means conforming to the social conventions of the classroom. The two social skills that matter most in school—unquestioning obedience to authority and conformity to peer pressure—are alien to my child's mind. Mark was never going to master either of these, no matter how many years he stayed in school.

Mark is a quiet, polite child, but deference to authority is not in his nature. He speaks to headmasters in exactly the same tone of voice that he uses with children his own age. As for peer pressure, he is completely unaffected by it. Right up until the moment when the bullies strike, he is unaware of the growing danger, because he doesn't see how he is perceived by others. He doesn't see and he doesn't care. He doesn't think it's important, because it is illogical. Nothing I can say or do will change his mind.

Because we are so happy at home, I sometimes forget how different we are from other people. I begin to think that we can go about our business as normal people do, and that nobody will notice anything wrong. Sometimes it works, but not always. Sometimes people react badly. In my experience, it's a matter of luck whether people regard Mark as disabled or gifted. It depends on the context.

We went to the theatre to see *The Tempest*, and stayed for the post-show discussion. Mark raised his hand and asked, 'Why did Prospero break his magic staff and throw his book into the sea? Think of all the benefit to society if he had used his magic for good when he returned to civilisation.' Philip Voss, who played Prospero, gave a long and thoughtful reply. Then another of the Royal Shakespeare Company actors spoke up, pointing to Mark. 'I see so many children dragged here to see Shakespeare, giggling and messing about in the audience, wishing they were somewhere else. This child has restored my faith in young people.' I glowed.

On another occasion, we visited the public library to get a borrower's card for Mark, which required his signature. He gripped the pencil awkwardly and struggled to write his name in the small space provided. Then he looked up at me and asked nervously, 'Is that correct?' The librarian looked at me with horror and pity. I cringed.

At times, I have been overly optimistic. One day, I took Mark to the dentist for a routine examination. When his turn was called, I let him go in on his own. He seemed so grown up, so totally normal. He had never had any problem with dentists. Some time later, the dental assistant came to look for me in the waiting room. She was confused and upset. 'I don't know what's wrong with him,' she said. 'He doesn't seem to understand anything I tell him. He's acting very strangely.'

'Mark is mildly autistic,' I heard myself saying. 'He'll be fine, but he does need very clear explanations. I can help if you like.' She looked relieved, but also a bit annoyed. 'Well, I wish I'd known that!' she said. 'Why didn't you tell me earlier?'

It suddenly seemed so simple. She needed an explanation. I had one I could give her. It helped her. It helped us. We could go forward.

These days, I usually tell people that Mark is autistic at the start of any encounter. As a result, they are prepared for the worst, and are often pleasantly surprised by how normal his behaviour is. Without the explanation, it is only a matter of time before someone asks, with some embarrassment, what exactly is wrong with him.

I wish there had been an explanation like that for me when I was growing up. I wish someone had been able to step forward and say to my teachers, my classmates, my employers, 'She can't cope with that, because her mind doesn't work that way, but the problem goes away when you stop expecting her to be normal.'

They kept expecting me to be normal, and I kept expecting myself to be able to cope with the things that other people coped with, simply because I saw that everyone else assumed that I could. But I couldn't, and I didn't know why. I was just normal enough to keep trying—and failing—to act normal. And I had no way of explaining to anyone what was going wrong.

As I learn more about the autistic spectrum, everything falls into place. It all makes sense to me now. My gifted, disabled son. My own childhood. My family.

I should have known there was something special about my family, especially after my younger sister was born. Unlike the rest of us, Christy didn't go to university. Even at a very young age, it was obvious there was something missing. We felt sorry for her, but there was really no need. She was by far the prettiest girl in our family, and she genuinely seemed to enjoy her bizarre way of life.

She was totally different from all her brothers and sisters. For one thing, she was unaccountably easygoing. Nothing sent her into a rage. She didn't seem to have any consuming interests or obsessions. The oddest thing about Christy, though, was her social behaviour. She always had friends over to play after school—not just one, but often two or three at a time. Once I saw her with a group of five friends all at once. She actually enjoyed going to concerts and parties. She was also capable of astonishing duplicity: she would say nice things to people to please them, things that might not even be true. Her behaviour was incomprehensible to me.

Now, years later, I have learned that there is a word for what's wrong with my little sister: Christy is normal.

Maybe Christy doesn't need a label. Mark needed his. The label of autism—or rather, the insight that it represents—has changed our lives. It may have saved his. It has liberated us not just from school, but from the misery and confusion of not fitting in and not knowing why.

It has been a strange journey of self-discovery for both of us. The terrible grief and pain I felt when we began has been transformed into a deep sense of freedom and even enjoyment. Life on the autistic spectrum can be good. Mark knows he's different, but he's happy to be the way he is. I love Mark, and somehow that makes it seem possible to accept my own difference, too.

I go up to Mark's bedroom. I tap on the door and open it as gently as I can, but he still jumps at the interruption. I go over to his bed and sit down next to him. 'I'm sorry I complained about your humming today,' I tell him. 'You have a right to hum if you want to. It's just that I'm very sensitive to sounds, you know, especially when I'm trying to think of what to write. I think it comes from my being a little bit autistic, too.'

He notices that I am sitting next to him and not going away. From this he correctly deduces that I wish to communicate with him. He turns to face me and carefully makes eye contact. He reaches out his hand and pats my shoulder three times, mechanically, in a stylised gesture of comfort.

He sees that this stratagem has not been effective, since I am still sitting there, waiting. He has known me a long time; it is clear, even to him, that nothing short of spoken language will satisfy me.

'That's all right, Mummy. It's like the pencils.'

'What pencils?'

'At school, when we were supposed to write stories, I could never think of anything to write, because the sound of all the pencils scraping against the paper kept distracting me.'

'Yes, it's exactly like that. I'm glad you understand.' I hug him. Generously, he puts up only token resistance. I return to my study and leave him in peace at last.

14

Living without the label

Jan Fortune-Wood

Home-based education: a positive choice

If you are a parent reading this book, you may well be looking for alternative educational provision for your child. This may mean that you are coming to the decision fresh, with a young child who has not yet encountered any educational system. It may (more likely) mean that you are urgently searching for an educational model that will not go on compounding the damage that you believe your child has already sustained. The sad reality is that many parents come to home-based education as a negative response to what is on offer within mainstream or special needs schooling. Sometimes it may even be seen as a last resort or an unwelcome necessity.

This is the time to revise that opinion. No matter what your motivation for considering home-based education, home education can always be a positive choice. It is a viable educational alternative, and not merely a reactionary expedient for those who feel they have run out of options (even if that is where you are starting from).

The primary responsibility for a child's education rests, in law, with the parents. The majority of people choose to delegate that responsibility to schools. Home educators are those who choose not to delegate the responsibility, but rather to take that primary responsibility for themselves. Moreover, they do so for a growing number of positive reasons.

Only home education allows for meeting the individual child's needs in a tailored learning environment. Families practising home-based education are free to pursue event-driven lifestyles rather than clock-driven lifestyles, giving them maximum flexibility and access to an increasingly event-driven society. The notion of a government-controlled curriculum is replaced with the more positive notion of learning that is specifically responsive to the intrinsic motivation of the child and the educational philosophy of the family.

The need for schools is becoming less and less obvious. We now live in an information-rich world. With growing access to a wide range of media, including television, video, music, radio, CD-ROMs and the Internet, it is both possible and desirable for parents and children to work together to foster personalised learning.

In a postmodern society, home education naturally promotes a sense of being in control and responsible, with children being not only partners or the leading protagonists in their own education, but also in charge of simple human functions (such as getting snacks or drinks or going to the toilet), thus promoting confidence and maturity. Education becomes part of a wider vision of developing and supporting moral and humane family and societal institutions. Furthermore, children remain a full part of local communities, with the ability to access community facilities, such as libraries, shops, museums, exhibitions, theatres, transport, art centres, etc., on a full-time basis. Social skills can be developed within the community across a full range of age groups.

Home education is as diverse as the people who practise it. There is no home education National Curriculum, but rather the opportunity to discover and optimise special interests and skills. Areas of learning can be studied and followed up to exactly the depth required in each instance. There is no compulsion either to cut short studies because of the demands of a generalised curriculum, nor to pursue subjects beyond the point of interest and value to the individual. Learning is focused on wanted and needed information.

Such individual responsiveness comes as a welcome relief for families who feel that their child has already sustained damage from the educational system, however well-meaning, whilst others feel fortunate to have had access to home education from the beginning.

A singular education

Any educational system that envisages working with groups of children must, by its nature, be aimed at some mythical typical child. It is perhaps remarkable that any child manages to comply with this level of standardisation, and perhaps very few remain completely undamaged by the demands of compulsory institutional conformity.

For many children, however, such demands are intolerable. The response of the educational machine to these children cannot be to change and adapt to take account of their individuality and intrinsic learning motivation. That is not how institutional structures work, no matter how well-meaning the individuals within them. All too often children, and sometimes their whole families, find that what is actually a problem of large institutions being unsuited to making humane, small-scale individual responses is redefined as a problem of individual child or family dysfunction.

With home-based education there is no one educational system to slot into. The child and parents mould the learning. The learning does not mould the child. This singularity of education sets home-based education apart from any other learning system. This singularity also makes for a wide diversity of educational styles, methods and philosophies among home educators, so that 'home education' becomes a vast umbrella term for an endlessly innovative variety of educational provisions.

Of course, all this applies equally to any child, but in this book we are looking at children on the autistic spectrum and, in this chapter, I am particularly addressing the rise in numbers of children diagnosed with or suspected of suffering from 'Asperger's syndrome'. Will all this individual, often highly informal learning suit them?

You may already have experience of the negative effects of school on your child, or fear that your child who has not yet gone to school will, at worst, be traumatised and labelled and, at best, be repressed by the demands of the educational system. Furthermore, you now know that there are many positive reasons for choosing home education, not least the overriding advantage of facilitating an individualised, singular educational environment for your individual child. You know that in theory the choices are legion and the educational style and philosophy you end up with can be unique to your family and child. All that said, where on earth do you start? How do you translate the positive reasons and the educational theory into the context of your particular child?

Labelling to mould

Two years ago, I had never heard of 'Asperger's syndrome'. Suddenly, it is a 'condition' that seems to be proliferating in classrooms everywhere. Amongst stressed young children who are not fitting in with the increasingly narrow definition of what it is to be normal in a highly structured regime, 'Asperger's' seems to have become a byword for coercing children towards an agreed political standard of normality, allegedly 'for their own good'. The assumption is that children are products—and a product, as we all know, has to meet certain standards and criteria before it can be acceptable.

Children who are labelled are often also involved in bullying. If they are perceived as the hyperactive inflictors of rage, the label is most likely to be 'attention deficit hyperactivity disorder' (ADHD), whilst their victims are also regularly perceived as dysfunctional and given the Asperger's label. The weight of expectations about how someone must look and behave in order to fit in is then added to this already distressing scenario.

In an ethos where the product mentality is operating, a child who waits until everyone has got started on the work the group has been instructed to do before asking, 'And what should I do?' attracts a host of 'faulty product' labels. Options are worked through. Should the child be seen as 'deaf'? Should the child be seen as 'deliberately annoying' and brought up to specification with behavioural modification? Should the child be seen as 'slow'? That is an apparently useful label when his response to instructions is sometimes to follow them literally. It does not take much imagination to conjure up the reactions parents would receive when a child who is told to undress for physical education does just that. Teacher product requirements are that children should be compliant and, at least to some extent, bright. School ground product requirements may vary from school to school, but it is not uncommon that a boy of six is expected to be tough, have good ball skills and not wear glasses.

Faced with the prospect that their child is being seen as a stupid or weak product, parents, far from questioning the fundamental assumption that children are products at all, will often go to great lengths to find other attributes that counter the 'faulty product' perception, objectifying the child not with labels like 'stupid', 'clumsy', *etc.*, but with others like 'highly articulate', 'idiosyncratic', *etc.*

Caught up in the product mentality and desperate to prove their child's worth, parents can easily compile their own list of labels or characteristics, which, on a good day, function as cute eccentricities of which to be fond and, on bad days, become an embarrassment, a signal of their own parental failure to produce the longed-for masterpiece. Faced with such a burden of angst and guilt, it is unsurprising that many parents are relieved when a scientific-sounding diagnostic label comes along to alleviate their worst fears that they have caused their child to be a faulty product.

Under the protection of 'diagnosis', the list takes on the authority of being not merely a group of commonplace and wrongly attributed labels that could be used to diminish the humanity of thousands of other children who display their individuality, but rather an explanatory framework for the child's inability to function within the demands of the institution. This does not give rational credibility to such diagnoses.

The world is full of children (and adults) who talk before others have finished their turn, who introduce *non sequiturs* into conversation or who use language very literally. Many children have apparently quirky fears. Not everyone responds to social signals and eye gestures. Not everyone likes to be hugged. There are hosts of people who can amaze us with memories all the way back to babyhood, but still forget the last thing that was said to them. Many people never conquer spelling and handwriting, but still soak up factual knowledge or become totally engrossed in specific topics to the exclusion of all else. It is not rare to find able people who seem to have great co-ordination in an activity like playing the violin, but nonetheless wander around with untied shoelaces, seeming clumsy, awkward and ill at ease in their bodies.

The list of differences, many of them subtle, some of them slightly surreal, could go on. Having a unifying label for the set of characteristics that make up a parent's perceptions of one child at just one moment in time does not make up for taking the child seriously as an autonomous individual in her own right, and it is this which home-based education offers, particularly for those families that choose a non-coercive model of parenting and education.

Taking Children Seriously (TCS) is an educational and parenting philosophy that believes that it is possible to bring up children without coercion. Starting from the assumption of personal autonomy for everyone, even children, it sets out a theory for living consensually, positing that with sufficient openness, rationality and creativity all parties in a relationship can reach common preferences. These are not compromises, but genuine win–win situations. Living without coercion is a radical undertaking for even the most liberal of parents. Being fallible, the families that attempt it are far from perfect, but the serious undertaking to strive continually for no coercion has major ramifications for every way in which a family interacts.

The road to assessment, labelling and therapy is no doubt paved with the good intentions of those who want to help 'different' children to fit in for their own good, but it inevitably diminishes individuality and autonomy. TCS enables parents to begin questioning the usefulness of the label *per se*. This is an emotive area. Many parents find it an enormous relief to have a label that makes sense of all the differences they have been experiencing. For them, the label is a useful description and a shorthand for a particular group who seem to share many similarities in behaviour or outlook. The label can also be seen as a highly effective way of attracting assistance. One person, for example, described the problems of Asperger's syndrome as being similar to those of wheelchair users in their need for help:

> There are some people who need special help. If someone can't walk, it doesn't mean they need someone else to take charge of their lives, but it does mean they need a wheelchair, and some ramps around so they can go to places. Asperger's people are like this: they are not different so that they need to be controlled, but they still have a disability, which on occasions means they need something like a wheelchair.

This sounds so reasonable, but is it? Many children are 'different' within the broad cultural terms which elevate certain characteristics and denigrate others, but what makes these cultural terms normative or right in the first place? Is having a tendency to become engrossed in particular subjects to the exclusion of other things objectively a bad thing, or is it merely that it doesn't fit with the school regime of dividing the day up into artificial subjects corralled into time allotments which are controlled by bells? Is a propensity to express extreme and (to others) seemingly bizarre anxieties a symptom of a recognisable disease, or simply a child's response to various coercive stresses? Is Asperger's syndrome a pathology comparable to spinal paralysis, or is it merely a convenient fiction, one which gives conventional parenting and education the justification for coercing highly individual children into conformity?

If we lived in a society that truly tolerated difference and idiosyncrasy in all its human glory, then we would not feel a surge of relief on hearing that our child has been given a label, which might at least mean some recognition of his difference. If we lived in a society that took for granted the premise that all education should be centred in the individual and should be intrinsically motivated by the learner, rather than extrinsically motivated by government or parents, then the pursuit of 'assistance' for children who are currently diagnosed as having Asperger's would have no meaning.

We do not live in such a society, of course, but that in itself is not sufficient reason to succumb to poor thinking. Home education offers the possibility that children diagnosed as having Asperger's can be brought up and educated solely on the basis of their own self-determined needs and interests, and not on the basis of a list of demeaning characteristics which may or may not happen to say something about how they are observed, but which certainly can never do justice to all that an individual is.

Faced with the diagnoses which seem to have scientific and medical currency, it can be easy for parents to succumb to labelling their child as a means of helping the child, little suspecting that what is really being offered is a humiliating means of control. The 'symptoms' of Asperger's are not a list of medical indicators, but a list of subjectively observed and often rather demeaningly phrased character traits. Within the list every so-called Asperger's child is a unique subset of the group, no child having exactly all the same characteristics or conforming to the list in its entirety. This is explained away by those defining the syndrome as being because the condition is a 'spectrum disorder', but is this meaningful? All that we actually have is a group of conventionally unwelcome characteristics, some of which are observed to greater or lesser degrees in a group of children who all resist mainstream conformity.

Children are not products

Just thinking about our children in this demeaning way distorts the relationship and tends to exacerbate a whole range of subtle coercion. How is this so?

One writer on the TCS e-mail support list has developed the very useful image of the iceberg, something which is huge and constantly changing, and only fractionally visible.

> I think of people as huge icebergs. When I look at my child and focus in on one aspect of him, I recognise that what I am seeing is not the whole person by any stretch of the imagination. It is only the part of the iceberg that happens to be above water and visible right now, or that I happen to be focusing upon. I am then better able to be aware that my perception is far from accurate or the whole picture; it is only my interpretation of a small aspect of the person based on very, very limited information. How can it be

anything else, when the bulk of that person is totally invisible to me?

The image of the iceberg is an enormously helpful one in ridding ourselves of the tendency to seek labels for our children or to see them as products of our parenting or education. It frees us from the need to construct our child as a perfect product and instead allows us to realise that what we see of another person is simply what is visible at that time. It is a small snapshot of a process, not a static definition.

If our children are not products, then what does it matter that at any one moment a child is consumed with a particular subject, that at another moment a child interrupts a conversation and that at another moment a child flinches away from touch? In a school environment it matters because an artificial environment with a determination to inflict a certain homogeneity of learning and behaviour is strongly in operation. This environment can be totally dispensed with in a home education setting where only the child's intrinsic motivation and autonomy govern what is learned.

This does not mean that an autonomously educating parent would never communicate information about what others might expect in given situations, but this can be shared as suggestions and opinions with no compulsion on the child to comply and no judgments that define and objectify the child.

The TCS writer adds, 'It is important to realise that "whatever is visible of the iceberg" is simply a matter of what I choose to see and how I choose to see it—that even looking at just what is above the surface is not definite—it is just my interpretation and is very subjective.' In a lifetime we are lucky if we come to understand ourselves well. Even if we do achieve this, we never really know the whole. It is presumptuous and demeaning to think that we can know another.

We make observations, always partial, even if sometimes helpful. There is nothing wrong with offering up observations which might help our children: 'If you don't look at people when you're talking, you might find that they think you're lying.' 'If you don't tie your shoelaces or ask someone to help you with them, you might have an accident on your bike.' This is reasonable and helpful, but it is not reasonable, helpful or necessary to coerce a child into making eye contact by placing him in some behavioural modification programme or by constantly barraging him with information that he has long since tired of hearing.

The point is to help the individual child live his own life by his own lights in the way that most pleases him, not to mould him into a new set of attributes which seem more functional and pleasing to parents who want a higher level of product satisfaction, even when it is dressed up in the insidious cloak of being for the child's 'own good'.

Once we have rid ourselves of the product mentality, then the question of how we can help our children to become more functional, more acceptable, more socially in tune, more rounded individuals becomes not only irrelevant, but meaningless. The only question that remains is the same question that we should apply to all children: 'How can I as a parent help my child to do the things he wants with his life in ways that will not impose anyone's agenda but his own, in ways that will not seek to define or control or modify my child against his will?' I am convinced that only through non-coercive interactions, only through home education that absolutely respects the child's autonomy, can we really be of assistance in our children's lives.

Living without the label

Children who are labelled with Asperger's syndrome do not need more structure and direction in their lives; they need considerably less. They need, primarily, to be freed from being seen as products or being objectified and defined by a list of subjective observations. They need parents who are unquestioningly on their side, not to impose their own or so-called experts' agendas on their children in the name of loving assistance, but simply to assist their children in carrying forward their own intrinsically motivated lives in process.

To do this requires a willingness to ask radical questions and to let go of many entrenched assumptions about education, psychology and parenting, to name but a few. It requires going against mainstream and often allegedly expert opinion. It is not an easy path. It is not a neglect-ful path. It is a moral path that puts the individual above any of our partial perceptions and involves parents in constant engagement on the child's terms. It is possible.

In a comic strip from the book *Hurray for B.C.*, one of Johnny Hart's characters is reclining forlornly on a rock. He muses,

> So one day when I was a little kid I got really hungry and I ate an ant. Some people saw me. One says, 'What's that?' And another one says, 'That's an anteater.' You eat one lousy ant and you're typed for life! (Johnny Hart, *Hurray for B.C.*, by permission of Johnny Hart and Creators Syndicate, Inc.).

Behind this humour is a poignant truth afflicting an increasing number of children who are ill served by those who label them 'for their own good'.

> So one day when I was a little kid I got scared of walking on grass and I didn't think the teacher was speaking to me when she talked to this bunch of kids in the class and I just wanted to learn about Genghis Khan. Some experts saw me. One says, 'What's that?' And another one says, 'That's Asperger's syndrome.' You have one lousy interest and you're typed for life!

15

I've decided to home educate—what do I do next?

Christine Waterman

If you are considering teaching your child at home, it will probably seem like a daunting prospect. It certainly involves a great deal of commitment, but the strength of home education is in being able to use your intimate knowledge of your child to do whatever really works for you, changing and adapting it as you observe what is helpful. This chapter will not tell you what to do, but it may help you find answers to some of your questions, and give you ideas about getting started. I hope that it will give you more confidence in your ability to be your child's teacher.

I'll begin by explaining a little about my background. Before I discovered home education, I was employed for many years by Hillingdon Education Authority, on the outskirts of London, as an advisory teacher for special needs. I taught in both special and mainstream schools, but worked mainly with families in their own homes. I left work when my own son arrived and, apart from a short and unrewarding few months when I sent him to nursery school, I have been teaching him at home ever since. He is now nine, and we have spent the last five years learning together, exploring the things that interest him and finding ways around anything that causes him a problem. It has been immensely satisfying.

Two years ago, I decided to put my experience to good use and volunteered to become the special needs contact for the home education support organisation Education Otherwise. This has brought me into contact with many parents who are home educating children on the autistic spectrum. The following are my answers to the questions they often ask as they take their first steps on the path of home education.

What on earth will we do all day?

When our children are small, most of us spend many days with them simply getting on with life: cooking, gardening and doing household jobs together; playing games, sharing books and watching TV; going out to the park, the shops or the library and dealing with any problems as they arise. If a child is not going to go to school, then there is no reason why this pattern should change. What has worked during the pre-school years can develop naturally into home education.

> Sometimes I might have a bright idea for some fun 'educational' activity I might do with Alex. However, when I went to him I would invariably find him doing something like reading a book, playing with Lego, making a cardboard model or playing with Polydrons. I could never see any point in interrupting the activity he had chosen for himself in favour of my idea.
>
> —Grace

The majority of people come to home education after their children have had a bad time in school, and approach their first day of freedom from the school routine wondering how they are actually going to spend their time. As you will have gathered from the stories in this book, there are as many styles of home education as there are home-educating families. The one thing they all have in common is that they are able to spend their days doing what is right for them as a family.

You do not have to turn your home into a classroom. You don't have to have lessons around the table, or confine what you do to 'school' hours—in fact, you don't even have to stay indoors! You have the flexibility to develop your child's learning in whatever way works for you. By providing a range of interesting books, stimulating experiences, learning equipment and toys, you can, if you so wish, make it possible for your child to direct his own learning, or you may prefer to teach him more directly in a manner that is enjoyable and relaxed.

If your child has suffered from a stressful time at school, then you may both need to recover and relax. Spend time enjoying what you do together—whatever helps your child to unwind and feel good about himself. From your knowledge of him, use whatever you can to help him feel calm. For one child, it may help to spend time on a special interest; another may need to find a quiet, peaceful room to be in. Some children find it relaxing to walk by the river or to play with water, or to listen to particular pieces of music. Others need exercise and movement in order to relax.

Don't feel guilty about spending time in this way: it will do your child more good than any lessons. Give him space, without pressure, to be himself. Where you can, try joining in with the things that give him pleasure, even if those things are unusual activities for you! Having fun together can bring you much closer and help you develop a better understanding of each other. You are your child's most valuable resource; through you, and with your support, he can explore whatever he wants to learn.

> When we started our programme, it was totally child-centred and child-led learning. Our first task was to establish contact between Greg and people, which we did by going with Greg and his interests (becoming autistic with him). We then built a bridge of love between Greg's world of autism and our world. With this bridge in place, we encouraged Greg to move towards people. We were then able to introduce more conventional teaching and develop his concentration, communication, self-help skills and, consequently, his ability to learn.
>
> —Alan

Home life in itself can be a rich resource for learning. Without the morning rush to get to school, there is more time for learning essential self-care and independence skills. There is also the opportunity to learn about the tasks that go into running a home. You can plan meals, shop and cook together, grow vegetables or flowers, load the washing machine and clean the house, or organise a daily or weekly budget.

Such activities have an immediate purpose and increase your child's independence and self-esteem, as well as making life easier for the rest of the family. They also involve using and practising other skills such as planning, making lists, using money, measuring, weighing, reading instructions, manipulative skills such as stirring and pouring, using tools, and learning how to ask for things in shops or order snacks in a café. Doing some of these things may even develop into a more involved project or hobby, such as tending a patch of garden or preparing meals.

What teaching materials do I need to buy?

Many parents prepare for their first week of home education by rushing out to buy a lot of school-type resources, but there is no real need to do this. Look around your home and rediscover the good books and toys that haven't been used for a while; some of these may well have a great deal of educational value, as well as being fun to play with.

Many board games can be used to develop maths and thinking skills. If your child likes construction kits, these can be very useful learning tools. Quite apart from the design and building elements, children using these are learning about size, number and shape. Lego, for example, can provide lots of opportunity for discovering number (how many bricks with two dots fit on the brick with eight dots?). K'nex is excellent for learning about angles, while both K'nex and Polydrons teach about shape. It may be worth arranging your room to make these things conspicuous and easily available to a child looking for something to do.

If you do want to splash out on some new educational materials, then the following are worth considering: Logi-blocks and Capsela, although quite expensive, can be very absorbing and thought-provoking. Simple magnet kits and electricity sets made up from a collection of bulbs, buzzers, batteries, switches and wires (available from catalogues or shops like Tandy or Maplin) can also be a worthwhile investment.

Other useful items include a good globe, maps and charts, binoculars, magnifying glasses and a compass. Look for colourful posters with information that interests your child: perhaps a history time line, or a chart of the planets. If this sounds like an alarming expense, rest assured that it is not intended to be a list of essential equipment; these are merely ideas for things you may wish to collect over time depending on your child's interests. Having things like this around will allow him to explore without experiencing any pressure.

Television programmes may spark off interesting conversations or provide new avenues for exploration. Documentaries cater for all kinds of interests, and it can be worth setting the video for Open University broadcasts. Some of the Schools TV programmes are informative and enjoyable, and both BBC 2 and Channel 4 will supply a free guide to what is on. You can also buy teachers' notes, videos and information packs to accompany the programmes. Television channels such as *National Geographic* or *Discovery* can also be useful, and English Heritage allows home educators to borrow a range of excellent history videos under their free 'teachers' loan' scheme.

> Television has been an excellent resource for Kevin. Cable TV has allowed him to learn about other countries, history, animals, world news, science and more.
>
> —Jackie

Most parents, though, say that the single most useful resource is the computer. Using the computer as a word processor can enable a child who finds handwriting difficult to produce a well-presented piece of work much more quickly. Computer games become many children's main hobby. Some of these, such as *Civilisation*, *Age of Empires* and *Sim City*, provide learning experiences as well as hours of entertainment. Interactive multimedia software is ideal for those who dislike being taught directly, as is the Internet with its vast number of information-based web sites. Electronic mail makes it possible for people who find it hard to make small talk to 'converse' with others who share their interests.

The computer is a necessity for Robert: it's the key to his learning, social life and independence. He uses it for all three. I am amazed at what he has taught himself since we got him his own PC; he is the 'techie' expert in our home. He watches DVDs on it, types on it, downloads all sorts of information on his specialist subjects, listens to music and also uses it to e-mail folk. Things have been easier since we managed to get unlimited Internet access.

—Andrea

How will we cope with being at home all day?

One of the common misconceptions about home education is that children are stuck at home all day, sitting at the dining table doing lessons. In reality, nearly all home educators use their local area as a significant part of the education they provide.

It is a great advantage to be able to enjoy the quiet times during the day. This can transform visits to normally busy places like parks and swimming pools. You can explore the local countryside and find the best places to go pond dipping or bird watching, or to see aircraft, trains, or farm machinery—or just to walk or sit, or use the playground equipment. Many museums and places of interest offer reduced, or even free, admission to home-educating families.

Planning in advance can do a lot to reassure a child who gets anxious about going out to new places. Asking questions over the 'phone or visiting the relevant web site can make the experience seem less like venturing into the unknown, and some places will happily send out information packs to help you prepare for your visit. It is worth gathering leaflets about places of interest such as historic sites, environment centres, museums or wildlife parks and aquariums in your area. Libraries often have a stand of leaflets, as do most museums. Notice boards and local papers will often carry adverts for events, talks or shows that may interest your child.

If you have local home education groups that meet together, you may find that they organise outings to suit a range of tastes. Many factories, police or fire stations and supermarkets will allow groups in for a 'behind the scenes' visit and some, such as the Body Shop, Ford, or power stations, do tours for the public. This is another way in which your child can be learning about the world around him without any pressure, and even if he doesn't seem to talk about it much at the time, he may well have quietly absorbed information for use at some later stage.

> Tristan doesn't love to be out; he would quite happily stay at home. He has never, ever asked, 'Can we go to...?' Once we're out, though, he does enjoy himself. He has never in his whole life pointed out something 'interesting'. In spite of that, he does learn from things he's seen on our outings; I know, because things will crop up later in conversation.
>
> —Anne

How will I know what to teach?

You may decide that you and your child would feel happier working in a more structured way, devoting a set time to more formal lessons. There is no requirement to do this, but many families choose to for a number of reasons. It may be that, as a parent, you feel more confident that you are providing your child with an education if you can be sure that you have covered certain aspects of the curriculum in this way, or you may all be more comfortable with a set routine to the day. Many families start off doing formal lessons at home, and then find that they adapt their style as they discover what works best for them. With your expert knowledge of your child, you will undoubtedly find an approach that is satisfying for both of you.

If you do want to do lessons at home, you may well be surprised at how much you can accomplish in a short space of time without any of the inevitable distractions of a busy classroom. Much time in school is taken with lining up, listening to whole-class instructions and waiting for everyone to be quiet.

At home, with one adult to a very small number of children, the work can be done quickly, leaving you with much of the day to do whatever you like. You can work at the time of the day when your child is most receptive and in whichever place he is comfortable. You can take breaks when you want, work while on the move if you wish, and cease work before your child gets tired or fed up or stops succeeding.

If you want to use workbooks, you can select those presented in a style that suits your child and, as there is no need to do every page in the book, you can pick and choose which sections to use in whatever order your child is ready for them. Autistic children tend to be much more able in some areas than others, and you can choose activities that reflect this.

> Books like *Horrible Histories* appeal to Stephen's sense of humour. We have used some textbooks, too. He has trouble following instructions unless they are very clear and unambiguous. He tends to read very fast but carelessly, so he misses subtleties or difficult points. He actually needs a highly skilled but traditional approach to get him motivated. My husband helps him with maths, and we have found that tutors can sometimes succeed where we fail. We used a distance learning pack for English GCSE from Open Learning Centre International, but I still had to keep a close eye on what he did.
>
> —Elizabeth

The day can be organised in such a way that the child's self-directed learning is supplemented with short sessions of more formal work, such as workbooks or activities from teachers' guides. Alternatively, you could encourage your child to make his own plan of activities and perhaps review later how it went. Another approach is to select a few activities and encourage your child to choose from that range, or to take a project or topic that you have chosen together and explore this in different ways.

Written work can be a problem for many autistic children, but when a child is learning at home, there is no need for everything to be written down. A teacher in a busy classroom will often need to see written work in order to know how much the children have learned, but you will know from your conversations with your child how much he has understood, so there is much less need for him to write about it.

If you wish to have something to show for what you have done, it may be helpful to keep your own diary of activities and conversations in which your child demonstrates his learning. There are other ways of recording work, too, such as making a scrapbook of cuttings, taking photographs, word processing, or using tape and video recordings. If you really want to encourage your child to write or type, then making lists or notices, leaving instructions for someone, filling in forms, writing letters or sending e-mails in order to get information are real reasons for writing. Children are more likely to write something when they can see a purpose to the task.

Do we have to follow a curriculum?

There is no need to follow the National Curriculum, but if you wish to do so, or to be aware of what it contains, then the web site of the Department for Education and Skills (DfES) contains all you need to know. In addition to the syllabus, there are suggested activities for various topics. Information about the National Curriculum is available in good bookshops, as are workbooks and CD-ROMs tailored to it. The Schools TV programmes and teachers' guides are also geared to cover the curriculum and many museums and historical sites have produced National Curriculum work packs for schools or families wishing to visit.

There are some published curricula available, mostly from the USA. You can find out about these by visiting the web sites listed in the *Finding support and information* section at the end of this book. Older children may wish to follow an established course such as a GCSE course. This can be done through distance learning, or possibly through a local college.

> Robert attends an adult education centre for two hours a week. He has now completed his third (adult) qualification. He has earned certificates in computer literacy, business studies and Internet technology. He has a passion for computers and loves the Internet: web page building and all that sort of thing. He was suf-

ficiently motivated to do the computer courses because it is a
subject he wants to learn.

—Andrea

For children who are not ready for such materials, developmental charts
covering the first five years of child development may provide a useful
guideline for skills to teach and activities to try. Alan Phillips describes
this process more fully in Greg's story. Again, you may well not want to
cover everything on the charts, preferring to pick and choose the items
that seem relevant to your child. This is particularly important, as
children with autism and Asperger's syndrome have very uneven
profiles on these charts, being far behind their age level in some areas
and sometimes far ahead in others. Montessori or High Scope materials
may also be worth looking at, particularly if they are available in your
local library.

Should we follow one of the treatment programmes
for autism?

Some families withdraw their child from school and follow one of the
treatment programmes for autism, sometimes with funding from their
local education authority. These programmes fall into two main styles: a
largely behavioural approach, represented by Applied Behaviour
Analysis (ABA) and Lovaas, or an attitudinal approach, represented by
Son-Rise (also called Option therapy), based on the philosophy of the
Option Institute in the USA.

ABA and Lovaas use similar methods. They both have a structured
approach based on rewarding behaviours and teaching new behaviours
one at a time. They can be very intensive, but are designed to be carried
out by the family at home, so that the child learns to use new skills in the
natural home setting.

Son-Rise operates from a quite different basis, described as going
with children rather than against them. Son-Rise practitioners believe
that the most effective way to teach children is to draw information,
understanding and insight from them, providing a variety of experiences which will help a child to discover and learn, with assistance from

a caring adult. The adult, in turn, learns about the child's world by observation, without judgments or attempts to direct the child as he explores.

> The strength of a Son-Rise programme is that it creates spontaneity, interaction and language development, whereas the strength of an ABA programme is that it promotes the child's academic abilities. ABA is much more representative of school life, but done in a distraction-free environment, with one-to-one teaching and far higher expectations of what the child can achieve.
>
> —Alan

What about social skills and making friends?

The first thing that many people ask when they hear that a child is home educated is usually 'What about socialisation? How will he make friends? Won't he be lonely?' Those who ask that question often overlook the fact that many children who attend school every day are very isolated. Spending all day among thirty other children of the same age does not guarantee that you will have friends.

Sadly, some children have great difficulties with the social life provided by school and find themselves being ridiculed or bullied by the other children. Being at home with one's family is less painful and lonely than suffering in this way, and it does offer children the opportunity to recover some of their self-esteem. Many children who leave school after having such a traumatic time may not wish to venture out into the world to meet other people for some time. When they are ready, if they are home educated, they will have the advantage of supportive adults to reassure them and give them some protection from further negative social experiences.

Once you leave the school system behind, it becomes easy to see that, away from the classroom, people mix with others of all ages. There is no reason why a child's main social contact should be with others of his own age. Just as very young children make their first relationships with adults, only beginning to interact with other children later, children with autism who have significant problems in making relationships will benefit from having more time to learn to relate to the most important adults in their lives before they have to deal with large groups of children. Even children with greater social skills are still likely to find large groups overwhelming, and are therefore likely to find one-to-one relationships more satisfying.

Educating at home means that you can help your child to develop the kind of social life that suits him, with enough time for privacy, too. For some children, this may mean spending time just with family and a few select family friends. Others might benefit from having one particular child to visit for short periods, to do a specific activity together (such as going to the cinema) or to use the computer. It is important to avoid situations that your child may find stressful. If he has strong feelings about not having his possessions moved around, for example, he may be happier playing in a family room, at someone else's house, or outdoors. On the other hand, a child with phobias may be better able to play in his own home.

Feeling socially isolated can be a big problem for children on the autistic spectrum, whether they go to school or not, as many of them wish to have friends but have not mastered the skills required to make and sustain relationships. As a parent, you may find that you feel isolated, too. If you are keen for your child to meet and mix with new people, it is worth finding out if there is a local home education group or a relevant support group (maybe one for children with autism, or one for gifted children).

It will not necessarily be easy to make friends, but these groups do have some advantages. It is likely, for instance, that you will be able to attend any organised activities with your child, offering support where needed, and you can leave before he has time to get restless or over-loaded. You can pick and choose the activities you attend and, if none seems suitable, you can always try organising something that is! Some of the other parents will have seen their own children experience problems in social situations and will perhaps be more tolerant. Many of us have found it helpful to explain something about our child's diffi-culties as, if other parents understand, they are less likely to be critical or judgmental and can instead work with us to support any developing friendships by explaining to their own children how best to deal with any difficult situations that arise.

> I get an enormous amount of emotional support from my friends, precisely because they understand that Alex has Asperger's syndrome. It also makes it so much easier for the other kids to know how to respond to Alex—not to have to be embarrassed if they need to speak to me about him, for instance.
>
> —Grace

While few children with autism seem to enjoy organised sports classes, activities such as swimming, cycling, bowling, skating or visits to parks can be fun to do with a group. There may also be an activity group associated with your child's special interests, such as a computer class or club, games shop, model or steam railway society, chess club, or local history or environmental group. If you are very lucky, you may find a suitable after-school club or holiday play scheme. Unfortunately, there is no magic answer to finding friends, and you may find that those your child does find do not live very close to your home.

How will I have time for myself?

You may well be thinking, 'What about me? How will I cope? Where will I get any space for myself?' I said earlier that home education is a major commitment. For most people, it involves giving up either some time that they previously had for themselves or their earnings. For the majority of us, the compensation comes from closer relationships with our children and the enjoyment of learning together.

Nevertheless, it is important to consider these questions, and to work out how you will cope financially. Some of you will be entitled to disability benefit, and it is certainly worth making enquiries about this. You may also find that you can earn money by using your skills to work at home, or in a part-time job when a partner, friend or family member can care for your child.

It is also vital to find some support for yourself. The home education organisations have advice lines and may be able to put you in touch with other parents or tell you about groups in your area. The Internet is a valuable source of information, and also provides access to e-mail support lists specifically for people who home educate.

If you need some time away from your child, but lack willing friends and relatives to help out, you may want to consider whether respite care would be appropriate. Alternatively, you may be able to find a child-minder who has the skills you need. You could try contacting a volunteer bureau or a local college that offers childcare courses, to see whether they have someone who wants to gain experience in working with a child with special needs. It is also worth finding out whether there are any activities or after-school clubs that your child could attend with support.

Will I have the patience to home educate?

Nobody would pretend that home education is a breeze. Whichever style you choose, you will probably have some bad days when everyone is arguing, the house is a mess, and the only thing your child wants to do is to play some endlessly repetitive game on the computer that seems to have no learning potential at all.

If this happens to you, take heart! We have all experienced bad days and difficult patches. Even the most enthusiastic learners seem to need some time off, if only to have the opportunity to absorb what they have learned.

If you and your child are having a hard time learning at home, then it may be useful to give yourselves a break, do something enjoyable and take the opportunity to talk to (or e-mail) other home educators for support. Looking after yourself is important, and it is worthwhile trying to find other things to do that make you feel good about life. You could try a new activity to see if you can get around any situations that are causing conflict. Talking to your child may also help, if he has the necessary communication skills. He may be able to tell you what he is finding difficult; it may even be that he is feeling tired or unwell.

Above all, don't be too hard on yourself on those days when your patience is short or when everything you do seems to go wrong. You don't have to be a saint to home educate, and you can learn from any mistakes that you make. Home education is not going to be perfect; it may not even be easy, but, for most of us, the bad days at home are not nearly as painful as the bad days at school—and the good days can be wonderful.

Happy home educating!

16

An Outline of the Law and Practice of Home-Based Education

Ian Dowty, BA (Oxon), Solicitor

This chapter, or one upon which it is closely modelled, first appeared in another book about home based education written a year ago[1] and started by asking why it was necessary. Why did anyone need to know anything about the law of home education? However, as you might find, home educators always seem to end up educating not only their own children but also the world at large. Although home-based education is receiving much more prominent publicity and general acceptance, it is still necessary to have a grasp of the legal basis to the answer to questions such as: 'Doesn't everyone have to go to school?' and: 'Don't you have to have a teaching qualification?' Unfortunately, it isn't enough to tell you that the answer to both these questions is: 'No.' If it were, this would be a short chapter. It is a shame, to put it mildly, that it cannot be. For many parents choosing to home educate in many areas of the country, they need have no greater knowledge of the law. For others it becomes absolutely essential.

While this book may be on sale in other countries, it is published in England. England and Wales have a unified legal system. The legal pro-

1   *Free Range Education*, ed. Terri Dowty, pub. Hawthorn Press Dec 2000

visions I set out below only apply within that jurisdiction, and reflect the law as at April 2001. Parents are able to home educate in many other parts of the world both near and far, where different legal systems operate, but their arrangements are beyond the scope of this chapter.

Finally, before I get going, I need to make it clear that this is only intended as an introduction to home education law and I have been asked not to include too many source references or, indeed, too many points of detail or contention. The general guidance I give is not designed to answer questions posed by a specific case. Law is not static and changes all the time, whether by will of Parliament or of the courts. As I cannot know the circumstances of any particular case, I cannot assume responsibility for the application to it of what I say here. If anyone gets into the position of having to argue chapter and verse, I would encourage them to take legal advice. I hope they will be able more easily to understand the advice they receive after having read this chapter.

To understand the legal position of the home educator, it helps to have a complete overview. Armed with this, I hope that home educators will be able to feel certain of their ground legally and comforted by that. However, I have to include, for example, what happens if a prosecution is mounted against a home-educating parent. There is a need to know the bottom line, but I do want to stress that the chances of this actually happening are very slim. If I give the contrary impression, it is probably because I deal with those for whom things have gone awry. Nobody goes to see a lawyer unless they really need to! There are those who encounter difficulties from officialdom, in the shape of their local education authority (LEA), and others who have a blissful relationship with theirs.

I know this is a controversial area, but it seems fair to say that some LEAs, or perhaps some of those employed by LEAs, do not appear to take kindly to the idea that supposedly 'unqualified' parents are able in law and in fact to home educate. Even down the telephone line, I have been able to feel the steam rising from some LEA representatives who find it incomprehensible that parents 'can just do it without our permission'. Too often have I heard representatives of LEAs claim for their authority 'local arrangements' which they appear to believe negate the law of the land. We no longer face the position of the early pioneers who were forced to move home repeatedly to keep one step ahead of the applications for care orders. I really do not know how they managed to persevere, but all those who home educate today are deeply indebted to them. Through their efforts, and in many cases their suffering, it has become accepted that parents are perfectly able in law and in deed to educate their own children. Nowadays, many LEAs are happy to support home-based education and I only mean any criticism to apply to those in other LEAs who are responsible for placing what I consider to be unreasonable and, on occasion, unlawful obstacles in the way of parents exercising their lawful freedom of choice.

The difficulty home educators face is the assumption that school is the only way. Certainly, it is very difficult for those who have been schooled to understand how home education works. For those whose models of education have been reinforced later by working in schools, this may be even harder. Given their experience, it is perhaps natural for LEAs to seek out a *structure* and, in so doing, fail to see the all-pervading presence of the learning process.

Moreover, recent research indicates that four out of five LEA representatives feel completely unprepared for their task and receive no training in home education, though they would welcome it. My experience leads me to believe that many of the problems faced by home educators in their dealings with their LEA would be avoided if LEA representatives were required to have studied the theory and practice of home education.

Sources of law

It might help, for those who have never had to consider it, if I outline where we get our law from. As I have said already, England and Wales form one legal jurisdiction in which the law of education (as with every other area) derives from legislation passed by Parliament and from decisions of the courts.

Legislation is primarily made up of Acts of Parliament, also referred to as statutes. Acts are divided into sections, abbreviated to an 's', and subsections which are shown in brackets. Thus section 437, subsection 3, is written 's437(3)' and referred to in speech most usually as 'section four three seven' (slight pause) 'three'. There are further subdivisions into paragraphs, first using lower case letters and then Roman numerals.

As with other acts, the Education Act 1996 contains provisions which delegate to the government of the day powers to make regulations about certain matters which can be changed from time to time, without the whole Act having to be reconsidered by Parliament. These regulations, called statutory instruments, are also referred to as delegated legislation and have the force of law.

Up to 30 June 1999 the government departments that dealt with education were the Department for Education and Employment (DfEE) and the Welsh Office. The relevant secretary of state who headed each Department had power to make delegated legislation which affected England or Wales. However, from 1 July 1999, the powers and responsibilities of the Secretary of State for Wales were taken on by the National Assembly for Wales, which is now able to develop and implement policy in education matters as they affect Wales, leaving England to the DfEE.

The legislation sets out how education is to be organised and who or what bodies have a duty, responsibility or power to act in certain ways or make certain decisions. Such actions or decisions (or failures to act or decide) are generally reviewable by the courts. This is done either by using procedures set out in the legislation itself, or under general principles which have been established that those in authority who make decisions have to make them lawfully, reasonably and rationally. They must take into account all matters they are required to consider and they must ignore matters that should not affect their decision. The courts will generally only review a decision on the application of any person specifically affected by that decision.

The DfEE issues Circulars which set out its guidance on matters of policy and interpretation of the law. These can be very useful in gaining an understanding of the viewpoint of the DfEE, but they do not have the force of law, and indeed can be challenged if the advice or instruction contained in them is contrary to the provisions laid down in the legislation.

At a local level, answerable to their electorate by way of elected councils, are the many LEAs whose officials and representatives carry out the duties imposed by the legislation, and the policy decisions made by the government and the LEA itself.

Whether they come from the DfEE or an LEA, those who carry out any function ordained as a result of policy or legislation can only do what in law they are empowered to do so. If they overstep their legal powers, even if they act in accordance with policy, any person affected can apply to a court to ensure that the law is complied with and any unlawful policy overturned. Similarly, if there is a dispute over what an Act or statutory instrument means, those affected can apply to a court to resolve the problem and the court will, if necessary, decide what Parliament meant when it passed the legislation in question. In doing so, the court effectively decides what the law is, and on occasion can be said to make law.

Legislation always refers to people in the masculine and I repeat that where necessary; however, if I cannot elegantly use a gender nonspecific term elsewhere, I have referred to a child in the feminine and anybody else in the masculine. This has the added benefit of aiding clarity of meaning.

The responsibility for educating children

I haven't investigated it scientifically, but if you ask most people who it is that has the responsibility for educating their children, they will probably answer: 'Their school.' It comes as a bit of a surprise to them to find out that is not the case. The law fairly and squarely places the responsibility for the education of their children on parents, and they are not absolved from that duty by sending their child to school. For the purposes of the Education Act 1996, the term parent embraces not only a natural parent, but also anyone with parental responsibility for a child or 'who has care of him'.

The cornerstone of educational provision is set out in section 7 (s7 from now on) of the Education Act 1996 which states [with my emphasis]:

'The parent of every child of compulsory school age shall cause him to receive efficient full-time education suitable;

(a) to his age, ability, and aptitude, and

(b) to any special educational needs he may have,

either by regular attendance at school *or otherwise.*'

It is the 'or otherwise' bit that makes it all possible. Although the somewhat confusing term 'compulsory school age' is used, it is *education* which is compulsory and *not* school. The draftsman needed a phrase which could cover children of a defined age and lighted upon 'compulsory school age', when it would have been more accurate to have said 'compulsory education age'. What that demonstrates quite well is that there is, without doubt, a bias towards school education; a bias which perhaps results from an assumption never challenged in the minds of those responsible for drafting the legislation, and which regrettably pervades officialdom.

The section states quite clearly that, in discharging the responsibility placed on them to educate their children, parents are faced with an equal choice: 'school', 'or otherwise'. No matter what their children's abilities or whether they have special educational needs (SEN), a phrase further defined as I set out later, all parents have this choice. Not all LEAs, or at least not all of their representatives, appear to see it this way. Too many seem to see their task as getting home educated children back to school.

If the rights of parents needed any reinforcement, it is provided by the European Convention on Human Rights. Although this was adopted by the UK in 1950, it was only on 2 October 2000 that the Human Rights Act 1998 came into force, requiring that the rights enshrined in the Convention be taken into account by English legislators and courts. Any legislation must be interpreted compatibly with Convention rights 'so far as it is possible to do so'.

The right of children to receive an education, and that of their parents to select it, is affirmed in Article 2 of the First Protocol to the Convention:

> 'No person shall be denied the right to education. In the exercise of any functions which it assumes in relation to education and to teaching, the State shall respect the right of parents to ensure such education and teaching in conformity with their own religious and philosophical convictions.'

The UK has entered a Reservation that it accepts the right accorded to parents: 'only so far as it is compatible with the provision of efficient instruction and training, and the avoidance of unreasonable public expenditure'.

Much is rightly made of the responsibility of the family in bringing up children to be valuable and contributing members of society. In my view it is important that, with this aim in mind, the family unit be not only free, but encouraged to take hold of that responsibility at its fundament and ensure that their children are educated in accordance with their reasonable principles, convictions and philosophy.

Indeed, who is better equipped than a parent to know what will best suit their child and what will best fit in with the arrangements that each family wishes to, and can, make? As a parent it is likely nowadays that, whether you are mother or father, you will have been present at your children's births, watched them develop into independent individuals and seen what they struggle with and what they find easier. Your knowledge and assessment of their abilities will be inherent in your appreciation of your children without any necessity to operate a system of 'tests'. Parents are in the best position to protect and give effect to their children's rights until they can speak (and are allowed to be heard by society) for themselves.

Home-based education allows parents to provide an education that is uniquely suited to the individual needs of each of their children, matching those changing needs as their children develop. The law not only makes allowance for a diversity of approach, I would suggest that it is the natural consequence of the proper exercise of the responsibility placed upon parents by s7 to ensure that their children are educated according to their individual attributes and needs. The section provides the only criteria that have to be met by parents who choose to home educate; none other applies.

You do not have to obtain anyone's permission or consent to home educate your children, except if your child is already registered at a special school or at any school as a result of the making of a school attendance order. You do not have to have any formal teaching or other qualifications. You do not have to follow any particular curriculum, or indeed any curriculum at all. The National Curriculum only applies to state schools, as does the requirement that any curriculum be 'balanced and broadly based'. You do not have to keep school hours or terms. In short, unless that is what you want, you do not have to reproduce a school at home. Provided you satisfy the requirements of s7 you can, in fact, do exactly as you choose.

The ingredients of s7 Education Act 1996

So what exactly does s7 mean, and how can you be sure that you will be able to meet its requirements?

The education that has to be received by a child is qualified by the words 'efficient' and 'full-time' but its linchpin is that it has to be suitable to the individual child. Those are the only qualifications imposed by the legislation on the word 'education'; it is a definition wide enough to encompass many different theories and practices of learning.

Apart from the phrases 'compulsory school age' and 'special educational needs', none of the terms used in the section is further defined, not even 'education'. When words in a statute are not defined, they are meant to have their meaning in ordinary usage, but that may still leave room for interpretation. Courts usually have recourse in this situation to the Oxford Dictionary and have done so in the past when considering what education is, finding there that it is defined as:

'1. The process of nourishing or rearing.

2. The process of bringing up.

3. The systematic instruction, schooling or training given to the young ... in preparation for the work of life. Also the whole course of scholastic instruction.'

'Compulsory school age'

The duty placed upon parents by s7 applies only in respect of their children of 'compulsory school age'. Broadly speaking, that is those aged between 5 and 16 years. However, there are provisions which establish exactly when the phrase applies to a child. The law defines when a child becomes of compulsory school age by relation to 'prescribed dates' in the year, which are 31 March, 31 August and 31 December. Your child reaches compulsory school age on the next prescribed date after her fifth birthday or the prescribed date itself, if her birthday actually falls on it. She ceases to be of compulsory school age at the end of a day called the 'school leaving date', which has been fixed as the last Friday of June each year. If a child attains 16 at any time before the beginning of the next school year after that date, she ceases to be of compulsory school age on that date. If her sixteenth birthday is after the start of the new school year, she is still of compulsory school age until the end of the last Friday in June of the following year.

That poses no difficulty for children who are at school, but what does it mean for the home educated? For them, it is a rather woolly definition of a date that has considerable importance, as it changes the legally enforceable responsibilities of the parents. The school year starts at the beginning of the next term after July in any year. There appears no ready answer to whether the home-educated child must abide by the date set by local schools, whether she can select dates used by any particular school in the country, or whether home-educating families can nominate their own terms and, therefore, starts of years. It is difficult not to see this as an example of the failure by legislators to take home education into account. There are also provisions for those in school to engage in education-related work experience in the last two years of compulsory schooling if arranged by the school or LEA. This would presumably apply to home-educated children, but the LEA would have to sanction any arrangement made.

'Efficient'

The word 'efficient' needs closer consideration, not only with regard to its meaning, but also the way in which it needs to be approached in consequence by the home educator. It is a word with a commonly known and accepted meaning, but it is helpful to bear in mind that a definition found useful by at least one court is that an education is '"efficient" if it achieves that which it sets out to achieve'.

This is important because it allows a subjective view of what is efficient, providing always that it meets the full criteria of s7. For this reason, I think it is essential that parents establish clearly what they seek to achieve by home educating, and how they are going to go about it. If you find this difficult, perhaps it might help to imagine how your child will be at 18 if her education has succeeded. What of your principles and beliefs do you hope she will value? How will she absorb them and how will she be equipped to make her way in life? What, for you, makes a good education? By what method is your child to learn? Does any characteristic of your child make it more difficult for her to acquire some particular learning of a life skill? If so, how do you propose to accommodate that?

Having thus clarified your aims and approach, you should be able to compose a written statement setting them out; for want of a better expression, I shall refer to this as your philosophy of education. It need not be cast in stone, and I would expect you will want to revise it from time to time as you and your children grow and change. It is in my view vital to have such a document because, when the efficiency of the education you are providing is under consideration, you will need your philosophy as the yardstick against which it will be measured. If you do not define 'efficient' for yourself, then by default you run the risk of being judged according to the precepts of your LEA, whose chief interest lies in the supply of school education.

Before leaving 'efficient', I need to mention that some LEAs, and indeed some legal textbooks, seem to suggest that its meaning is qualified by reference to the National Curriculum, and that an education can only be efficient if it incorporates the requirements of the National Curriculum. I am at a loss to understand this, because it is made abundantly clear in the Education Act 1996 that the National Curriculum applies only to state schools. Neither independent schools nor home educators have to use it, so how then could they possibly be judged against it?

'Full time'

'Full time' at least should not provide any problem; home based education is just that, in a way that school cannot be, and is not designed to be, so any comparison with its hours, days, weeks or terms is not a relevant one. Home based education starts when your child awakes and ends when she goes to sleep. Even if you choose to adopt a school-like approach, you may find that stopping at the end of 'term' is not possible, and 'relentless' is perhaps a more apt description!

'Age, ability and aptitude'

You would think that 'age' might be an easy word to define, and it is, when purely a description of calendar achievement. However, what does 'age' mean in educational terms? Many home educators see an advantage in freeing themselves from learning based upon age banding, preferring instead to match it to what their child is ready to do. This may especially be so if a child has any SEN.

Perhaps this causes no problems of definition if age is coupled with the words that follow it: 'ability and aptitude' – yet they might seem to highlight its redundancy. What if your 11 year old wants to occupy herself with the finer points of astro-physics, or some other equally esoteric subject, or even a more mundane subject but to a high level of expertise? Would an education which failed to meet such a need be suitable for her simply because it would have met the needs of the majority of 11 year olds? I venture to suggest that most home educators would not regard it as doing so. If your child has a particular and consuming interest which suits well her abilities and aptitudes, would that not justify its being concentrated upon, even at the expense of some topics in which she has no interest? Is this not in accordance with s7 itself? The obligation to have a broad and balanced curriculum has no application to home educators, but is a statutory requirement imposed by the Education Act 1996 upon state schools only.

'Special educational needs'

Finally, in terms of definitions, there is the phrase 'special educational needs' (SEN). This topic on its own is worthy of a much more detailed analysis than is possible here. SEN, in respect of a child, is a phrase defined by the Education Act 1996 as a 'learning difficulty which calls for special educational provision to be made for him'. A child has a learning difficulty if he has 'significantly greater difficulty in learning than the majority of children of his age' or 'a disability which either prevents or hinders him from making use of educational facilities of a kind generally provided for children of his age in schools'.

The relevant provisions concerning SEN are to be found in Part IV Education Act 1996, the Education (Special Educational Needs) Regulations 1994 and the Code of Practice on the Identification and Assessment of Special Educational Needs. The Code which was issued in 1994 is undergoing revision at the time of writing (April 2001).

The legislation provides for an LEA, in consultation with parents, to assess a child if it considers she has, or probably has, SEN. This procedure can be instigated by the parents. If special educational provision has to be made for a child, a statement of SEN setting out that provision must be maintained by an LEA. Not every child with SEN has to be statemented; only those for whom it is necessary for the LEA to make some additional provision to augment that provided by a school.

There is no doubt that a child with SEN, statemented or not, can be home educated, as there is reference to it in s7 itself; a parent has to take any SEN into account as it qualifies the suitability of the education to be provided. Whether parents of a home-educated child with SEN feel that their child should be statemented may depend on whether it would make any difference to them, or to the child, or whether it might simply impose further constraints upon them. They might be swayed if it would result in the provision of some assistance, practical or financial, by a local authority, and they would need to make their own enquiries about this.

The whole procedure and purpose of statementing is to enable a child with a special need to be able to be educated in a school by the provision of additional assistance at the expense of the LEA. While it would be in the power of LEAs to provide the same assistance to home educators with statemented children, this appears only to be exercised in exceptional cases where a child has considerable needs. Parents may find it takes a great deal of time and perseverance to obtain any assistance even in these circumstances.

Other than in those exceptional cases, it would seem that LEAs are not prepared to assist if the child is home educated. If the parents do not meet the child's SEN, the LEA has a duty to do so, but is likely to say that the most appropriate way of doing so is in a school environment, and so it is not obliged to make any provision for a child who is home educated. If the LEA forms this view, it may be unlikely that any appeal by the parent to the SEN tribunal or to the courts would succeed. In any event this might be a dangerous argument for home-educating parents to advance, as it might indicate a failure by them to provide suitable education. Perhaps success is only possible when the LEA sees that it is less costly to support parents than to have to make full provision itself.

Accordingly, in the great majority of cases, home educators may rightly come to the view that statementing has no application, and is generally of no relevance to their child. Its only effect is to provide a further layer of officialdom with which they have to deal.

If your child is at school and is statemented that, as I shall explain later, does not prevent you from removing her to home educate, although this may be more difficult if she is placed by the LEA in a special school. It may be that the difficulties faced by your child and which led to the making of the statement are much alleviated or even eradicated by her being educated at home. If it is no longer necessary to maintain it, an LEA may cease to maintain a statement, and parents meeting the needs of their child may be able to argue that the statement should cease. However, if the new draft of the SEN Code is enacted in its present form, it requires that the statement continue, but be amended to show that the child is home educated if the parents are able to satisfy the LEA that they are making the educational provision the statement specifies (in Part 3). How this would be interpreted by LEAs, should it come into force, remains to be seen, but it may have some considerable effect upon those in this position.

If the statementing procedure is started by the LEA while the parents are home educating and they do not want it to be completed, they can argue that as they are making full provision for their child's SEN and the LEA is not required to provide anything, it is not necessary for there to be a formal assessment or statement. If the statement is made, the parents may appeal it by application to the SEN tribunal. Once made, the statement has to be reviewed annually, although it can be reviewed at any time if the LEA wishes to do so.

The full picture

That deals with the meaning of the constituent parts of s7, but while an understanding of them is needed, it is important also not to lose sight of the whole definition and the way in which the parts link together; an 'efficient full-time education' has also to be 'suitable' to the child's age, abilities and special educational needs. Courts have concluded that this is established if the education provided equips a child to live in a modern civilised society; or in a particular community within it, as long as it enables the child to adopt a different way of life, if she wished later on to do so. For those with children who have any SEN, this definition would be modified to take into account their needs and expectations.

These, then, are the criteria you will need to have in mind when deciding to home educate. Once you have made your decision, how you put it into practice depends first on whether or not your child is a registered pupil at a school.

What do you do if your child has never been to school?

If your child has never been to school you need do nothing; nothing more, that is, than you have probably been doing already. The only difference is that once she reaches compulsory school age you have to provide an education which meets your obligation under s7 Education Act 1996.

When your child attains this milestone, there is no legal requirement to notify anyone, your LEA included, that you are home educating. There is no provision for registering with your LEA. If your child already has a statement of SEN, that does not prevent you from deciding to home educate. Anyone who says anything to the contrary is simply wrong.

It is entirely up to you whether you let your LEA know that you are home educating. Some LEAs say that they prefer if home educators would let them know they exist, which quite properly leaves it up to the individual parent. However, it is a matter of regret that others misrepresent the position and imply, if they do not say, that you are required by law to do so. Many people, lawyers included, believe this to be the case; it is counter-intuitive to them for it not to be. Some LEAs appear to believe, from the documentation that they send out, that parents have to make an application to home educate which the LEA can decide whether or not to allow. This is not the case. LEAs have no determinative say in whether you home educate; it is your decision. LEAs can only consider the educational provision you make and at worst, if they remain dissatisfied with it, bring the matter before a court in ways I describe below. They themselves cannot stop anyone home educating.

So, how do you decide whether to tell them or not? Well one of the ways is to balance what you get out of it against what you have to do. I have already discussed the general lack of assistance and financial provision for children with SEN. For other children, the LEA is most likely to provide absolutely nothing, not even advice. Although some home educators do enjoy contact with their LEA, many others find that the lack of understanding of home education brings nothing but a struggle, is a substantial intrusion into their privacy and actually distracts them from their task. How you exercise your choice may well depend on where you live and how other home educators in your area experience contact with the LEA.

You may find that other professionals with whom you are involved, doctors, nurses, health visitors and so on, may inform the LEA, which then contacts you. It is to be regretted that we have not got past the stage of people prejudicially viewing home education as a welfare issue, notwithstanding the lack of any evidence to support that view.

What must you do if your child has been to school?

Children nowadays can be registered at school prior to compulsory school age. If you decide to home educate before they reach that age, you can simply remove them from school and your only constraint is one of courtesy. However, it is important that their name is not on a school register after they have reached compulsory school age, and for that reason you might feel that it is wise to follow the steps I set out below.

The parents of a child of compulsory school age whom they have sent to school, and as a result whose name is entered in the register at the school, must ensure that she attends at the school regularly. If they do not ensure that she does, they can be prosecuted by the LEA in the magistrates' court. Even a short absence can be treated as failure to attend regularly. When you decide to home educate a child who is a registered pupil at a state or independent school, it is therefore of the utmost importance that you ensure that her name is removed from the school's register. Even if everybody accepts that you are home educating satisfactorily, if your child is still on a school register you are committing an offence if she is not at school.

If your child has been registered as a pupil at a school but for some reason is not actually registered at the time you start home educating, perhaps because you have moved to a different area, you do not have to do anything. You are in the same position, effectively, as if your child had never been to school.

Deregistering your child is in most cases straightforward and, whether or not your child has a statement of SEN, you can do so simply by sending a letter, unless your child attends at a special school or at any school in accordance with a school attendance order.

Child registered at a 'mainstream' school

A statutory instrument, the Education (Pupil Registration) Regulations 1995, sets out the grounds upon which a school, in the state or independent sector, has to remove a child's name from its register. All you need to do is keep your child at home, and at the same time send a letter to the 'proprietor' of the school requiring him to take your child off the register on the basis that she has ceased to attend the school and is receiving education otherwise than at school. It is important to ensure that this is couched in this way; it is sad to have to tell you that there is one LEA which will not allow a child to be deregistered if it can possibly construe the letter as evincing a future intention to home educate. On receipt of the letter, the proprietor is required by reg. 9(1)(c) of the 1995 Regulations to remove your child's name from the register. He does not have any discretion; he *has* to do it.

The proprietor of the school is the person or body of people responsible for the management of the school. If you do not know who this is, send the letter to the head and ask for it to be forwarded to the proprietor. You should seek confirmation that this has been done. You do not have to write to the LEA.

Regrettably, it would seem that some schools in the state sector and LEAs still believe that they have some say in whether a child is removed from the register in order to be home educated. This was the position before the 1995 Regulations came into effect; that some LEAs have missed this change in the law is not so surprising when yet others (and the DfEE) still refer to the 1944 Education Act, which was replaced completely by the 1996 Act.

When they get the deregistration letter, some schools or LEAs may say that they will not remove the child's name from the register until the LEA has approved the arrangements that the parent is making for her education, and they may even send out an application form. Just write again telling them why they are wrong in law and, when doing so, you might like to point out that the 1995 Regulations are made in accordance with what is now s434 Education Act 1996 which makes it a criminal offence not to comply with them. An intransigent proprietor risks a prosecution and a £200 fine if he continues to demur.

Once you have written to the school notifying it of the position, you cannot commit the offence of failing to ensure that your child attends regularly. The letter you send is therefore an important one and you would be wise to keep a copy of it, obtain and keep confirmation that it was sent and, if you can get it, that it was received. You may at a later stage need to prove that you notified the proprietor, if the LEA does not accept that the letter was sent. So, if you hand-deliver it, make a note of when, where and to whom you handed it over, and get them to sign and date a receipt if you can. If you post it, send it recorded delivery and get the Post Office (or Consignia, or whatever other embodiment exists) to confirm it was received. In the letter, ask for confirmation to be sent to you in writing that it has been received and that your child has been removed from the register. If you do not get a reply, pester the school for confirmation in follow-up letters which again say what you are doing. Do not stop until you have an acknowledgement; this is your protection against prosecution.

The 1995 Regulations require the proprietor to tell the LEA that you have withdrawn your child from school to home educate and to supply it with your address within ten days of removing her name from the register. You yourself do not have to take any further steps and do not, for example, have to tell anybody else that you are home educating, not even your LEA, unless you want to do so. I cannot emphasise this point too much; anyone seeking to criticise you for failing to do so is, plain and simply, wrong.

If your child has a statement of SEN naming the school, you can still deregister her in this way. I have discussed above the steps you may then wish to take with regard to the maintenance of the statement.

Child registered at a special school

Special schools are those established specifically for children with SEN whose needs cannot be met in mainstream schools. If your child has become a registered pupil at such a school as a result of arrangements made by the LEA, her name cannot be removed from the register without the consent of the LEA. This restriction only applies if the child has actually attended the school as a registered pupil; the mere fact that the school might be named in a statement is not enough.

It would appear that some LEAs, when asked, are quite happy to allow the parents to start home education, making enquiries later to ensure that s7 responsibilities are being met. LEAs do this either by giving consent at the outset, or by first allowing time for the parents to establish satisfactory home education before finally doing so. Both courses respect the parents' right to home educate.

There are, however, other LEAs which require a parent to satisfy them in advance, by showing planned arrangements, that they will be able to provide an education that meets all the criteria of s7. As s7 is only satisfied if a suitable education is *received by* a child and not *provided by* a parent, this exercise has to be a purely hypothetical one which may very well prove little, but which can allow full rein to the prejudices of those giving consent. I cannot avoid saying that many parents who have difficulties with their LEA are those from a background which does not fit a stereotype lodged in the minds of the LEA.

In these circumstances parents can always advance proof that they are effectively home educating when their child is out of school. It may be that friends will be able to confirm this and the parents can thereby build up a body of supporting evidence in just the same way as I discuss elsewhere in this chapter. Many parents find that they are dissatisfied with the provision being made at school for their child, and no doubt can profitably compare this with the provision they are able to make.

It would seem to me that if an LEA had any doubts about the educational provision the parents would make, it can easily resolve them by allowing the parent to home educate on a provisional basis. The child is marked as 'absent with leave' until the final decision is reached. If the LEA concludes that the parent is not educating adequately, it can ensure that the child is returned to school by informing the parents that no further leave will be granted.

Some LEAs will refuse to give consent at any price. They should be challenged immediately; home education is a right possessed by parents and preserved by s7, and nobody should be discriminated against because of a perceived disability. The fact that a child has SEN is not a reason to refuse consent to home educate.

If the LEA refuses to consent, the Regulations provide that the Secretary of State can direct that the child's name be removed from the register. Before taking this step, parents should consider getting the help of a solicitor if they have not done so before. If the Secretary of State were to refuse to make the direction, it might be possible to seek judicial review of his decision, but any parent contemplating this should without doubt take legal advice.

It might be understandable if a parent, faced with a refusal to consent, were to remove their child from the school and start home educating. In that way they could certainly show whether their child would receive a suitable education at home, but the parent risks being prosecuted for failing to ensure that his child attend at school regularly. It is no defence to that to show that she was being adequately educated at home.

An alternative to full-time home education which suits some families is to combine both school and home education as discussed under the heading 'Flexi-schooling' below.

Child registered in accordance with the requirements of a school attendance order

I set out below what a school attendance order (SAO) is and how it comes to be made. If the parents of a child registered at a school as a result of the making of an SAO wish to withdraw her from the school to home educate, they will first have to apply to their LEA for the order to be revoked 'on the ground that arrangements have been made for the child to receive suitable education otherwise than at school'. The LEA has to revoke the order 'unless it is of the opinion that no satisfactory arrangements have been made for the education of the child otherwise than at school'. It is only when the SAO is revoked that the child can be removed from the register.

As I have discussed in the last section, LEAs will approach matters such as this in different ways. Parents here, though, may find that they will have the added difficulty of having to explain how their situation is now different from when the SAO was made. If the LEA refuses to revoke the SAO, an appeal lies to the Secretary of State, and the remarks I make above apply.

Flexi-schooling

Some parents prefer to combine attendance by their child at school on a part-time basis with home education. Their child might, for example, go to school for two or three days a week, or even for certain lessons, and for the rest of the time be educated at home. This has the effect of using school as just another resource available to the home-based educator, from which they can take what is needed and combine it into the overall learning process.

The agreement of the school is necessary, and they are under no obligation to give it. The child remains a registered pupil at the school, but she is given leave of absence for the days on which she is home educated. Leave can be given by any person authorised by the governing body of the school and, once given, operates to prevent a child being 'taken regularly to have failed to attend at school' (see s444(3) and (9) Education Act 1996).

Some parents find that schools are resistant to the concept, and may even believe that it cannot be done. It is perfectly legal and is recognised as such by the DfEE. It does not affect the school's funding provisions and there are no insurance problems. Quite often, a written agreement is entered into by the parents and the school, which makes it clear when the child will and will not attend.

A child who is flexi-schooled has to follow the same path as any other child registered at the school including, if it is a state school, the National Curriculum. The LEA will almost certainly want to inspect the home education element, and may be in a position to insist upon a greater involvement in view of the circumstances of the arrangement. While it is a matter entirely for the school as to whether leave is given, most state schools will consult their LEA and are likely to be guided by it; a constraint that does not apply to an independent school prepared to participate.

There are references in the 'UK-Based Home Education Resources' section of this book, should anyone want further information on this subject.

Who do you have to show that you comply with s7?

Now that you have embarked upon home-based education, you need to have some idea of what will happen next. You may not hear from your LEA at all, and this should not worry you. Unless you decide to tell them, your LEA may remain unaware that you are home educating; there are certainly numerous home-educating families not known to their LEAs. As I have said, if you have taken your child out of school, the school must tell the LEA that you are now home educating, and there are other ways it might find out. Most commonly, someone might contact the LEA just to let it know; doctors, midwives, health visitors and nextdoor neighbours have all been known to do this.

Although home educators do not have to notify their LEA or be registered with it, the 1996 Act makes provision for LEAs to require parents of a child of compulsory school age to satisfy them that their child is educated in accordance with their duty under s7 of the Act. The Act makes no direct provision for LEAs to supervise home-based education, and what provision exists is phrased in the negative. Section 437(1) of the Act provides:

'If it appears to a local education authority that a child of compulsory school age in their area is not receiving suitable education either by regular attendance at school or otherwise, they shall serve a notice in writing on the parent requiring him to satisfy them within the period specified in the notice (which must be not less than 15 days including the day of service) that the child is receiving such education.'

This provision applies equally to all parents, whether they home educate or their children attend at school. It might be argued that if a school fails its OFSTED inspection, the LEA should contact every parent with a child at the school with the enquiry envisaged by s437. Of course that does not happen; well not at least if it is a school which is the responsibility of the LEA. (LEAs ought, perhaps, also to consider serving such notices upon their own local authority following the findings of the House of Commons Select Committee on Health which reported in July 1998 that 26 per cent of children in local authority care were receiving no education and 75 per cent of 16 year olds in care left school without any formal qualifications.)

But to return to reality, s437 is commonly used only in respect of those who home educate, and it is used by LEAs when they come across anyone who is home educating, to check on the educational provision that is being made. This is a task that some LEAs acknowledge is not an easy one. It is not surprising if they find it difficult; the Education Act provides little help and the DfEE gives no guidelines whatsoever to an LEA as to how it should reach any decisions. The DfEE's view is that LEAs should decide for themselves how to cope with home educators which, not unsurprisingly, gives rise to differing approaches from area to area.

An LEA will take action under s437 if is not satisfied that your child is receiving a suitable education. This does not mean that it is left to the LEA to decide what are suitable methods of education. The phrase 'suitable education' is defined by the Education Act 1996 as an 'efficient full-time education suitable to [the child's] age, ability and aptitude and to any special educational needs he may have'; in other words, in terms identical to s7. Effectively, therefore, the LEA will want to satisfy itself that you are fulfilling your s7 duty when educating your child at home, and the definitions I have already discussed apply. If it is not satisfied, the LEA must consider whether it should make a SAO which effectively requires that parents send their child to the school named in the order.

The order remains in force while the child is of compulsory school age, unless it is revoked by the LEA or directed by a court to cease to be in force.

How does an LEA satisfy itself?

What then is likely to happen once an LEA learns that a child of compulsory school age is being home educated in its area? Effectively, it is up to the LEA to decide, but if it contacts a parent, what does that parent have to do? The only power the LEA has is derived from s437 of the Act. It is only if the LEA can bring that section into operation that it has any function at all with regard to home-based education. The section is triggered into action if it appears to the LEA that no suitable education is being received by a child in its area. What that actually means has been the cause of some difficulty, and continues to be so.

Some parents contend, with apparent reasonableness, that this means that the LEA must be possessed of some piece of knowledge or evidence from which the appearance of lack of provision can be suspected or deduced. Only then should the LEA be able to ask a parent about the educational provision being made. However, the matter has been tested in court in 1980 in the case of Phillips v Brown. There, the parents declined to supply to the LEA any evidence of the educational provision they were making. The LEA made an SAO and eventually prosecuted the parents, as they failed to comply with it (I have described the procedure in more detail below). In the magistrates' court, the parents still declined to give any evidence that they were providing suitable education as they said that the SAO should not have been made. There was, they insisted, nothing known to the LEA from which it could conclude that there was an appearance that no suitable education was being provided. The LEA said, on the contrary, that was indeed the appearance, precisely because it did not know anything about the child's education and whether it was suitable for him. The magistrate convicted the parents and they appealed to the Divisional Court (Lord Justice Donaldson) which decided that, while it sympathised with the parents' approach, the LEA had acted perfectly properly and in accordance with a duty, which the court said LEAs had, 'to be alert in order to detect the possibility' that there was the appearance of no suitable education.

When the LEA came across a child about whom it knew nothing, the Divisional Court suggested, the LEA ought to ask the parents about the provision being made. It would then be up to the parents to decide whether they responded to this request for information. The court made it clear that they would be under no obligation to reply, but if they did not tell the LEA anything, the LEA might reasonably feel it had no option but to conclude that there was no appearance of a suitable education. If the LEA were to come to this view, it would have to start the procedure set out in s437 and send a formal notice requiring a parent to supply evidence which satisfied the LEA that a suitable education was being provided.

LEAs frequently refer to this decision if they are called upon to justify making immediate contact with the parents of a child when they learn that she is being home educated.

How will your LEA contact you?

Many LEAs make their first contact by sending you a letter but, for some reason, quite a number of LEA officers think that there is nothing wrong with turning up unannounced on your doorstep, even, it appears, on bank holiday weekends. It seems to me that some LEA officers forget that the premises into which they demand entry or invite themselves is someone's home, not a school or place of work. I often wonder how many would like it if, when you had a question, you turned up at their homes? Is it any wonder that parents approached in this way doubt that their LEA sees them as equals? Perhaps parents also object to being made to feel as if they are doing something wrong, to prevent which the LEA needs to mount a surprise visit to catch them out. Too many LEAs see home-based education as a potential welfare problem and need to see how insulting that is.

If the invasion comes, it will most likely be carried out by an education welfare officer (EWO), an officer of the LEA whose function, according to the DfEE, is to help parents and LEAs meet their respective statutory obligations in relation to school attendance. In some LEAs, EWOs are known as education social workers. The practice is growing of describing the LEA officers who deal specifically with home educating families as advisers, although they are not the ones who usually make these initial calls on families.

You might find it helpful to have thought out in advance what to do if someone does turn up out of the blue like this. You will already be armed with your philosophy, but will you choose to talk on the doorstep, let them in or bid them goodbye?

At the risk of stating the obvious, you first need to find out who they are and check their identification. Sometimes, they come not from the education department but from social services; some of those who might report you are apt on occasion to exaggerate. Annoyed and upset though you may be, you might feel that it is wise to let social workers see your children, so that any welfare issue is dispensed with immediately. If social workers are denied access by you, however innocently, their department can become very concerned and may feel the necessity to take further action. This, you may feel, is common sense and applies whether or not you home educate. Any quite justifiable sense of grievance can be addressed to the whistleblower or their professional body later.

Once you have ascertained that the door-stepper is only interested in your children's education, it is up to you how you proceed. One thing you do need to bear in mind is that, while it could be an enlightening visit, if it is not, it could be a disastrous start that will haunt your first years of home education. Too often, it would seem, initial contacts with home educators by an LEA are heavy-handed, aimed at finding out why your child is not at school and with the agenda of getting her into, or back into, school.

I am left to wonder if some LEAs intentionally make home educators run the gauntlet to earn the right to home educate. Some parents seem to have to face an onslaught designed to break their resolve, rather than meeting understanding and support for their decision. These LEAs point out how difficult they believe it is to home educate and sometimes demand to see curricula, timetables, lesson plans, yearly plans and the like. Many give the impression that it is necessary to have a separate room or area of the house dedicated to the learning experience, much like a classroom, and some even ask about fire escapes and first aid provisions. None of these is necessary, let alone a legal requirement.

Regrettably, some LEA representatives are not beyond distorting the law to support contentions about needing permission, having to follow the National Curriculum, or having to be inspected or visited. When a parent who knows the law stands their ground and points out that this is not correct in law, their assertions are sometimes countered by 'well, I think it's just been changed recently'; although they are a little fuzzy, when pressed, as to when and by what provision.

As a result of this bombardment, many parents find themselves forced to believe that they have to adopt the model envisaged by their LEA, or they will not be allowed to home educate. This is not the case, and LEAs that cling to such notions have simply not taken the trouble to acquaint themselves with any of the literature on the subject.

All this may perhaps convince you that the best course of action is to turn away the intruder, telling them to write to you if they have any concerns or questions about your child's education and saying you will reply in writing. This will allow you time to compose yourself, as well as your letter, and enable you to present a complete picture to the LEA that cannot suffer from any misunderstandings of what exactly you were saying.

If you experience difficulty in convincing your LEA that entry to your home is by your invitation only, you might like to remind them that they now need to take account of the impact of the European Convention on Human Rights, Article 8 of which affirms the 'right to respect for private and family life'. The European Court has observed that 'the object of the Article [8] is "essentially" that of protecting the individual against arbitrary interference by the public authorities' and stated that this 'does not merely compel the State to abstain from such interference … there may be positive obligations inherent in an effective "respect" for family life'.

This would seem capable of applying not only to unannounced visits, but also to those where parents are told that they will be visited, rather than asked if they would agree to accept a visit at a convenient time. Some LEAs fail to understand, or actively ignore the fact, that they cannot insist upon visits even as the law stands at the moment. If parents choose to invite them into their house, that is an entirely different matter, as long as the parents have done so in the knowledge that they are under no compulsion.

It is worth reminding ourselves here that LEAs can only act in accordance with s437, and their only task, in the final analysis, is to decide whether or not parents have satisfied it that they are providing suitable education. All an LEA can do is to say that it is not satisfied. It cannot stop parents home educating; the worst it can do is to issue an SAO and then prosecute if it is not complied with. Only a court can make an adverse finding about whether a parent is providing suitable education.

I am not advocating that parents adopt a confrontational attitude when dealing with their LEA, but rather hoping to redress the imbalance that too often appears when LEA representatives and others say to home educators that they *have* to do *this*, or they *have* to do *that*. It is simply not true. What parents do at all times is up to them, as long as they know the consequences that might follow. Parents may end up doing what their LEA has asked, or demanded, but only as a result of their own choice, as their LEA should be told.

There is no provision that allows LEAs to specify the way in which they are to be satisfied, or what sort of evidence is acceptable to them and what is not. Parents can choose what evidence they wish to supply in accordance with their philosophy. In assessing such evidence, LEAs must act reasonably. In particular, the Divisional Court has held that LEAs cannot as a matter of policy insist on a home visit as the only method of being satisfied. If formal assessment of children's learning is contrary to a parent's philosophy, LEAs should not attempt to carry it out. Indeed, if you decide, as many home educators do, that you are happy to have the LEA visit, there is no need for a formal assessment, as much more can be gleaned from playing and chatting with children. Some home educators enjoy visits such as these.

When your LEA does write, you may find that you receive a request to complete a questionnaire which asks questions of the sort I have outlined above, and others such as: At what times will education take place? How long will the lunch break be? What is your weekly timetable? Often ending with one along the lines of: When will your child return to school? If you choose to answer this letter, do not feel under any obligation to complete the questionnaire. While you do not have to answer this sort of general enquiry, you might consider it wise to supply the LEA with a copy of your philosophy and a report in general terms setting out how you go about home-based education on a day-to-day basis, what resources are available to you, how you make use of them and anything that would show that you are providing a suitable education. If you wanted, you could also complete and return the questionnaire, filling out answers to those questions that apply and marking those that do not accordingly. Alternatively, you could use the questions to prompt matters to which you can refer in your report.

A note of caution is needed here, as some LEAs refer to their department which deals with home-based education as 'Education Otherwise', and letters to you may bear that description. You should not confuse that with the support organisation of the same name, commonly abbreviated to EO. EO has copyrighted the phrase 'Education Otherwise' to prevent the possibility of misunderstandings as to who is writing to you. If your LEA uses this phrase, I know that EO would appreciate your letting them know so that they can contact the LEA. EO's address can be found under 'UK-Based Home Education Resources' at the back of this book.

If you have just started to home educate, whether that be because your child has just reached compulsory school age or you have just taken her out of school, the courts have made it clear that your LEA should not ask you for any information until a sufficient time has passed to enable you to establish your own arrangements. How long that is may well depend on your circumstances, but it needs to be a reasonable time. If, for example, your child has had the misfortune to be bullied at school and has had her confidence badly dented, it may take a while for her to relax before settling down to any kind of pattern. If you are contacted by your LEA during such a period of readjustment, explain the position and be prepared to negotiate. You may find that there is no real difficulty; it is only if LEAs find that their enquiries are ignored that they can become understandably concerned.

Much may depend on being able confidently and in sufficient detail to say how your child is learning at home, and how you are accommodating any difficulties your child is having. Some parents find this difficult to quantify for themselves, as the beauty of home education is that knowledge can be gained almost imperceptibly. Often, if you sit and analyse what your child is doing, you will see that she has gained various skills, simply as an adjunct to finding out what she was actually interested in, which might at school be divided into different 'subjects'. For instance, an interest in something like volcanoes might include science (which itself might be general or more detailed and involve geology, seismology, etc.), history, social studies, anthropology, language, geography, and would also utilise various skills such as reading, writing, drawing, painting, using reference books, atlases, the internet, asking others for information and discussing conclusions. This analysis can be carried out with any interest your child has, and you may find that she naturally encompasses all the subjects she would cover if she were at school, but not in the abstract nor for their own sake.

Those parents who have a more formal approach to their child's learning may find it easier to describe what they do, and also to convey it to the representatives of the LEA, than parents who adopt a more autonomous approach. Because of their grounding in school education, LEA representatives might find it more easy to understand the effectiveness of an education which resembles something they recognise. The younger your child, the easier it ought to be to satisfy the LEA, particularly when you consider that in many European countries, formal education, even in state-run schools, does not commence until children reach seven years of age. Indeed, our apparent obsession with lowering the age at which formal education begins is regarded in the rest of Europe as at best counterproductive. Steiner schools have existed in Great Britain and in other countries, notably Germany, for many years now and are likely to receive State funding here. They do not countenance teaching anything, including reading and writing, until after a child is seven. If a parent espouses the philosophy of Rudolf Steiner (or just this part of it), an LEA should have no difficulty in accepting his right to do so. The parent will need to carry out some research and would, in my view, be wise to refer to its results in his philosophy of education.

On receiving your report, the LEA may write to say that everything is satisfactory, or that you will be contacted at some time in the future, or indeed both. However, you may be told that an LEA representative, an adviser, will call to see you, perhaps to discuss how you intend to educate your child. At the risk of sounding like a broken record (which probably dates me, anyway), what you do is your choice. I do feel I need to warn you that sometimes such a discussion is not the friendly chat about the ups and downs of home education that it appeared to be at the time. Too many parents have found out later that some innocent aside or a question about some difficulty they experience is blown out of all proportion and appears as an adversely critical reference in the adviser's report. Wait until you know and trust your adviser before confiding your fears, worries and difficulties; until then, reinforce the positives. I appreciate this may well offend some LEA officers, but they have only their professional colleagues to blame. It may be that disarming frankness causes no problems most of the time, but when it does you might in retrospect wish that you had been cautious.

So, for those who are about to have trouble, I need to set out the position clearly. There are still LEAs who believe that you need their permission to home educate and their letter to you will state exactly that. Other LEAs, if they do not actually state it, seem to hint that they will allow you to home educate if they can be satisfied that the arrangements you have made are approved by them. Both are wrong. What it does mean, however, is that you will have to be very careful in all your dealings with the LEA. While your decision to remove your child and take full responsibility for her education causes no difficulty with many schools and LEAs, some find this hard to accept.

You would be best advised when dealing with such LEAs to keep a diary of your contact with their representatives. How you maintain this contact is for you to decide and if you prefer it always to be by letter, tell the LEA this and do not feel obligated to give them your telephone number, or to use this method of communication, if you do not want to. If you do speak to anyone from the LEA in person or on the telephone, make a note straightaway, or as quickly as you reasonably can, of what was said. If you can, follow up each such contact with a letter to the LEA setting out the discussion and any important points. Keep a copy of all letters you send, as well as any that are sent to you. This will minimise the opportunity for any misunderstandings about what was said or agreed and will hopefully prevent confrontation, as both you and the LEA will know exactly where you stand and there will be no room for dispute.

It is always a good idea, essential in fact, to have a friend (or two) with you if you decide to meet any representative of the LEA. This is not only for moral support, although that may very well be needed, but also so that the friend can make a note of the conversation and ensure that you do not get pressured into agreeing to something that you do not want to do. By making notes, you will always know the exact sequence of events and, if it came to it, you would be able to use these notes to jog your memory if you had to give evidence in court. To be able to use them in this way, they have to be what lawyers call 'contemporaneous notes': that is, notes of meetings and events made either at the time of the meeting or event, or at your first opportunity afterwards, when everything was fresh in your mind.

Visits do not have to be at your home. You can choose to meet your LEA representative at any convenient place; for example, the LEA's premises, the local library or playground, or a friend's house. You may choose to have your children present for all, part or none of the time. I understand that one parent and LEA representative used to meet regularly in a local pub.

If you decide that you do not want to meet an LEA representative, you will need to consider whether you should take some other action instead. If you do nothing, your LEA may move towards making an SAO. You might feel it best to write setting out your reasons for not wanting to have a meeting, and consider supplying a more detailed report. Have in mind that you need to supply sufficient evidence to satisfy a reasonable authority that it is more likely than not that your child is receiving a suitable education. You may not want the LEA to meet or assess your children, but you may have friends who are well aware of the educational provision you are making and the abilities of your children. A very useful way of bolstering a report in these circumstances, if not generally, is to include references from such friends, particularly if they have qualifications which the LEA might appreciate. Some parents keep a diary of their children's activities and, if it accords with your philosophy, you could supply copies of entries to your LEA.

You might have more of a struggle with your LEA if you adopt this course, but many do successfully negotiate with their LEA to achieve a formula acceptable to both.

What happens after you have satisfied your LEA?

After you have satisfied your LEA that your children are receiving suitable education, you may not hear further for a long while. If you do hear, it may be with the same sort of enquiry that you received when you were first contacted. Even if you encountered difficulty on that occasion, you will be in a much better position this time as you will be more experienced, your child will be more able to say for herself what she does and, most importantly, the LEA knows about you and has already satisfied itself once about the educational provision you are making.

Your philosophy may by this time be a more detailed document, if you have chosen to update it as you go, and answering questionnaires and preparing reports should present less of a problem than before. If you invited your LEA to visit you previously, you are perfectly free to consider whether you want this to happen again should your LEA suggest it. If you did not want another visit, you might reasonably say that, as the LEA was happy with the arrangements seen before, a report on this occasion should be sufficient to satisfy it. Again, what you do is a matter of your choice, informed as it is of the consequences of the LEA saying that it is not satisfied.

If it has been a sufficiently long time since your LEA last contacted you, you may feel that it is reasonable if you are contacted again. Some LEAs ask for periodic reports and you need to consider whether this is acceptable to you. It might depend on the frequency and, perhaps, the purpose. You might feel that a request for an annual report is reasonable, but that any more onerous suggestion is unreasonable. I have heard that some LEAs try to insist upon quarterly reports or visits, which would seem to me without any justification. I would doubt whether a court would say such frequency was reasonable, or indeed necessary, unless there was some good reason.

There is no provision, as I have already remarked, in the legislation which explicitly requires or indeed empowers LEAs to supervise or monitor the provision of home-based education. The duty that is placed upon the LEA by s437 Education Act 1996 is a continuing one and it might be that it justifies regular attention by an LEA. When Donaldson LJ approved (in Phillips v Brown) the actions of the LEA in making enquiries to ascertain the position with regard to a home-educated child, it was against the background that the LEA knew nothing what-soever about the child. However, once the LEA has satisfied itself that the child is receiving suitable education, it knows a considerable amount about the parents, the child and the educational provision. Consequently, it might be argued that it cannot again 'appear' to the LEA that she is not receiving a suitable education unless there is some specific piece of evidence which indicates to the contrary.

Some LEAs rely upon s443(3) Education Act 1996 as justification for regular contact with home-educating families. However, in my view the wording of this provision is, on the contrary, capable of strengthen-ing the argument I have just advanced, as it contemplates an LEA only being able 'to take further action under s437 if at any time [the LEA is] of the opinion that, *having regard to any change of circumstances,* it is expe-dient to do so' (my emphasis added).

There does not seem to have been a case in which the issue of ongoing monitoring by an LEA has been raised. This may be because no parent has ever decided to challenge the legality of it, or because

LEAs have always reached an acceptable compromise with any parent who objected to it.

What happens if a school attendance order is made?

Unless parents have been unwise enough to bury their heads in the sand when contacted by their LEA, it is unlikely that they would reach this stage without the exchange of a considerable amount of correspondence and discussion between them and their LEA. Some LEAs might tend to act precipitately, but generally they seek to avoid confrontation in court, unless they believe there is no other option. If parents maintain a supply of information to their LEA, this ongoing communication can often lead to a resolution of any problems.

However, if all else fails and an SAO is made, it requires parents to register their child at the school named in the order. It is an offence contrary to s443 Education Act 1996, triable in the magistrates' court, not to comply with an SAO, unless the parents can prove to the court that they are providing suitable education. If the parents wish to continue to home educate, they should consider how they would go about proving this to a court, should it come to that, and they should not register their child. This is important because, if they do register their child, they will lose the opportunity of relying on this defence.

This is because, as soon as the parents register their child at a school, they then have the duty to ensure that she attends regularly. If the child does not, the parents can be prosecuted for her failure to attend under the provisions of s444 Education Act 1996. This is what might be referred to as the truanting offence and it is not a defence to this charge to show that the child was receiving suitable education at home. Some LEAs, on making an SAO, also take the step of registering the child. This cannot have legal effect and, if the child does not attend at the school, can lead an LEA into the error of prosecuting the parents for failing to ensure that the child attends regularly contrary to s444. This charge can only be correctly laid if the parents have registered their child at a school, otherwise, the *parents* are entitled to be acquitted.

If parents fail to comply with an SAO, the LEA must consider what next it is to do. It has a limited number of options, and if it still considers that it is not satisfied that the child is receiving a suitable education, at the head of the list is a prosecution of the parents for the offence of failing to comply with the SAO contrary to s443 Education Act 1996.

To commence proceedings, the LEA has to apply to the magistrates' court for a summons, which the parents will receive from the court, most likely by post. The summons will state the date upon which the parents have to attend at court. If they have not seen a solicitor already, it is important at this stage that parents go to see one, so that they are fully aware of their position and choices, and what preparation is necessary to present any defence. This is, in effect, a criminal prosecution and the LEA has to comply with various matters, including disclosing certain material that it is not using as part of its case. Legal advice, which may be without cost to the parent depending upon their level of income, is available from solicitors. The cost of legal representation in court can be covered by the grant by the magistrates' court of a representation order, which is now not means tested. The parents will have to inform the court in some detail of the complexity of the matter and stress the importance to them of the outcome, and would be best advised to seek the assistance of a solicitor in completing the application form.

The LEA has to prove that the SAO was made and that the parents failed to register their child at the school named in the order. The parents can challenge the making of the order itself, but that inevitably will mean they have to show that they were providing their child with suitable education, which will in any event entitle them to be acquitted. It is a statutory defence set out in s443(1) Education Act 1996 for the parents to prove on a balance of probabilities that they are 'causing the child to receive suitable education otherwise than at school'. Another way of putting the 'balance of probabilities' test is that the parents must show it is more likely than not that they are educating suitably. To succeed, the parents need to prove that the required education is being provided at the date of the hearing, whether or not it was being provided at any other time, including when the SAO was made.

In order to establish this to the necessary standard of proof, the parents should consider calling evidence from experts as to the efficacy of home-based education and as to the provision being made for their child. How much that might resemble an assessment of their child's education will depend on the philosophy of the parents. If reports from experts are to be relied on, some consideration can be given to whether they should be disclosed in advance to the LEA. The fact that an SAO has been made does not mean you should stop supplying your LEA with information about your child's education. The LEA should take account of anything with which it is provided, and if it becomes satisfied about the suitability of your child's education, the prosecution should be discontinued and the SAO revoked.

If the matter goes to trial and the parents do succeed in proving their case, they will be acquitted and that is the end of the prosecution. It would be logical to think that it was also the end of the SAO but, somewhat curiously, s443(2) provides that if a parent is acquitted, the court *may* direct that the SAO cease to be in force. The effect of this is that, when acquitted, parents must apply to the court for such a direction. They may also be able to apply for a defence costs order to meet any expenses they have incurred in preparing their defence or attending at court.

If the parents do not succeed in proving to the court that they are providing a suitable education, they will be convicted. The most likely sentence, certainly on a first conviction, is a fine and an order made that the parent pay some or all of the LEA costs in bringing the prosecution. The maximum fine that can be imposed is a 'level 3' fine which at the moment is a maximum of £1000. If, as is usual, both parents have been summoned for the offence, on conviction both can face the maximum fine. I need to stress that maximum fines are rarely, if ever, imposed and the court will weigh the seriousness of the circumstances of the offence with the means of each parent before reaching a decision, which in most cases will be very much less than the maximum. Other sentences are available to a court, including a parenting order. However, space does not allow me to expand further and I can in any event only reiterate that anyone facing this situation would be best advised to consult a solicitor, as they should if they wished to appeal against any decision.

One further provision needs to be mentioned. Before mounting a prosecution, an LEA must consider whether it should, instead of, or as well as, a prosecution, apply to a family proceedings court for an educational supervision order (ESO) under the Children Act 1989. The court might sit in a magistrates' court, but it is not constituted in the same way as the court which would hear any prosecution under the Education Act, and the two cannot be heard at the same time.

An ESO can be made by the court if it is satisfied that a child of compulsory school age is not being educated properly. This has the same meaning as 'suitable education' in s437 Education Act 1996 and is in the same terms as the requirements of s7 of that Act. It would help if the same phrase were used in all statutes, but then who would need lawyers? An ESO places the child under the supervision of the LEA, which appoints a supervisor, usually an EWO, whose duty it is 'to advise, assist and befriend, and give directions to' the child and his parents 'in such a way as will, in the opinion of the supervisor, secure that he is properly educated. The supervisor has to 'ascertain [their] wishes and feelings ... including, in particular their wishes as to the place at which the child shall be educated' before making any direction, but there is no requirement even to take them into account. If parents persistently fail to comply with a direction, they commit an offence unless they show that they have taken all reasonable steps or that the direction was unreasonable. If the child persistently fails to comply, social services will become involved.

In order to get an ESO, the LEA has to produce evidence to prove a negative: namely that the child is not receiving proper education. This might be a difficult task to accomplish were it not for the fact that if an SAO has been made, and it is not being complied with, there is a statutory assumption that the child is not being properly educated, unless the parents prove to the contrary. If it applies, this effectively removes from the LEA the burden of proving its case and places the parents in the same position, and with the same considerations, as when they contest a prosecution for failing to comply with an SAO.

If parents are convicted of failing to comply with an SAO, the court may direct that the LEA commence proceedings for an ESO unless, in consultation with social services, the conclusion is reached that 'the child's welfare will be satisfactorily safeguarded' without one being made.

Before the enactment of the Children Act 1989, courts could make care orders in the same circumstances as they can now make ESOs. The law was changed, as it was not felt that this drastic step was appropriate simply if a child was not receiving a suitable education. However, if a parent repeatedly failed to educate suitably or was repeatedly convicted of failing to comply with SAOs or ESOs, this might well result in a care order being made on the application of the local authority's social services department, if it was believed that this was causing 'significant harm' to the child. It would seem likely, if this situation developed, that social services would have other concerns about the child's parenting and it would not be purely an education matter.

Conclusion

I hope that this chapter has been informative and will be useful to those contemplating home-based education, without making it seem that they have a frightening task. Many officers in many LEAs do understand and support home-educating families, and those families and those officers have no need to consider the matters I have dealt with. I have not intended to offend officers such as these. However, other families are not in such a fortunate position and I see the suffering that can be caused by an insensitive and sometimes bullying approach. Even that approach can be mollified by discussion and explanation, and I hope I may have been able to give some structure and material for that task. Home educators all too often have to take on the education of those around them to defeat an unthinking response and gain acceptance. It can be galling in the extreme to have gained the understanding of one LEA representative, only to find that the 'convert' moves on and is replaced by another for whom the process has to start again.

Home educators ought to be able to expect that LEA officers appointed to deal with them are alive to the practice of home-based education, appreciate its effectiveness and acknowledge and respect the rights of parents and their children to find a way of learning that uniquely suits them. LEAs need to be open to the advantages that home-based education can offer: advantages that are increasingly understood by parents. The experiences of those who have contributed to this book demonstrate amply the benefits which have accrued to their children.

The number of families home educating in this country is growing, but nobody knows just how many home-educated children there are in the UK at the moment. All the available evidence points to it being a very significant and rapidly growing number which may be as much as 1 per cent of the school age population. As political and economic entities grow ever larger, it is of vital importance that variety and diversity are acknowledged as the healthy signs of a successful and tolerant society. There is seldom one right way to do anything, and in the field of education it is especially important to recognise that there are many different ways of learning. Home-based education originates within the family, the building block of society, and that it is flourishing should be seen as a hopeful sign for the future which richly deserves every encouragement and support.

17

Finding support and information

Sources of support and information are listed below in three categories: home education resources, information about autism and Asperger's syndrome, and other useful addresses. Within each category, organisations with a regional base are grouped into three geographical areas: the United Kingdom, the United States, and Australia.

HOME EDUCATION RESOURCES

UK

Spearhead is an independent charitable organisation which offers free advice and support to all parents of children with special educational needs who are, or are considering, educating their children at home. We offer expert advice relating to parental and LEA rights and duties with regard to all aspects of educational issues, including elective home education, LEA-funded provision at home, statutory assessments, statements, reviews, returning to school or funded provision, and appeal to the SEN tribunal.

Tel: 0161 799 7244
E-mail: advice.spearhead@lineone.net

The HE-SPECIAL-UK e-mail list provides a supportive meeting place for families who home educate children with special educational needs, where we can offer encouragement to one another, share our difficulties and celebrate our successes. For information about how to join the mailing list, as well as home education articles, resources, and links, please visit our website.

Website: www.he-special.org.uk

Independent Panel for Special Education Advice
6 Carlow Mews
Woodbridge
Suffolk IP12 1DH
Advice line: 0800 0184016 or 01394 382814
Tribunal appeals only: 020 8682 0442
General enquiries: 01394 380518

The Free Range Education Website
Use the 'Ask FREd' e-mail service on this website to get in touch with an experienced home educator who can answer practical questions, help you decide whether home education is for you, offer you personal support and point you towards other sources of information and help. An experienced legal team answers queries about the law. You will also find links to other home education websites, resources, reading suggestions, educational links, information about local groups and much more besides.

Website: www.free-range-education.co.uk

Choice in Education is a publication produced by a co-operative group of home educators who seek to promote and publicise the alternative to mainstream schooling in our society. Choice in Education produce Truancy Information Cards to help give children confidence when out and about during school hours. They also organise the Home Educators' Seaside Festival (HES FES) every May, which is the biggest gathering of home educators in Europe. It is a week of camping, workshops for adults and children, and HE discussion groups, as well as lots of fun, games and entertainment. For more information on any of the above, subscriptions or sample copies of the Choice in Education newsletter, please contact

Choice in Education
PO Box 20284
London NW1 3WY
Website: www.choiceineducation.co.uk

Education Otherwise (EO) is a membership organisation which provides support for families whose children are being educated outside school, and for those who wish to uphold the freedom of families to take responsibility for the education of their children. EO is not committed to any 'correct' system of education, and it does not undertake to provide educational syllabi or materials. Rather it tries to help families establish what is suited to the needs of their own children, in accordance with their own beliefs. For further information, visit the EO website or send an A5 SAE to

Education Otherwise
PO Box 7420
London N9 9SG
Urgent helpline: 0870 7300 074
Website: www.education-otherwise.org

Herald offers its members a stepping stone between the rigours of schooling and the autonomous approach which many home-based educators strive to achieve, by suggesting a structured yet flexible framework as a basis for study. For more information, write to

Herald
Kelda Cottage
Lydbrook
Glos GL17 9SX
Tel: 01594 861107
Website: www.homeeducation.co.uk

Home Education Advisory Service (HEAS) is a registered charity which supports and advises families who wish to educate their children at home instead of sending them to school. HEAS produces information leaflets, *The Big Book of Resource Ideas* and *The Home Education Handbook.* Subscribers receive the quarterly Bulletin, access to the Advice Line and the Dyslexia Helpline, a concession card and a list of local contacts. The organisation offers information about educational resources, GCSE, special educational needs, information technology, legal matters and curriculum design.

HEAS
PO Box 98
Welwyn Garden City
Herts AL8 6AN
Tel/fax: 01707 371854
E-mail: enquiries@heas.org.uk
Website: www.heas.org.uk

Schoolhouse is a national Scottish charity which offers information and support to home educators and those with an interest in home education. Services include an enquiry line, a young people's newspaper project and a home educators' newsletter (both published quarterly), and a teenage peer support network. Individual or family memberships are by voluntary donation; membership is also available to organisations.

Schoolhouse Home Education Association
311 Perth Road
Dundee DD2 1LG
Tel: 0870 0968
Information Line: 0870 0967
E-mail: info@schoolhouse.org.uk
Website: www.schoolhouse.org.uk

Travellers' School Charity (TSC) is dedicated to helping travellers with the successful education of children. If you wish to subscribe to TSC, you will receive the quarterly newsletter and help us with funding, fuel and communications. Please send a £5 cheque or postal order payable to 'TSC' to

TSC
PO Box 36
Grantham NG31 6EW

Advisory Centre for Education (ACE)
1b Aberdeen Studios
22 Highbury Grove
London N5 2DQ
Tel: 0207 354 8318
Advice line: 0207 354 8321
Website: www.ace-ed.org.uk

Information on Flexi-schooling
There is an extensive chapter by Kate Oliver describing flexi-schooling in *Free Range Education* (ed. Terri Dowty, pub. Hawthorn Press ISBN 1-903458-07-2).
Website: www.warwick-district.org.uk/flexi

USA

The National Home Education Network exists to encourage and facilitate the vital 'grass roots' work of state and local homeschooling groups and individuals by providing information, fostering networking and promoting public relations on a national level.

NHEN
PO Box 41067
Long Beach, CA 90853
Fax: (413) 581-1463
Website: www.nhen.org

Growing Without Schooling magazine was founded by John Holt in 1977 as a way to support homeschooling families and to provide a forum for them to communicate with one another. It continues in this work to this day. For more information, contact

Growing Without Schooling
Holt Associates
2380 Massachusetts Ave, Suite 104
Cambridge MA 02140
Tel: (617) 864-3100
Fax: (617) 864-9235
E-mail: info@holtgws.com
Website: www.holtgws.com

Jon's Homeschool Resource Page is full of resources and links to other homeschooling websites.
Website: www.midnightbeach.com/hs/

AUSTRALIA

Canberra Home Education Network
230 Taylors Creek Road
via Tarago NSW 2580
Tel: 02 4849 4662
E-mail: aun@tpg.com.au
Website: www1.tpgi.com.au/users/aun/homeschool/index.html

Home Education Network
8 Bardia Street
Carlingford NSW 2118
Tel: 02 9871 3482
E-mail: garratts@zipworld.com.au

Home Education Coalition
4 Bruce Street
Stanmore NSW 2048
Tel: 02 9564 5086
E-mail: pstrange@atu.com.au

Brisbane Natural Learners
PO Box 2157
Tingalpa QLD 4173
Tel: 07 3348 8287

Home Based Learners
22 Hillsea Avenue
Clearview SA 5085
Tel: 08 8260 5229
E-mail: smlang@space.net.au

Tasmanian Home Education Network
155 Main Road
Austin's Ferry TAS 7011

Western Homeschoolers
PO Box 688
Werribee Vic 3030
Tel: 03 9742 7524

Home Based Learning Network Inc.
PO Box 1356
Subiaco WA 6008

INFORMATION ABOUT AUTISM AND ASPERGER'S SYNDROME

Autism-Europe is a European association whose main objective is to advance the rights of people with autism and their families, and help improve their lives.

Autism-Europe
Avenue E. Van Becelaere 26B, bte 21
B-1170 Brussels, BELGIUM
Tel: +32 (0)2 675 75 05
E-mail: autisme.europe@arcadis.be

The World Autism Organization aims to help improve the quality of life of autistic people and their families throughout the world.
Postal address as for Autism-Europe
Website: www.worldautism.org/

OASIS

On-line Asperger's Syndrome Information and Support
Website: www.udel.edu/bkirby/asperger/

Autism Resources Page
Website: www.autism-resources.com/

Tony Attwood's website
Website: www.tonyattwood.com

On-The-Same-Page is a website with a large number of links and resources on autism and Asperger's syndrome.
Website: amug.org/~a203/index.html

Wendy Lawson's Home Page
Website: www.mugsy.org/wendy/index2.htm

jypsy's links
'More autism-related links than you can shake a stick at!'
Website: www.isn.net/~jypsy/autilink.htm

UK

PEACH
(Parents for the Early Intervention of Autism in Children)
School of Education
Brunel University
300 St. Margaret's Road
Twickenham
Middlesex TW1 1PT
Tel: 0208 891 0121 ext. 234
Website: www.peach.org.uk

High Scope
Copperfield House
190–192 Maple Road
London
SE20 8HT
Website: www.high-scope.org.uk

The National Autistic Society
393 City Road
London EC1V 1NG
Tel: 020 7833 2299
Fax: 020 7833 9666
E-mail: nas@nas.org.uk
Website: www.oneworld.org/autism_uk/

Autism-UK e-mail list
Website: www.autism-uk.ed.ac.uk

Autism Research Centre
Douglas House
18b Trumpington Road
Cambridge CB2 2AH
Tel: 01223 746113
Fax: 01223 746122
Website: www.psychiatry.cam.ac.uk/arc

USA

Son-Rise
The Son-Rise Programme at the Option Institute
2080 S Undermountain Road
Sheffield, MA 01257
Tel: (413) 229-2100
Website: www.son-rise.org

High/Scope
600 North River Street
Ypsilanti, MI 48198-2898
Tel: (734) 485-2000
Website: www.highscope.org

Asperger's Syndrome Coalition of the US (ASC-US)
PO Box 351268
Jacksonville, FL 32235-1268
Tel: 1-866-4-ASPRGR
Website: www.asperger.org

The Autism Society of America
7910 Woodmont Avenue, Suite 300
Bethesda, Maryland 20814-3067
Tel: (301) 657-0881 or 1-800-3-AUTISM
Fax: (301) 657-0869
Website: www.autism-society.org
Clickable map of local support chapters at
www.unc.edu/~cory/asa/chapter_map.html

ASPEN of America is a national non-profit organization providing information and support to individuals, families and professionals dealing with Asperger's syndrome, nonverbal learning disabilities (NLD), and related neurologically-based social and communication disorders on the high-functioning end of the autistic spectrum.
Website: www.aspennj.org/

AUSTRALIA

OzAutism Support Mailing List
Website: www.hunter.apana.org.au/~cas/ozautism.html

Autism Association ACT
PO Box 717
Mawson ACT 2607
Tel: 02 6286 8887 (office)
Parent line: 0419 223 357
Fax: 02 6286 4475
E-mail: AutismACT@bigpond.com
Website: http://autism.anu.edu.au

Autistic Association of New South Wales
PO Box 361
Forestville
Sydney NSW 2087
Tel: 02 94 52 5088
FREECALL 1 800 06 99 78
E-mail: aanswnet@ozEmail.com.au

Autism Association Queensland
PO Box 363
437 Hellawell Road
Sunnybank Hills
Queensland 4109
Tel: 07 3273 2222
Fax: 07 3273 8306
E-mail: mailbox@autismqld.asn.au
Website: www.autismqld.asn.au

Autism Tasmania
PO Box 1552
Launceston
TAS 7250
Tel (South): 03 62 44 2540
Tel (North West): 03 64 23 1086
Website: www.autismtas.org.au

Autism Victoria
PO Box 235
Ashburton
Victoria 3147
Tel: 03 98 85 0533
Website: www.vicnet.net.au/~autism

Autism Association of Western Australia (Inc)
987 Wellington Street
West Perth WA 6005
Tel: 08 9481 1144
Website: www.autism.org.au

OTHER USEFUL ADDRESSES (UK)

BBC Educational Publishing
PO Box 234
Wetherby
West Yorkshire LS23 7UE
Tel: 01937 541001
Website: www.bbc.co.uk/education/schools

Channel 4 Learning
PO Box 100
Warwick CV34 6TZ
Tel: 01926 436 444 (Customer Services)
Website: www.4learning.co.uk

RELATED SPECIAL NEEDS

ADHD Family Support Group
Gill Mead
1a The High Street
Dilton Marsh
Westbury
Wilts
Tel: 01373 826045

Dyspraxia Foundation
8, West Alley
Hitchin
Herts SG5 1EG
Tel: 01462 454986

National Association for Gifted Children
Suite 14, Challenge House
Sherwood Drive
Bletchley
Milton Keynes MK3 6DP
Website: www.nagcbritain.org.uk

PRACTICAL HELP

Disability Living Allowance
Tel: 0845 7123456

Financial help may be available from

Family Fund
PO Box 50
York YO1 1UY

Support for Carers

Shared Care Network
Units 63–66 Easton Business Centre
Felix Road
Bristol BS5 OHE
Tel: 0117 941 5361
Website: www.sharedcarenetwork.org.uk

Crossroads Association
10 Regent Place
Rugby CV21 2PN
Tel: 01788 573653
Website: www.crossroads.org.uk

Contributors

Anne Bedish lives near London with her husband and son, whom they have been home educating for over 12 years. Shortly before her son was born, Anne decided to give up paid work to become a full-time mother and housewife. Prior to that she had had a variety of experiences and jobs, including au pairing, grape picking, computer operating, clerical and administrative work.

Grace Carpenter is a single parent with two teenage sons, one of whom has Asperger's syndrome. Her sons attended school for six months when they were 11 and 9. Other than this, their education has always been home based.

Rachel Cohen lives with her family on Long Island, New York. With an M.A. in music and an M.B.A., education has always been important to her. She continues to learn, along with her child, as they home educate. Rachel finds that the flexible hours that she has as a piano teacher fit in well with their home education choice.

Ian Dowty started legal life in 1976 as a barrister, transferring to become a solicitor in 1980. He subsequently managed his own firm in London for 14 years before becoming a consultant with Goodall Barnett James in Brighton. He lives in London and is married to Terri Dowty; together they home educate their two children, aged 9 and 13, and have done so for 5 years.

The Rev. Dr. Jan Fortune-Wood is a parish priest at St Barnabas Church in Birmingham, England. She and her husband Mike home educate their four children in an autonomous style. Jan is the author of two books on non-coercive parenting and autonomous education: *Doing It Their Way* and

Without Boundaries, both published by Educational Heretics Press. Her family's education website is found at www.home-education.org.uk.

Karen Marsh is a qualified driving instructor, which has given her patience and a flexible approach when home educating her son Matthew. Her husband William is a microbiologist, which has been particularly helpful in devising and adapting home science lessons. They have two other children, Natalie (14) and Ben (10). The commitment to home educate Matthew was a family decision, with all family members helping, including Matthew's grandparents.

Mark's Mum is a former corporate lawyer who now stays home full time to educate her son. Her engineer husband helps out at weekends with technology lessons and practical science experiments.

Margaret Paton and her husband home educated their two grown-up sons for significant periods of time. Both boys had special education needs, David because of severe brain damage, and Jeremy because he was academically and musically gifted. She believes that academic qualifications will never provide the principal factor in an ability to bring children to their full potential, but that love and common sense, given adequate support, can enable any parent to achieve the apparently impossible.

Alan Phillips and his wife Helen have two children, Lee and Greg, aged 21 and 19. They have home educated for 13 years and continue to run a programme to support Greg. They have always tried to help other families by sharing their knowledge. Eventually they were persuaded to set up a consultancy, which enabled them to give direct support to other parents in the practicalities of home teaching and helping their children, especially those at the severe end of the ASD spectrum. They are also known for helping families to prepare cases for SEN tribunals and helping to obtain funding for home-based education programmes from LEAs. To contact Alan, log on to www.autism.pwp.blueyonder.co.uk.

Lise Pyles is a parent of a child with Asperger's syndrome. Her family's journey has encompassed living on three continents and following many paths dealing with therapy, diet, medication and several schooling options.

Although she has been a freelance writer for several years and is the author of *Hitchhiking Through Asperger Syndrome*, her primary concern is raising good, decent and happy kids.

Andrea Stephenson is 43 years of age, married with 2 children, and lives in the North of England. Andrea was a police officer for 14 years, but retired from the service soon after her son's developmental difficulties were identified. Andrea now works part time from home for a registered charity, providing support and advice to parents of children with special educational needs. Having recognised the benefits of home education for her eldest son, Andrea now also home educates her youngest son.

Jackie Stout is a painter living with her husband Rick in Carmel, Indiana. Mother to three teenage children, she has home educated Ben (14) since early childhood. Laryn (16 ½) attends high school half days and takes classes at a local university. Kevin (18) currently studies chemistry and anthropology at the university. Jackie moderates an Internet group for parents, relatives, and friends of children with AS who are home educated. To join *As You Like It*, log on to www.asyoulikeit@yahoogroups.com.

Christine Waterman is a qualified teacher of children with special needs. Her experience spans several years of teaching in special and mainstream schools, and working as an advisory teacher with schools and families. Since leaving full-time employment to care for her own son, Christine has worked as a freelance lecturer and has also provided respite care for children with a disability. She has one son and has been teaching him at home for the last five years. She is currently involved with Education Otherwise as the contact person for families home educating a child with special needs.

Book list

Tony Attwood
Asperger's Syndrome (Jessica Kingsley Publishers 1997 ISBN 1853025771)

Linda Dobson
The Homeschooling Book of Answers (Prima 1998 ISBN 0761513779)

Terri Dowty (ed)
Free Range Education—How Home Education Works (Hawthorn Press 2000 ISBN 1903458072)

Echo Fling
Eating an Artichoke (Jessica Kingsley Publishers 2000 ISBN 1853027111)

Jan Fortune-Wood
Doing It Their Way (Educational Heretics Press 2000 ISBN 1900219166)

Uta Frith
Autism and Asperger Syndrome (Cambridge University Press 1991 ISBN 052138608X)

John Taylor Gatto
Dumbing Us Down (Anthroposophical Press 1991 ISBN 086571231X)

Gunilla Gerland
Finding out about Asperger Syndrome, High-Functioning Autism and PDD (Jessica Kingsley Publishers 2000 ISBN 1853028401)

Stanley Greenspan
The Child with Special Needs (Addison Wesley Publishing Co 1998 ISBN 0201407264)

Mary Griffith
The Unschooling Handbook (Prima 1998 ISBN 0761512764)

David Guterson
Family Matters—Why Homeschooling Makes Sense (Harcourt 1993 ISBN 0156300001)

Matt Hearn (ed)
Deschooling Our Lives (New Society 1995 ISBN 0865713421)

John Holt
How Children Learn (Penguin 1991 ISBN 0140136002)
How Children Fail (Penguin 1990 ISBN 0140135561)
Teach Your Own (Lighthouse 1997 ISBN 0907637094)
Learning All the Time (Addison Wesley 1990 ISBN 0201550911)
Escape From Childhood (Holt Associates ISBN 0913677043)

Patricia Howlin
Autism; Preparing for Adulthood (Routledge 1996 ISBN 0415115329)

Carol Stock Kranowitz
The Out of Sync Child: Recognizing and Coping with Sensory Integration Dysfunction (Skylight Press 1998 ISBN 0399523863)

Mary Sheedy Kurcinka
Raising Your Spirited Child (Harper Perennial 1992 ISBN 0060923288)

George T. Lynn
Survival Strategies for Parenting Your ADD Child (Underwood Books 1996 ISBN 1887424199)

Roland Meighan
The Next Learning System (Educational Heretics Press 1997 ISBN 1900219042)
Learning from Home-Based Education (Education Now 1992 ISBN 187152606X)
Learning Unlimited: the Home-Based Education Case-Files (Educational Heretics Press 2001 ISBN 1900219182)

Brenda Smith Myles and Jack Southwick
Asperger Syndrome and Difficult Moments: Practical Solutions for Tantrums, Rage and Meltdown (Autism Asperger Publishing Co 1999—available from Jessica Kingsley Publishers in UK and Europe ISBN 0967251435)

Jasmine Lee O'Neill
Through the Eyes of Aliens (Jessica Kingsley Publishers 1998 ISBN 1853027103)

Freda Painter
Living with a Gifted Child (Souvenir Press 1989 ISBN 0285626272)

Madeleine Portwood
Developmental Dyspraxia (David Fulton Publishers 1999 ISBN 1853465739)

Lise Pyles
Hitchhiking Through Asperger Syndrome (Jessica Kingsley Publishers 2002 ISBN 1 853029378)

Mary Ann Rose and Paul Stanbrook
Getting Started in Home Education (Education Now 2000 ISBN 1871526426)

Alan Thomas
Educating Children At Home (Continuum 2000 ISBN 0304701807)

Liane Holliday Willey
Pretending to be Normal (Jessica Kingsley Publishers 1999 ISBN 1853027499)

Donna Williams
Nobody Nowhere (Jessica Kingsley Publishers 1998 ISBN 1853027189)